To my mother and to the memory of my father

VICTORIAN BIOGRAPHY

Intellectuals and the Ordering of Discourse

David Amigoni

Lecturer in English Studies, University of Sunderland

HARVESTER
WHEATSHEAF

NEW YORK   LONDON   TORONTO   SYDNEY   TOKYO   SINGAPORE

First published 1993 by
Harvester Wheatsheaf
Campus 400, Maylands Avenue
Hemel Hempstead
Hertfordshire, HP2 7EZ
A division of
Simon & Schuster International Group

Typeset in 10/12pt Ehrhardt
by Pentacor PLC, High Wycombe

Printed and bound in Great Britain
by Biddles Ltd, Guildford and Kings Lynn

British Library Cataloguing in Publication Data

A catalogue record for this book is available from the British Library

ISBN 0–7450–0771–6 (hbk)

---

1   2   3   4   5   97   96   95   94   93

Contents

Acknowledgements

This book grew out of a Ph.D. thesis, so I am grateful to Roger Webster, Mike Pudlo and Brean Hammond for their patient and thorough supervision, as well as their friendship. Liverpool Polytechnic and Liverpool City Council (the two were once thus linked) provided me with NAB funding to pursue this research. The Picton Library in Liverpool provided me with materials on which to base the research. My interest in the nineteenth century derives from an earlier, fruitful period spent at Keele University, where Charles Swann, David Vincent, Anthea Trodd, James McLaverty and John Briggs provided stimulation and encouragement. A number of readers looked at various manuscript versions and provided me with helpful comments and suggestions which I have gratefully worked into the text; particular thanks to Simon Dentith, John Goode, and my colleague at Sunderland, John Storey. I would like to thank others for their comments, support and encouragement, particularly Tim Ashplant, Jeff Wallace and Joe Simm. Needless to say the mistakes are mine. Jackie Jones at Harvester Wheatsheaf has been exceptionally supportive and encouraging – as well as very patient. I am very grateful to her. Finally, many, many thanks to Karen Ellis.

Introduction: Historicising academic disciplines

This book is about the relationship between Victorian biography and the disciplines of literature and history. It will not, primarily, be concerned to demonstrate that biographical narratives which purport to be factual are comprised of conventions that owe much to fiction; Victorian biography has already been tellingly surveyed from this angle.[1] Instead, it will explore how Victorian biography assisted in the construction of those academic disciplines which, since the nineteenth century, have come to be demarcated as 'literature' and 'history' – often in oppositional and antithetical terms. This will involve historicising the emergence of these disciplines, or orders of discourse. In turn this necessitates a discussion of the simplifications and oversights displayed by recent influential historical accounts of the emergence of academic disciplinarity in the nineteenth century – simplifications and oversights which a focus on the intertextually complex tradition of Victorian biography can help to redress.

Biographies are stories in which the life of a particular individual is narrated. It has become a commonplace that the characteristic Victorian biography was not only a story about a life, but also about the 'times' which moulded the life, and which the life in turn shaped. John Morley's monumental *Life of Gladstone*, in which the subject is presented as being shaped by 'an agitated and expectant age', while at the same time 'propelling, restraining, guiding his country at many decisive moments' illustrates this cult of exemplarity. The example of the Victorian 'life and times' biography has affected perceptions of the entire tradition of Victorian biographical writing, which has come to be seen as a monolithic contribution to master-narratives with much broader ambitions.[2]

So what enduring role did Victorian biography play in forming those master-narratives of Victorian culture, which came to celebrate on the one hand a political and constitutional tradition, and on the other a literary tradition? A look at the contours of the academic disciplines in which these master-narratives came to be embodied would suggest that the role of biography was considerable. University courses in English history stressed the individual role of major figures who, it was claimed, developed the institutions of the English state; this despite social history – history 'with the politics left out' as G.M. Trevelyan tellingly put it[3] – gaining a foothold. Similarly, university courses in English literature told the story which Victorian culture narrated about the history of English writing as manifested through the lives of its authors: beginning with Chaucer, the story focused on every major poet, dramatist and novelist who, it was claimed, had made a significant contribution to the development of literature and the language.

However, things have begun to change, and the narratives that had sustained the traditional structures of 'literature' and 'history' have been challenged. During the last two decades these traditional disciplines have been subject to the scrutiny of a body of discourses which have either been vilified or celebrated under the name of 'theory'. Amongst other things theory has undertaken an analysis of the social and intellectual forces which brought these disciplines and their master-narratives into being: so much so that a significant body of writing has been produced, exposing the selectivity of these disciplinary narratives.[4] Influential critical writings that attribute considerable ideological power to the master-narrative of 'literature' have argued that the discipline itself was the product of an irresistible rise, a rise that they have related in another powerful narrative. Yet if theory has played a role in deconstructing the master-narratives of Victorian academic culture, it is surely important to employ it further in questioning our own cherished master-narratives about the rise of the academic disciplines that helped to set them in place.

A theoretical re-reading of the function and significance of nineteenth-century biographical writing will be placed at the centre of this act of questioning. I shall argue that, far from constituting a seamless field, Victorian biographies were the products of ideologically antagonistic intellectuals with radically different strategies for disordering and ordering cultural discourse. My argument will focus on a selection of biographical texts which contributed to this cultural contest, in order to question the rise of a homogeneous ideology of 'English literature' which, it has been claimed, dominated throughout the course of the nineteenth century. The argument contends that the emergence of the authoritative discipline of history in the nineteenth century was crucial in determining the subordinate space occupied by literature.

First it will be necessary to examine critically some recent influential accounts of the emergence of academic disciplines in the nineteenth century. Of particular relevance here is Terry Eagleton's account of 'The rise of English' in his influential book *Literary Theory: An Introduction* (a story that paved the way for his book *The Function of Criticism*).[5] Eagleton narrates a compelling story about the rise of 'English literature' – the decisive moment being the early nineteenth century. I shall contrast Eagleton's account with Ian Small's recent account of the professionalisation of literary criticism and other forms of knowledge in the later part of the nineteenth century.[6] Small's account is very helpful because he widens the purview beyond the literary, seeking to grasp the relations between different academic disciplines as they emerged. He is also alert to discontinuities between nineteenth-century discourses on 'literature'. Yet my argument moves beyond Small's, suggesting that disciplines need to be grasped as political and institutional acts of resistance to the power, materiality and mobility of rhetoric. It is in this sense that this book will explore the different attitudes to the power of rhetoric displayed by Victorian biographers such as Thomas Carlyle and John Morley. Eagleton's story in *Literary Theory* ends with the rediscovery of rhetoric (*LT*, pp. 205–7). In practice rhetoric has never disappeared from the embattled history of the ordering of English cultural discourse, despite attempts to make it disappear. Had this been realised, the story that Eagleton came to tell in respect of the nineteenth century would look rather different.

The fortunes of 'literature' in the nineteenth century: Terry Eagleton

Terry Eagleton's account of 'the rise of English' in the nineteenth century is an integral part of the argument he advances about literary theory. For Eagleton, literary theory is a vacuous framework of explication because the 'knowledge' which it serves is so tenuously grounded in the first place. Literary theory can only prolong the dubious project of 'English literature', the emergence of which is charted in Eagleton's compelling narrative.

Eagleton's narrative on 'the rise of English' is an attempt to answer his opening question: 'what is literature?' In answering this question, Eagleton adopts an historical perspective and argues that the term has undergone transformation. In the eighteenth century, literature meant the whole body of valued writing in society (*LT*, p. 17). The end of the eighteenth century marks a watershed: 'the final decades of the eighteenth century witness a new division and demarcation of discourses, a radical reorganising of what we might call the "discursive formation" of English society' (*LT*, p. 18). Eagleton is here describing the emergence of 'the Romantic imagination', and so simultaneously, the appearance of the autonomous category of 'literature' which was perpetuated throughout the nineteenth century. If the imagination of Wordsworth and Coleridge was inward, contemplative and spiritually nourishing, then the writing to which it gave rise would have a unique effect on the reader who came into contact with it – an effect like no other form of communication.

We should pause for a moment to look at the language and sense of periodisation that Eagleton uses to construct this 'break' in his story, for it gives us a sense of the theoretical and narrative sources that he has drawn upon in constructing his account. In referring to the 'discursive formation' of English society, Eagleton is drawing on the writings of the French theorist and historian Michel Foucault, for whom 'discursive formations' are organised domains of statements – in the example that we are pursuing here, statements about the imagination and poetry and their effects on readers. A great deal of Foucault's writing focuses on the late decades of the eighteenth century and the early decades of the nineteenth, and it explores – as Eagleton explores here – a momentous shift in the relations between discursive formations.[7]

Eagleton's use of Foucault has been grafted onto a narrative formulated by a major English cultural historian, Raymond Williams. Eagleton's *Literary Theory* is jointly dedicated to Williams, and 'The rise of English' quite clearly draws on Williams's work, especially *Keywords* and *Marxism and Literature. Keywords* is Williams's investigation into the semantic shifts evident in words that comprised a 'culture and society' vocabulary; 'literature' was one such key word, along with other related words such as 'criticism'. The conclusions that followed from these semantic investigations were to be assimilated into the historical arguments of *Marxism and Literature*, particularly the chapter entitled 'The multiplicity of writing'.[8] In common with much of Foucault's work, this chapter deals with the late decades of the eighteenth century, and the early decades of the nineteenth. And in the same way that Foucault (and latterly Eagleton) characterise that period in terms of a shift in the relations between discursive formations, Williams describes a shift in the relations between the elements that comprised the multiplicity of writing, or different styles of inscription, that were in circulation. Williams makes a further claim: that the disciplines of grammar and rhetoric were superseded by the bourgeois discipline of literary criticism, the latter displaying a distorting orientation towards the act of reading which occluded the materiality of writing. The implications that follow from this are twofold; first, rhetoric was expunged from the array of post-Romantic intellectual practices, and second, as a consequence of the former, the chance to formulate an adequate social theory of inscription was lost for the remainder of the nineteenth century. I shall return to Williams's contention later in order to question the conclusion he draws from it. For the moment I shall point to two openings that it provides for Eagleton's narrative: first, it enables him to close his story by reclaiming rhetoric as a 'lost' practice; and second, it enables him to tell a racy story about the nineteenth century in which 'literature' figures in the character of a reified, bourgeois grotesque.

Eagleton explicitly reclaims rhetoric at the end of his book, but it is fairly clear that he is deliberate in using narrative as a rhetorical device in the early chapter on 'the rise of English': 'if the reader is still unconvinced, the narrative of what happened to literature in the later nineteenth century might prove a little more persuasive' (*LT*, p. 22). What does Eagleton assemble before the reader in order to secure their assent to his story about English studies in the nineteenth century and its aftermath? For a start, Eagleton's history is monocausal: 'If one were asked to provide a single explanation for the growth of English studies in the later nineteenth century, one could do worse than reply: "the failure of religion"' (*LT*, p. 22). The celebrated disappearance of God that the Victorians experienced is thus made responsible: if the ideological function played by religion in maintaining a system of class domination was threatened by the collapse of the reign of the pulpit, then literature, the unique form of communication and source of nourishment to the imagination, could be called upon to fill up the authority vacuum that was left. It follows from this that certain figures stand at the centre of this drama: 'the key figure here is Matthew Arnold [author of *Literature and Dogma* and *God and the Bible*]' (*LT*, p. 24). This is an ideological project that extends from the Romantics through to the famous *Newbolt Report on the Teaching of English in England*, published in 1921. It enables Eagleton in his book *The Function of Criticism* to homogenise the meaning of 'literature' in the nineteenth century in the following way:

> From the writings of the later Coleridge, through to Carlyle, Kingsley, Ruskin, Arnold and others, literature is extricated from the arena of *Realpolitik* and elevated to a realm where, in the words of one commentator, 'all might meet and expiate in common'.[9]

On the question of 'literature', Eagleton makes no distinctions between Coleridge, Carlyle, Kingsley and Arnold, yet all of these intellectuals *write* about the term in markedly different ways. Furthermore, Eagleton's sense of Matthew Arnold being the key figure obscures Arnold as an intellectual writing against liberal intellectuals who were formulating different discourses about 'literature' and 'criticism'. Late Victorian biographers such as John Morley, Frederic Harrison and Leslie Stephen can be seen as a grouping or formation of intellectuals who cannot be seamlessly incorporated into Arnold's discourse on 'literature'. Furthermore, when these biographers and men of letters enter the frame then Eagleton's contention that 'literature' was a substitute religion is difficult to endorse: Morley, Harrison and Stephen celebrated the collapse of organised theist religion and were deeply anxious when confronted with signs of its resurgence.

Eagleton's narrative can be objected to in one more respect, and this is more of a methodological point – and one which will lead us to a consideration of the more recent work of Ian Small. In the extract quoted above, Eagleton refers to *Realpolitik* as 'literature's' Other. As I shall go on to demonstrate in the course of this book, 'literature' and 'politics' did indeed come to be opposed in this way, and the opposition was discursively linked to a more fundamental opposition, that of 'literature'/'history'. What is striking about Eagleton's narrative in *Literary Theory*, as Jonathan Culler has pointed out, is that this opposition comes to function as a rhetorical device, so that an attempt to historicise the literary privileges history, or the arena of the real source of all power where authentic politics takes shape.[10] If Eagleton were Sir Geoffrey Elton, then I should disagree with his view of the workings of power in the world and put it down to his disciplinary training as an historian. But Eagleton is not Sir Geoffrey Elton, and is instead a theorist who at other points in his narrative draws upon Foucault's vocabulary for analysing the ordering of cultural discourse, and this mode of analysis is premised on the assumption that discourse itself generates power through its assertion of authority. That discourse which we have come to see as history, and to which Eagleton appeals as an authority, is as amenable to this kind of analysis as any other. The point is that Eagleton's narrative is methodologically underdeveloped when it comes to critically considering the relations between different and historically situated modes of cultural discourse, and the forms of authority to which they lay claim. It is at this point that we can turn to Ian Small's work.

Ian Small: 'literature', authority and difference in nineteenth-century cultural discourse

Ian Small's recent *Conditions for Criticism: Authority, knowledge and literature in the late nineteenth century* is an argument against accounts which attempt to historicise and explain the emergence of the discipline of literary studies, and which then use these explanations as commentaries on the current 'crisis in English studies' engendered by theory. Small's argument is multi-layered; not only is it a contribution to the current debate about the impact of theory on literary studies, it is also a reassessment of Walter Pater, Oscar Wilde and the Aesthetic Movement. According to Small, the individualist aesthetics of Pater and Wilde need to be seen as a form of intellectual resistance to a process of disciplinary specialisation and authoritarianism. Small summarises this in the following way:

> Authority became the central issue for disciplines of knowledge after 1870, because these disciplines were in competition with each other and offered different explanations of human society. Moreover, the manner

in which authority was to be established itself became problematic after 1870 because, as there were competing epistemologies, so there were competing models of authority.[11]

This is the conclusion to a narrative in which conceptions of literature are represented as changing. Small argues that, up until the 1840s and 1850s, literature meant a certain set of qualities that could be located in a diverse range of texts: 'texts by authors as diverse as Spinoza, Shakespeare, Adam Smith, Walter Scott, and Macaulay could be described . . . as possessing literary qualities' (*CC*, p. 136). This has echoes of the eighteenth-century meaning of literature excavated by Williams, thus suggesting that it persisted beyond the break (1790s–1800s) suggested by Williams. However, from around the 1860s Small locates a break which was not even initiated from within the 'sphere' of the literary (if such a sphere were so formalised); rather, it was initiated from within the field of classical political economy. According to Small, the theory of marginalist economics was revolutionary in that it transformed political economy from an amateur pursuit into a disciplinary specialism with a clearly demarcated epistemology, and model of authority which it used to explain human society (*CC*, pp. 35–45). Small argues that this structural transformation was replicated across the range of Victorian intellectual practices (historiography, sociology, aesthetics, psychology and biology) until 'literature' also became disciplined: that is, institutionalised and professionalised around the practice of philology, with a clearly demarcated epistemology which enabled it to make authoritative claims, but which simultaneously put it into competition with other similarly constituted practices (*CC*, pp. 25–6). Small argues that it is in this context that Pater and Wilde's 'unscholarly' and 'non-serious' writing practices make sense, as strategies of resistance to professionalisation (*CC*, pp. 91–130).

Small's account of the emergence – notably not the 'rise' – of English literary studies supersedes Eagleton's in two senses: first, it attempts to grasp the emergence of a discipline through its contestatory relations of difference to other disciplines; and, second, it sees the process of emergence as complex and discontinuous, arguing that there was not a homogeneous ideology of 'literature' spanning from Coleridge to the Newbolt Report. In short, Small offers a more convincing account of the place of disciplines (not just a discipline) in the process of ordering cultural discourse in the nineteenth century.

Small's account suggests that we need to look at the emergence of disciplinary configurations rather than the emergence of one discipline, and I shall argue that it is important to look at the emergence of the discipline of history in nineteenth-century England in order to gauge the discursive space that conditioned intellectual enquiry into literature. Some of Small's arguments still need to be questioned, especially on the relationship between intellectuals and institutions, and their relationship to disciplines and discourse. It can be argued that Small's account fails to appreciate a crucial function of disciplinarity, and that Victorian biography gives us an insight into this.

Unlike Eagleton, Small does not surreptitiously privilege one discipline (history) over another in order to make it authoritatively non-discursive and independent of the institutional conditions which generate its authority and power. Small is clear about the relationship between discourse, power and institutions: 'notions of power . . . have little meaning beyond the institutions which sanction them, and these sanctions may in their turn only be understood in terms of the operation of intellectual authority in institutions' (*CC*, p. 132). For Small, institutions play an extremely important role in the process that he is trying to describe. It is curious then that this position should start to blur when his focus shifts to the present 'crisis in English' that has followed in the wake of the emergence of theory. Small's account of the emergence of the discipline of English literature in the later part of the nineteenth century is simultaneously a perspective on the present and an argument with leading commentators on the so-called crisis in English studies:

> The purpose of this book was to describe the crisis in the late nineteenth century in *intellectual* rather than in institutional terms, a characterisation equally applicable to the present dilemma in English studies. Most critics have tended to describe the current crisis in institutional terms, but the fact that there is a wide divergence of opinion within English about what is to count as an appropriate theory of literary studies suggests that the nature of the current crisis is also fundamentally intellectual, and hence the reasons for its occurrence will be the same as any intellectual crisis, including my nineteenth-century example, namely those of intellectual authority and epistemology. (*CC*, p. 133)

Small's claim that the emergence of a disciplinary academic culture in the late nineteenth century was an intellectual phenomenon rather than an institutional phenomenon is directed against a number of critics – Terence Hawkes, Terry Eagleton and Peter Widdowson – who have argued that the current 'crisis in English' needs to be understood primarily in institutional terms.[12] It is somewhat surprising that Small should have made this into a matter of 'either/or'; how valid is it to say that a process is 'fundamentally intellectual'? Surely the intellectual and the institutional were and are interwoven forces? A consideration of the cultural significance of Victorian biographical texts enables us to appreciate this; it encourages us to interrogate assumptions about the categories of the 'intellectual' and the 'institutional' and the relationships between them; it also grants us an insight into a crucial function of disciplinarity which Small's account tends to overlook.

Biography, institutions and intellectual formations: resisting 'rhetoric'

Small does not engage with biography as a genre that has a bearing on the development of his argument, but here and there he draws upon biographical narratives as evidence for localised points. In dealing with H.T. Buckle, the materialist historian and author of the influential *History of Civilization in England* (1857–61), Small discusses the hostile reaction to Buckle's work, concluding that 'the rejection of Buckle's historiography owed more to the fact that he possessed no institutional authority for his views than to allegations of their internal incoherence' (*CC*, p. 51). Small's point is that Buckle – a Victorian writer who had not attended either ancient university and who had devised his systematic philosophy of history from a basis in self-education – became a victim of the common tendency to confuse the intellectual (coherence) with the institutional (prestige). As evidence for this conclusion, Small cites the entry on Buckle included in *The Dictionary of National Biography* (*DNB*), written by the then sole editor of this massive late Victorian cultural project, Leslie Stephen. As Small points out, Stephen's entry attributed Buckle's 'faults' to his lack of a university education (*CC*, p. 50):

> Buckle's solitary education deprived him of the main advantage of schools and universities – the frequent clashing with independent minds – which tests most searchingly the thoroughness and solidity of a man's

acquirements. Specialists in every department will regard him as a brilliant amateur rather than a thorough student . . . . Nor can it be said that Buckle fully appreciated the significance of the historical method . . . . But his literary power was very great . . . and though his conclusions are neither very new nor valuable to serious thinkers, they are put forward with rhetorical power admirably adapted to impress the less cultivated reader.[13]

Thus the habit of mistakenly using institutional parameters to assess intellectual validity received support from a collective biographical project which serviced the development of specialist university disciplines in the 1880s and 1890s.

But how are we to read this judgement of Stephen's? This in turn begs a larger question: how are we to frame his text? and what sort of status are we to assign to it? Do we follow Small and read Stephen's biographical discourse on Buckle as simply a reflection of a timeless category mistake which erroneously conflates the intellectual and the institutional? Or do we instead conceptualise Stephen's text as a release of cultural energy which, at the same time as judging the intellectual in terms of the institutional, actively constructs the intellectual through its institutional conditions of existence? I would argue that the latter is the most appropriate way to frame the text in the light of the medley of institutional determinants that produced the *DNB* and its intellectual stance.

Stephen's negative judgement of Buckle can be seen in terms of Stephen's own continued allegiance to the institution of Cambridge University where he had been both student and teacher. However, at the time of writing this (1886) Stephen's position was not formally 'validated' by Cambridge (he was no longer a university teacher); so Small's implicit understanding of an appeal to the authoritative role of *the* institution does not really grasp the forces that are generating Stephen's text. As such, we need to cast a wider net and consider the role that was played by such periodicals as the *Athenaeum*, which invited 'educated' readers to participate in the nomination process that led to the formation of the biographical project in the first place. This connects the *DNB* to key institutions of high culture in the late Victorian period, including the 'higher' journalism (through which Stephen earned his living as a writer and editor), and the physical spaces of the gentlemen's clubs that perpetuated the ideology of the gentleman-scholar; all of these institutions were hostile to the sort of popular-radical constituency to which Buckle's theory of history appealed, and this hostility can be felt in Stephen's counter-appeal to 'serious thinkers'.[14] It is clear that Stephen's judgement was not supported by one institution; instead, Stephen's biographical critique of Buckle needs to be seen in the context of an intellectual formation as defined by Raymond Williams, or a conscious movement of like-minded writers that existed between a number of different institutions, which produced a particular kind of ideological stance.[15] This also suggests that we need to substitute Small's sense of the 'intellectual' as the principle of coherence in a system of thought, with Antonio Gramsci's sense of intellectuals as specific organised individuals who perform a social and ideological function of discursive elaboration and refinement.[16]

The intellectual and institutional function of Stephen's biography of Buckle for the *DNB* was to elaborate and refine a particular exclusionary practice of discourse characteristic of disciplinarity. Stephen's judgement on Buckle's intellectual and institutional shortcomings viewed from the point of view of 'serious thinkers' is followed by a statement on the properties that Buckle's writings actually possessed. Stephen comments on Buckle's 'literary powers' which he then goes on to equate with 'a rhetorical power admirably suited to impress the less cultivated reader'. The connections that can be established between on the one hand the authoritative source of disciplinarity – characterised as 'the historical method' – and its Others – 'literary power' and 'rhetorical power' – are instructive for two reasons. First, they provide us with an important perspective on disciplinarity which does not emerge from Small's account but which has been one of Foucault's main insights into this theme; that is to say, they point to the way in which the disciplines of modernity have attempted to regulate and police a rhetorical insight into the workings of discourse on the construction of social practices – I shall say more about this theme in Chapter 1. And second, the connection between 'rhetorical power' and 'literary power' provides us with a more complex perspective on the 'literary' than that suggested by Eagleton's account of the 'rise of English' in the nineteenth century. Eagleton's account of 'literariness' presupposes a monolithic ideological discourse that spans the period from Coleridge to the Newbolt Report, and which was designed to pacify its users. I shall argue that for a late nineteenth-century intellectual formation of which the biographer Leslie Stephen was a part, 'literariness' was a source of cultural and political anxiety.

The question of how we are to read Stephen's biography of H.T. Buckle, which I raised above, needs to be theorised. Every act of textual selection presupposes a theory of reading, so it follows that theories of reading select and group textual canons. The texts that have been selected for inclusion in this book range from Thomas Carlyle's *Sartor Resartus*, his biography of Oliver Cromwell and Charles Kingsley's *Alton Locke* to J.R. Seeley's biography of the Prussian statesman Stein, and to the two series of short biographies published towards the end of the nineteenth century entitled 'Twelve English Statesmen' and 'English Men of Letters'. This is a diverse spread of biographical or quasi-autobiographical texts – and some readers may object to 'factual' biographies being grouped alongside 'imitations' of autobiographies. So how did an account of the forms of intellectual and institutional argument generated between these texts come to be constructed? Which theory of reading underwrites this argument?

A theory of reading

Late in his career, the Russian cultural philosopher Mikhail Bakhtin wrote a richly suggestive essay on the centrality of the idea of the text to cultural history. Bakhtin's essay might be used as a way of explaining how readers come to construct selective canons of texts. Bakhtin's essay theorises the text's inbuilt awareness of its passage through layers of time and different cultural contexts. His view of the rhetorical function of texts holds that all texts situate themselves and their institutionalised values in relation to a contemporary, socially identifiable addressee. Simultaneously though, texts also address a complex 'presence' which Bakhtin calls the 'superaddressee'; that is to say, texts imagine themselves arriving in the domain of an ideal reader situated in a desired distant time and position beyond the ascertainable social addressee inscribed in the textual event. Bakhtin recognises that although the text may target an ideal superaddressee – 'God, absolute truth, the court of dispassionate human conscience, the people, the court of history, science' – the actual reader who identifies this address and assumes the superaddressee position in history may have an interest in the text that is different to the imagined, ideal superaddressee.[17]

Because Bakhtin envisages all linguistic and textual activity as part of a great and never-ending dialogue, it follows that the actual superaddressee cannot be a passive recipient; the actual superaddressee is an active participant in the transaction, and is involved in reshaping the rhetorical materials of the text, and organising them into a hierarchy from an institutional and intellectual position in the present. Bakhtin's theory of reading can be used to reflect on the presence of superaddressee positions contributing to the formation of another master-narrative – this being Harold Nicolson's narrative of the development of English biographical writing, written in the late 1920s. This will be used to reflect on the intellectual and institutional position that has led me to construct the narrative of Victorian biography that will follow.

Harold Nicolson: a story about English biography

Harold Nicolson wrote *The Development of English Biography* in 1927. Nicolson set out to establish a selection of biographical texts as representative of the central English tradition of life-writing by discriminating between 'pure' and 'impure' forms of biography.[18] In Nicolson's story of the development of English biography, the long period initiated by the English Civil War, challenged by Johnson, Boswell and Lockhart, but for the most part dominated by 'impure' biography, ends in the later part of the nineteenth century when biography of literary subjects acquired a complete maturity. Nicolson's developmental story about biography is thus constructed from a point which participates in this mature transcendence; it has to deal with the chaff but it is eminently qualified to identify with and praise the wheat.

The *Dictionary of National Biography* is one biographical project that Nicolson praises as wheat or, as he describes it, a nourishing form of 'biography for students'; another is the 'English Men of Letters' series published by Macmillan between 1878 and the first two decades of the twentieth century.[19] In claiming that 'English Men of Letters' are 'biographies for students', Nicolson informs us that the project was implicated in the business of pedagogy, and consequently knowledge-producing institutions. In this sense, these late nineteenth-century biographies can be seen in the context of the rise of disciplines in the humanities, such as English literature and history. For Nicolson, these biographies exemplify the values of balance, detachment and objectivity. In reaching this judgement, Nicolson occupies a superaddressee position responsive to the discourses of literary criticism and historiography that were founded on a positivist epistemology and institutionalised in the later part of the nineteenth century. These were the very discourses which, I shall argue in Chapters 4 and 5, were in part constructed by and legitimised in biographies such as those comprising the 'English Men of Letters' series.

Nicolson's *The Development of English Biography* is thus an example of the sort of history of biography that might be written when the ideal superaddressee position inscribed in a selection of texts finds an agreeable superaddressee in a distant but sympathetic position of cultural influence and power. However, Nicolson's innocent complicity in this superaddressee position makes him a rather 'blind' reader in two directions: first, the complex diachronic relations of intertextuality that his supposedly 'pure' biographies are involved in – meaning that Nicolson's 'pure' biographies are inextricably linked to the 'impure' subtradition from which Nicolson's history seeks to distance his canonical texts; and second, the synchronic arrangement of discourses in which the 'pure' biographies are immersed – that is, Nicolson is positively unconscious of the constructed nature of the disciplinary framework that allows him to reach his judgements and to write his history in the way that he does.

To be able to draw these conclusions about Nicolson's 'blindness' as a superaddressee of the biographies comprising 'English Men of Letters' assumes, however, that I am reading and writing from a particular position; this position needs some theorisation. The institutional and intellectual position that I have occupied in writing the book that you are reading has played a formative role in determining the actual superaddressee position that I have read into the biographical texts that comprise its primary focus. In turn, this has shaped, first, the selective canon of nineteenth-century writing that I am constructing and, second, my sense of the patterns of epistemological and institutional conflict woven through this canon.

I started to conduct 'interdisciplinary' research in a British institution of higher education in the middle of the 1980s. The territory that the research was commissioned to explore lay between the disciplines of English literature and history, which in the institution concerned had been taught in relation to each other for around ten years. Pedagogically, the arrangement meant that each discipline was taught for itself, but brought into tentative proximity with its Other on limited occasions; these occasions would comprise a wary discussion of a certain amount of exposed common territory, but they would always conclude with a tacit withdrawal to the safe and peaceful heights of disciplinary autonomy. Clearly, though, a vigorous debate was going on which this practice had barely glimpsed. It was propelled by the writings of – amongst others – Foucault, Bakhtin, Williams and Hayden White. Their writings initiated a thoroughgoing theoretical critique which challenged the positivist epistemology and the 'literature' and 'history' opposition which it supported.[20]

Indeed, all of these theorists shared a deep interest in the constructive properties of language or discourse. Strikingly, it was the very issue of the status of language and its powers that caused so many discussions of disciplinary parity to founder. The experience of sitting around a course-planning table, listening to historians vehemently denying the importance of language and discourse to historiographical writing, opened up an area of anxiety and blindness that invited exploration.[21] Puzzlement with this reaction prompted me to seek, in what is generally agreed to be a formative moment for the modern humanities, nineteenth-century manifestations of this anxiety. I would stress that this account should not be seen as the product of a transcendent hermeneutics which ends in a celebratory intellectual autobiography. Sitting around a course-planning table, my sense of puzzlement was a product of institutional pressures; the intellectual has proved impossible to separate from the institutional.

Accordingly the actual superaddressee position that is occupied by this research has been alert, first, to the rhetoric of Thomas Carlyle's biographical texts, and their foregrounding of linkages between those ways of thinking and interpreting which a certain ordering of discourse has projected as separate; and, second, to the rhetoric of biographical texts from the later part of the nineteenth century, which attempt to police and regulate such links. Clearly, the superaddressee position from which I am conducting my dialogue with the biographies that form the basis of this study is not precisely identical to the superaddressee position originally inscribed in these biographies. However, the concern here – a political concern with the mobility, reception and use of discourse – is addressed by all the texts, and is one to which they devote a significant proportion of their rhetorical energies.

Chapter 1 will involve a more detailed consideration of the conceptions of discourse outlined by Mikhail Bakhtin and Michel Foucault, and the light that these cast on the different kinds of rhetorical and cultural energy released by Victorian biographical texts, focusing particularly on the contrasting styles of Thomas Carlyle and John Morley. Chapter 2 comprises a major re-reading of aspects of Thomas Carlyle's biographical writing, demonstrating its transgressive relationship to an early nineteenth-century ordering of discourse. Chapter 3 focuses on the positivist philosophical system of Auguste Comte and its appropriation by a later Victorian intellectual formation, which sought a new disciplinary framework for re-establishing order at the level of language – particularly the language designated 'political'. This theme is further developed in Chapter 4, where J.R. Seeley's use of biographical writing to popularise the nascent university discipline of history is explored – history for Seeley being the discipline with a social mission to reform public opinion and the popular language of politics. A major theme of Chapter 4 is Seeley's highly negative conception of 'literature', a conception shared by John Morley and other biographers writing out of this intellectual formation. Finally, Chapter 5 reconsiders the political practice of late nineteenth-century literary criticism in the light of this negative conception of 'literature' by focusing on the influential series of pedagogic biographies 'English Men of Letters'.

1

□

Biography and the ordering of discourse

In this chapter I will explore the relationship between biography as a form of ideological rhetoric and theories of the historical field of cultural discourse elaborated by Mikhail Bakhtin and Michel Foucault. I will discuss the significance of these Bakhtinian and Foucauldian perspectives for our understanding of the intellectual differences between two Victorian biographers, Thomas Carlyle and John Morley. These differences help to explain a vigorous contest over the ordering of English nineteenth-century cultural discourse, a contest which helped to form 'literature' and 'history' as disciplines. I shall begin with Raymond Williams's account of the way in which the ordering of cultural discourse was settled in the early part of the nineteenth century, for this offers a perspective on the segregation of 'literary' and 'historical' discourses.

'Literature' and 'history' and the multiplicity of writing

The replacement of the disciplines of grammar and rhetoric . . . by the discipline of criticism . . . is a central intellectual movement of the bourgeois period. Each kind of discipline moved, in the period of change, to a particular pole: grammar and rhetoric to writing; criticism to reading. Any social theory, by contrast, requires the activation of both poles.

This is a key claim made in Raymond Williams's book *Marxism and Literature*, where he attempts to account for 'the multiplicity of writing'.[1] Williams's concept tries to account historically for the many different styles of inscription that were being formed, organised and ranked from the early part of the nineteenth century. However, it also attempts to analyse the emergence of certain metalanguages which inscribed hierarchical relationships of value and difference between these styles. Williams describes these metalanguages as disciplines.

The eventual effect of these disciplines was the ordering and grouping of styles of writing into bodies of 'knowledge' which could be possessed, especially bodies of knowledge which we have come to call 'literature' and 'history'. In the quote above, Williams is describing the basic interpretive disciplines that have conditioned the bourgeois possession of 'literature', and by extension, all that is 'other' to 'literature', like 'history'. As we have already seen in the Introduction, Williams argued that in the seventeenth and early eighteenth centuries the term 'literature' denoted an educated acquaintance with all manner of printed texts – education being defined as a condition of humane and polite learning. From around the middle of the eighteenth century, the term 'literature' started to relate to questions of taste and sensibility. It also started to narrow around certain types of 'aesthetic' or 'imaginative' writing which, it was held, worked on the 'inner' sensibilities of the reader; the precise identity of this writing was arbitrated upon by the practice of 'criticism'.[2] At the same time, other forms of writing became marked out as 'factual', which were 'external' in their workings and had 'practical' effects in the world.[3] In his other writings addressing British cultural history, Williams has demonstrated how these distinctions have come to organise and delimit our very understanding of 'literature' and 'history' as restricted ways of seeing.[4] Furthermore, these disciplines separate criticism and reading from rhetoric and writing and polarise the opposition between them. As I have argued in the Introduction, this view of things was very influential upon Terry Eagleton's account of the rise of English literary studies. However, there are grounds for arguing that the ordering of discourse which Williams presents as a monolithic settlement was in fact subject to a more complex process of contestation and counter-assertion.

Williams points to rhetoric as a discipline, and as a discipline its function has been to instruct users of language in specific techniques for addressing, affecting and persuading audiences into accepting a particular path of action or set of beliefs. Indeed rhetoric has a very long history as a discipline used in the education of elites from classical times onwards.[5] However, as I shall go on to show, theorists like Foucault have argued that, since the Enlightenment, Western societies have displayed a deep cultural suspicion of rhetoric, which has been seen as an aberrant dimension of language use.[6] According to this construction, rhetoric is not so much a discipline as something that is in need of discipline and cultural policing. We have already seen an example of this in Leslie Stephen's biography of H.T. Buckle which appeared in the *Dictionary of National Biography*. This is an example of a certain kind of biographical writing which was produced in late nineteenth-century Britain to discipline the distinction between 'literature' and 'history', and this impulse to discipline was intimately bound to a fearful, politically motivated understanding of rhetoric. There is something rather paradoxical in this, because biography has been seen as a genre of discourse with strong rhetorical properties.

Biography: rhetorically double-voiced discourse as ideology

Williams claims that biography was one of the new written forms whose conditions of existence were transformed by the revolution in the ordering of writing that occurred at the beginning of the nineteenth century. I will argue that biography was a form of writing which was used to disseminate the metalanguages which organised the new ordering of writing, and so promoted the cultural acceptance of the categories of 'internal' and 'external' writing, and 'literary' and 'non-literary' writing. One of the striking characteristics of biography to which cultural historians like Richard D. Altick have pointed, is that a biographical mode of address was able to transform sensational conventions into culturally acceptable forms of meaning for certain communities of readers. Evangelical readers in the early nineteenth century who would not have looked at a 'novel' were happy to consume the conventions of gothic and romance fiction when wrapped in the narrative of an exemplary life.[7] This made biography useful as a pedagogic tool.

Nineteenth-century Britain saw a number of pedagogic drives initiated by intellectuals and organised around the production of popular biographies. Some of these, such as the efforts of Samuel Smiles in the 1860s to teach the nation to think in an enterprising way through his *Lives of the Engineers*, are well known. Less well known, perhaps, are the range of formations and initiatives that prepared a readership for Smiles. Here one could cite the enormously prolific Society for the Diffusion of Useful Knowledge (SDUK), an organisation set up in the 1830s between establishment figures like Lord Brougham and the journalist-publisher Charles Knight.[8] Publications such as *The Penny Cyclopedia* and *The Penny Magazine*, which were aimed at instructing a working-class readership in the values of self-improvement, sobriety and industry, relied heavily on biographical exemplars whose model lives were constructed for readers through brief narratives. In 1842, the Society started to produce a monumental *Biographical Dictionary* which aimed to include the instructive life of every worthy in British history. In 1846, the over-ambitious project went bankrupt, and it led to the dissolution of the Society; and a completed biographical dictionary of the scale planned did not appear until *The Dictionary of National Biography* (*DNB*) (1885–1900), under the editorship of Sir Leslie Stephen and Sir Sidney Lee.[9] As we have seen, looking back on the history of English biography from the 1920s, Harold Nicolson assimilated the *DNB*, along with another prominent biographical project from the late nineteenth century, 'English Men of Letters', to this powerful tradition of biographical pedagogic initiatives.[10]

These pedagogic initiatives were ideological, though their ideological aspirations addressed different communities of readers. This is hardly a controversial contention; any study making claims about the aspirations of a textual genre to instruct must back such claims through a framework that links texts to competing systems of values, beliefs and practices which either sustain or challenge the inequalities and power relations that exist between conflicting groups in society.[11] But having said this, there are a number of competing theories of ideology. I do not propose to enter into a lengthy discussion of the relative merits of these various theories. Indeed, it is possible – though, I admit, risky in hard-line theoretical company – to handle these theories eclectically. Thus my approach to biographical writing as an ideological force has been shaped by a number of theoretical positions. Louis Althusser's theory of the ideological moment as the (mis)recognition or interpellation of address has been valuable.[12] Antonio Gramsci's view of ideology as the ceaseless struggle between intellectuals to construct relations of hegemony, or consent to a set of values or a strategy with a bearing on the direction of culture, has been very important.[13] However, Bakhtin/Volosinov's view of ideology as the production and contestation of social and cultural meaning through the collectively held sign, has proved to be foundational.[14]

One feature connects these theorists of ideology both in themselves, and to my view of biography as a form of writing that played an important pedagogic role in elaborating disciplines that ranked and ordered nineteenth-century cultural discourse. That is, all of these theories of ideology take language to be central to their analysis. This is important because a biography shapes its reader's relationship to certain views of spoken and written language in quite systematic ways that have not received prominent attention in previous studies of the genre. To illustrate this contention, it will be helpful to look at a text from the 1840s, from that formation known as the SDUK mentioned above, a biography by Charles Knight entitled *William Caxton: The first English printer*:

> In these days, when the same language with very slight variations is spoken from one end of the land to the other, it is difficult to imagine a state of things such as Caxton describes in which the 'common English which is spoken in one shire varieth from another'. Easy and rapid communication, and above all the circulation of books, newspapers, and other periodical works, all free from provincial expressions [have created a national language] . . . . When there were no books amongst the community in general, there could be no universality of language.[15]

The extended narrative from which this localised detail is taken is about the life and times of Caxton. However, there is more embedded in this narration than just a statement on Caxton's life. Following Bakhtin, the narration might best be approached as an instance of rhetorical double-voicedness.[16] For Bakhtin, rhetorical double-voicedness is a special property of biography which is, in his typology of genres, a subspecies of that family of textual types which Bakhtin describes as 'the rhetorical genres'. The rhetorical genres have their origins in ancient forms of public rhetorical delivery (the panegyric, or encomium) which took as their topic the life and deeds of a particular individual. Because the individual was invariably dead – the funeral oration was an occasion for the use of rhetorical genres – the delivery took the form of one speaker representing the 'voice' of the subject of the address, and topics with which that subject's 'voice' had been associated. Knight's statement on Caxton's life could be said to be an instance of this genre of discourse.

Bakhtin also argues that rhetorical double-voicedness constitutes 'an analysis of the ideas that are parcelled out in [the voice], an analysis that exhausts it'.[17] Bakhtin is arguing that rhetorically double-voiced prose is a form of analysis that is ideological in the sense of forcing closure; that is to say, it can close down the potential for argument (dialogue) with the ideas contained in it. There are, however, difficulties with Bakhtin's formulation. To begin with, there is the implication that language is a 'container' that parcels out ideas – an instrumental view of language that Bakhtin's entire view of discourse seeks to combat. Also the role that readers or listeners are invited to play is not specified, and questions of contextual relations to other discourses are not raised. It might be said that Bakhtin's conceptual ambition seems to be running ahead of his critical vocabulary. We need to go back to Knight's statement on Caxton to see what Bakhtin might be driving at.

Knight's analysis constructs a view of the present (1840s), and juxtaposes it with a view of the past which Caxton's voice brings before the reader. The past is characterised by the heterogeneity of language communities, whereas the present is characterised by its linguistic homogeneity. Of course Caxton's life and observations are not simply a record of the past, and we need to be aware of a political interest. The reason that Knight – journalist, publisher, educationalist and champion of the role of the printed word as purveyor of a reformed culture – is celebrating Caxton's biography is that he established the first printing press in England. As such Caxton is projected as the decisive figure who enabled the heterogeneity of speech in the past to become the homogeneity of speech in the present. This is where Knight's rhetorically double-voiced text seeks to inscribe the reader in a singular and closed relationship to the multiple modes of discourse ('books, newspapers, and other periodical works') that are circulating about it. Knight's text is ideologically exhaustive in that it asks the reader to accept that the multiplicity of printed discourse is bonded by a national language. The text thus attempts to establish an image of the modern English language in print as a hegemonic image, or something that defines the boundaries of the community and specific conditions of belonging.

It is important to conclude this phase of the argument by stressing that the ideological dimension of biography is not simply a distortion to which we can restore a sense of 'balance' (say, substituting a more recent biography of Caxton for Knight's). Rather, biographies are ideological rhetoric, or productive discursive events which both respond and shape attitudes to the myriad forms of cultural language in which they are embedded.[18] Thus Knight's biography of Caxton is formally ideological in that as a textual event it produces a closed analysis which attempts to impose images of unity on the multiplicity of writing and the language.

It is relevant to link this ideological image of a national language to a broader set of contexts that are currently being interrogated in nineteenth-century cultural studies. One such context is Tony Crowley's recent work on the question of standard language in British cultural debate. In Crowley's account, during the 1830s and 1840s, a discourse emerged that generated a new discipline, 'the history of the language', which attempted to chart the development of certain standard or legitimate forms of English usage through time.[19] Crowley argues that a singular pressure urging the formation of this discipline was the working-class Chartist movement, which posed a significant threat to the British state in the 1830s and 1840s.[20] Crowley goes on to show how the assumptions that constructed this disciplinary terrain in turn had an important influence on the development of 'literature' as a discipline of study – taken to mean those printed texts that manifested those forms of writing which contributed to a sense of the 'history of the national language'.[21]

Bringing Knight's biography of Caxton into contact with the context established by Crowley's work on the discipline of the history of the language enables us to see two important cultural connections between Victorian biography, the emergence of disciplines and the ordering of cultural discourse. The first is that biographical writing was used by intellectuals for mediating the workings of disciplines that had been developed through influential cultural and political institutions. The second is that Victorian biographies attempted to instruct readers in conventions relating to the 'disciplined' appreciation of language.

I shall now go on to look in more detail at the work of two cultural theorists – Michel Foucault and Mikhail Bakhtin – who have attempted to map conceptual histories of European cultural discourse and to theorise the tensions between disciplines and contrary energies at work in language. It is particularly important to stress the role of these contrary energies. In the account of rhetorically double-voiced discourse which has been given above, biography was said to work for ideological closure. However, some uses of biography in the nineteenth century – particularly the writings of Thomas Carlyle –

were not premised on achieving this disciplinary effect, and were instead open to the contrary energies at work in language. The work of Bakhtin and Foucault on this question has important consequences for my account of the relationship between different styles of Victorian biography and their place in the emergence of the disciplines of 'literature' and 'history'. Both Bakhtin and Foucault have contributed forcefully to the debate about the position and function of 'literature' in the ordering of cultural discourse.

Foucault and Bakhtin: discourse in culture and disciplinary strategies

For both Foucault and Bakhtin, language is not an instrumental tool that expresses or reflects a culture; instead, it is actively constitutive of that culture. Discourse is both an act and an event. In addition, both conceive of discourse as a field of social and cultural struggle. In the discussion that follows, I shall deal first with Bakhtin, whose account of disciplinary forces in the discourses of early modern and modern European society is perhaps secondary to a much stronger interest in linguistic forces of transgression and resistance. Foucault, on the other hand, has elaborated a detailed system for theorising the strategies through which transgression and resistance are managed. Both theorists are concerned to establish a place for 'literariness' in their acts of discursive mapping. Bakhtin's sense of 'literariness' helps to explain the relation of Thomas Carlyle's biographical writing to the ordering of nineteenth-century cultural discourse by emphasising its transgressive potential. On the other hand, Foucault's construction of 'literariness' as a set of thresholds and limits helps us to frame the disciplinary counter-assertion against Carlyle which was produced by a later generation of Victorian biographer-intellectuals, such as John Morley.

Bakhtin on the centripetal disciplines of discourse: authority and transgression

Bakhtin's conceptual work often appears to be tidily schematic in the way that it generates oppositions to advance its arguments. The essay 'Epic and Novel' is a case in point. Epic is represented as a closed or 'monological' form of discourse in which action is complete and set apart at a distance in 'the absolute past', preserved exclusively by a 'national' tradition, and where language is coterminous with its subject matter.[22] On the other hand, the novel is an open or 'dialogical' form of discourse which, far from being bounded by tradition, is relentlessly innovatory, and which uses the full range of discourses in circulation to create its effects.

It has become something of a commonplace that the biographies of Thomas Carlyle, perhaps the best-known biographical practitioner and theorist of the earlier Victorian period, were epic in aspiration, proportion and design. Carlyle's epic biographies, most prominently *Oliver Cromwell's Letters and Speeches* and *Frederick the Great*, worshipped the forcefulness of a powerful central hero. Bakhtin provides us with another dimension to consider here, for if we accept his discursive definition of epic, then it would seem that Carlylean epic biography implies that closed form of rhetorical double-voicedness which was characteristic of Charles Knight's biography of Caxton and the ideological image of a homogeneous national language that it purveyed. Knight was certainly writing at the same time as Carlyle, so did their biographies share identical aspirations with respect to the ordering of cultural discourse?

In order to answer this question and to demonstrate Carlyle's difference from Knight, it is necessary to go into a more detailed analysis of Bakhtin's work on the history of discourse, and its relationship to early twentieth-century attempts to explain 'literariness'. For Bakhtin, the rhetorical genres like biography form against the backdrop of more complex linguistic and disciplinary developments, and this for Bakhtin is constituted by a continuous social conflict between centrifugal forces at work in language and centripetal forces which attempt to govern them. This broader cultural and historical canvas inevitably complicates any attempt to impose an idealist typology of values, functions and effects upon particular genres. The conflict between the centripetal and centrifugal forces in language is felt more acutely at some historical moments in the formation of a culture than others. For instance, it is non-existent in some contexts: Homeric Greek reflected the self-enclosed world-view of its speakers; it was 'monoglossic' in the sense that it did not have to compete with any other languages.[23] This places Bakhtin's view of 'epic' in an historical perspective. By contrast, by the time of the Renaissance, there were a whole range of competing languages in circulation – the Latin and Greek of official culture, but also the European vernaculars, which were themselves divided into 'high' and 'low' forms of discourse. For Bakhtin a writer like Rabelais brought these competing forms of language together into a carnivalesque form of prose writing.[24] At this stage, Bakhtin would claim that language is 'heteroglossic', and a writer like Rabelais a productive exploiter of the heteroglossia of French Renaissance culture.

The effects of heteroglossia, which is itself a centrifugal cultural phenomenon, have been historically checked by the opposing centripetal forces of cultural organisation. Thus in European cultures, the 'dead' languages of Latin and Greek came to assume an important 'policing' function. However, it was particular strains and tendencies within the classical tradition that came to assume this role; as Bakhtin has demonstrated, classical writing developed its own 'low' or carnivalesque strain.[25] Accordingly there came to the fore a number of policing disciplines within the classical tradition, one of which was the Aristotelian discipline of poetics. As Tony Crowley has suggested, Bakhtin singled out Aristotelian poetics as a key centripetal constraint attempting to discipline the contrary centrifugal energies of discourse.[26]

Successive versions of this discipline have been built upon Aristotle's insistence on the categoric separation between artistic discourse and rhetorical discourse. The Aristotelian conception of art in the *Poetics* is an attempt to autonomously categorise 'artistic' discourse and its internal, 'cathartic' effects. The *Rhetoric* is focused on a form of discourse which is taken to be systematically different in kind; rhetoric is delivered to a specific audience gathered for a specific purpose (legal, political), and the composition of the piece is calculated to have an effect on that audience.[27] The *Poetics* can be seen as a contribution to the formation of a regulatory discipline in which art was separated from rhetoric. In many ways, the early nineteenth-century moment that Raymond Williams identifies as an unprecedented break – the separation of rhetoric from criticism – can be seen as the effect of another reworking of this categoric distinction.

Bakhtin's initial project defined itself in relation to an early twentieth-century reworking of Aristotelian discipline, when Eastern European intellectuals started to try to systematically theorise 'literature'. In an essay on the relationship between Bakhtin, Russian Formalism and Marxism, Graham Pechey sets Bakhtin's early writing in a context organised primarily by 'the separation of poetics and rhetoric, with their strictly segregated fields of competence'.[28] For Pechey, Bakhtin's early writing can be seen in terms of a *dialogue* with the Russian Formalists.

The Russian Formalists effected their isolation of the literary, identified by a laying bare of the device, defamiliarisation and foregrounding, by attempting to forge a connection between rhetoric (devices of persuasion grounded in discourses of the ethical, political, legal and social) and poetics (the privileged discourse of art). According to Pechey's reading of Bakhtin, Bakhtin viewed the connection as inadequate because the Formalists had taken rhetoric into poetics on the latter's terms only. At one very obvious level, this meant that the Formalists had just taken the categories used for analysing poetry and applied them to prose. However, it also meant that rhetoric was subordinate to poetics in a hierarchy of functions and effects; the Aristotelian legacy in Formalism can be seen as another ordering of discourse in which the energy of rhetoric is regulated. It remains to be seen, however, how this latent Aristotelianism works as a centripetal disciplinary effect in discourse, and how Bakhtin provides a way of seeing which challenges it.

Pechey traces a crucial move in Bakhtin's early dialogue with Russian Formalism. In essays such as 'Discourse in life and discourse in poetry', Bakhtin/Volosinov inverts the relationship between poetics and rhetoric; whereas the former takes up the latter on its terms in Formalism, Bakhtin makes rhetoric embrace poetics under the terms set up by rhetoric. The fact that Bakhtin is involved in a dialogue with the Russian Formalists over this point is significant, both from the point of view of Bakhtin's intellectual practice, and with respect to the implications for poetics. As commentators on Bakhtin, like Michael Holquist, point out, Bakhtin's critical axioms can be seen to be formed out of a rhetorical dialogue with an opposed position.[29] The opposed position shapes Bakhtin's critical utterance, and Bakhtin's utterance, like all other utterances, is intertextually charged with *dialogism*. In its turn, the implications of dialogism confront poetics with the primacy of rhetoric, and challenge the centripetal tendencies – Aristotelian poetics can be seen as a centripetal discipline of discourse in the way that it generates a taxonomy which reifies the *criticism* of particular poets and texts[30] – in this Aristotelian discipline.

Bakhtin's work on this theme complicates any view that he appears to adopt with regard to tidy oppositions such as 'epic' and 'novel', 'monologic' and 'dialogic'. What appear to be static polarities are actually made complicated, first by Bakhtin's view of the historical battle between centrifugal and centripetal linguistic forces; and, second, by his insistence on the all-inclusive effects of dialogism – the rhetorical energy of all discourse – in culture. In fact Bakhtin's view that the cultural word itself is suffused with dialogism has led Graham Pechey to argue that 'there are no monological texts properly speaking, only monological readings', and his point is that our readings of texts – weavings of many cultural voices by definition – have been historically organised by centripetally inclined disciplinary systems whose function is to perpetuate a monological or disciplined reading frame.[31]

If there are no monological texts properly speaking then it remains the case that some texts are more truculently dialogical than others. In fact, Bakhtin's conceptual history of discourse provides us with ways of identifying those texts which have sought to dismantle the centripetal cultural drives embodied in disciplines at different moments in history. Bakhtin refers to these texts as 'novelistic', and as Katerina Clark and Michael Holquist have argued in their critical biography of Bakhtin, 'Bakhtin assigns the term "novel" to whatever form of expression within a given literary system reveals that system to be inadequate, imposed or arbitrary'.[32] I would broaden this formulation to argue that the term 'novel' might be assigned to an utterance displaying the characteristics of any given genre of writing that argues against the disciplinary system which defines those characteristics.

Bakhtin's argument with the Russian Formalists – during which he inverted and went beyond the conventional relationship between poetics and rhetoric in constructing the nature of 'literary' discourse – was formative in relation to his own theoretical practice. The position that it enabled Bakhtin to reach can help us in reassessing Thomas Carlyle's practice as an intellectual and biographer. This brings us back to Carlyle, and the reason that his biographical writing is different from the ideologically 'closed' biography of Caxton by Charles Knight. Carlyle's epic biographies can be seen as novelistic because they deploy a practice of writing that argues against the system which ostensibly grants the writing its conditions of existence. As a biographer, Carlyle writes life histories which foreground the primacy of the rhetorical or dialogical nature of the discourses from which biographies are written and through which they are read. In turn, they disrupt the authority of the very disciplinary protocols that, for Williams, established an ascendancy at the beginning of the nineteenth century.

Biography as novelistic discourse: Carlyle's
Life of John Sterling

We can see how this works if we look at an episode from Carlyle's *Life of John Sterling* (1851). This text usefully brings us back to the question of intellectuals and their use of biographical writing; as Ben Knights has demonstrated, the biography needs to be seen as part of an intense debate that was conducted in the 1840s and 1850s on the function of intellectuals in culture, and their influence on the formation of the next generation of intellectuals.[33] It also suggests the difficulty that we might face in trying to make Carlyle into a simple 'descendant' of Coleridge's on the matter of 'literature'; a lineage which, as we have seen, Eagleton constructs in *The Function of Criticism* (see Introduction).

Carlyle wrote his *Life of John Sterling* in response to a memoir of Sterling put together by J.C. Hare, an archdeacon of the Anglican Church – a biography which prefaced a set of collected writings authored by Sterling, so that Hare's biography of Sterling can be seen as an aid to interpretation aiming to align diverse readers in an authoritative relationship with a multiplicity of writings and contemporary concerns. Sterling had been a restless figure in the cultural and philosophical politics of the 1830s and 1840s, devoting himself at various times to the Anglican Church, Spanish liberation politics and the calling of 'literature'. The first and last of these commitments could be seen in the context of Coleridge's writings on a national 'clerisy', and accordingly, J.C. Hare's biography interpolates letters written by Sterling regarding Coleridge's intellectual ascendancy.[34] In these letters, Sterling uses poetic discourse to represent the sovereign power of Coleridgean philosophy – Coleridgean philosophical conversation is compared to the sea, its power to move being conveyed through the images of 'sparkling lights' and 'oceanic ebb and flow'.[35] The biographer inflects this poetic discourse in a special way; in Hare's biographical commentary Coleridge is represented as a unique centre of intellectual authority, and the alliance between poetics and philosophy works to advance a centripetal ideological effect.

Carlyle's prose asks the reader to interpret Coleridge differently:

> To sit as a passive bucket and be pumped into, whether you consent to or not, can in the long run be exhilarating to no creature; how eloquent

soever the flood of utterance that is descending. But if it be withal a confused unintelligible flood of utterance, threatening to submerge all known landmarks and thought and drown the world and you! — . . . . He began anywhere: you put some question to him, made some suggestive observation: instead of answering this, or decidedly setting out towards answer of it, he would accumulate formidable apparatus, logical swim-bladders, transcendental life-preservers and other precautionary and vehiculatory gear, for setting out.[36]

Carlyle builds upon the association between Coleridgean philosophical conversation and the poetic imagery of water, though Carlyle's rhetorically double-voiced prose positions the reader in a more diffuse and playful relationship to this association. In the first place, readers are asked to contemplate that, as the addressees of Coleridgean philosophical conversation, they might simply function as 'buckets' to be filled up; this extends the water imagery while radically transforming it. The image of the bloated and drowning addressee is set against the parodic representation of the 'life-saving' discursive equipment which 'rescues' Coleridge the speaker. Clearly, this parody undermines the authority of the connection between poetic language and philosophy effected in Hare's text. However, the formal manner in which it does this is important; Carlyle's 'list' of life-saving discursive equipment throws, first, a strange collage of vocabularies together, like philosophy ('transcendental') and biological science ('swim-bladders'), and, second, arranges them in the parodied style of the quack-inventor's advertising blurb. In other words, the authority of poetry and philosophy are undermined because their centripetal linguistic tendencies are not allowed to stand by themselves; instead they are opened up to the heteroglossia of other cultural discourses and their centrifugal effects.

Carlyle's novelistic discourse parodies and argues against Hare's biography of Sterling, and through that the orders of discourse that grant conditions of existence to Hare's writing and its manner of constructing Sterling's significance for the reader. It does not do this by producing a literary effect that preserves the positions of autonomy which Hare assumes for literature and philosophy; on the contrary, 'literary' or novelistic effects are created by a transgressive mingling of discourses which effects another transgressive insight: the exposure of the primacy of rhetorical energy, or discourse as an act. But what sort of transgression did this pose to the disciplinary order that Williams describes in *Marxism and Literature?* In order to understand this dimension of the politics of discourse, we need to turn to Michel Foucault's conceptual history of the ordering of discourse since the late eighteenth century, which stresses the role of regulating institutions.

Michel Foucault on the order of discourse

The constitutive energy of discourse is asserted by Foucault in an important essay which, in English translations, became attached to his thesis on discourse analysis, *The Archaeology of Knowledge*: '[discourse] prophesied the future, not merely announcing what was going to occur, but contributing to its actual event, carrying men along with it and thus weaving itself into the fabric of fate'.[37] This remark, taken from the essay variously translated into English as either 'The discourse on language' or 'The order of discourse', is insistent on the interrelationships between the dimension of 'language' and the dimension of 'events' – in fact, the remark is striving to dissolve these dimensions into one another through its metaphor of 'weaving'. It should be noted, however, that Foucault is writing in the past tense. The implication is that discourse was once perceived as being able to perform this weaving operation, but not at the moment when Foucault is addressing the topic. This is important, in the sense that 'The order of discourse' is simultaneously a piece of historical writing, and an attempt to make clear the unperceived institutional lines traversing the interwoven discursive and non-discursive order, which divide this order into zones. Foucault's point is that while our culture is still organised by the power and play of discourse as an act, it was the ancients who were more prepared to understand and fully engage with the power of rhetoric. In the ancient world, it was accepted that the fabric of an event was saturated with discourse. But why, as Foucault implies, have modern Western cultures tended to repress this insight?

This is where we come to Foucault's version of the history of discourse, and the role in time that institutions have played in distributing discourse and granting subjects access to its powers. It will necessitate looking at Foucault's work up to 1970 as an ongoing project investigating the techniques and practices supporting a *disciplined* society. Foucault's earliest writings, including *Madness and Civilisation*, *The Birth of the Clinic* and *The Order of Things* are organised around – although they do not necessarily explain – an historical juncture. According to Foucault, ways of conceptualising and dealing with human madness, sickness and the diseased body, and the whole representational structure of philosophy, enquiry and knowledge, underwent change in the late eighteenth century. This is a moment in time which is commonly identified as the beginnings of 'the modern period', an emergent epoch which is dramatically 'announced' by the French Revolution. Although Foucault's work displays a fascination with this historical moment, he did not see anything quite so unproblematically homogeneous as the spirit of the modern inherent in it. Foucault's work is constantly wary of such totalising judgements.

Foucault's work traces the emergence of new institutions and techniques for organising the non-discursive through new discursive formations: the historicist 'sciences of man', which provided new discourses for projecting 'man' as simultaneously the developing subject and object of the sciences of language, biology and labour (economics); and the discourse of mental illness, practised in and disseminated by the asylum; and the discourse of modern medicine, practised in the clinic. It is at this point that we should return to 'The order of discourse' in an attempt to explain the unfolding ideological consequences of this transformation. In this essay, Foucault draws attention to the repression of a rhetorical conception of discourse that has been performed by these new institutions of discourse production and distribution. Foucault's view of discourse is rhetorical and materialist – discourse is thus constitutive of the 'object' it beholds and thus socially and culturally constitutive. However, the philosophies and systems of thought that he is describing needed a measure of 'objectivity' to guarantee their authority or acceptability. To put it another way: man could be both subject and object of the sciences of man, but discourse itself could not comfortably be seen to be rhetorically implicated in, for instance, the production of the object constituted by the 'science of language'.[38] It might be said that what Foucault explores and describes in 'The order of discourse' are ideological strategies that attempt to resist the disruptive effects of discourse upon the supposedly empirical 'object'.

Foucault does not suppose that an ideological strategy – itself formed through discourse – can make discourse magically disappear. Rather, in 'The order of discourse' what Foucault describes are a set of compensatory technologies of limitation produced by institutions that monitor the delivery, distribution and reception of serious statements. These include 'disciplines' proper – frameworks for regulating the production of statements; commentaries – which claim to find depth and the hidden but 'not said' in statements; 'author functions' – a technique for limiting the proliferation and transformation of meaning by attaching statements to an author or source; and 'fellowships of discourse' – hierarchical communities of authoritative speakers and passive listeners, or hierarchical communities of authoritative writers and passive readers.[39]

The delineation of the functions of these technologies helps Foucault to pose a question which, according to his own assessment, became increasingly urgent to him: 'what is the threshold beyond which . . . a discourse begins to function in the field known as literature? . . . How is this discourse modified in its efforts by the fact that it is recognised as literary?' In asking questions about the movement of discourses across and between limits and thresholds, Foucault could be said to be framing a question about 'literariness' which examines the other side, so to speak, of Bakhtin's conception of novelistic discourse. Foucault gives us the means for analysing the way in which transgressive discourse is policed, domesticated and made into 'literature' – an object of study – by a complex set of disciplinary transactions worked out between the thresholds and limits set by cultural institutions and intellectuals.[40]

Broadly speaking, Foucault postulates an opposition between the classical period, when a rhetorical understanding of discourse and its effects pervaded European cultures, and the modern period when a range of disciplinary technologies were developed in an attempt to regulate the effects of the former understanding. Obviously, Foucault's broad generalisation does not account for details and complexities that have to be accounted for in any period- and culture-bound analysis. However, it is possible to see the English critic and intellectual John Morley appealing to these technologies when writing about Carlyle in the later part of the nineteenth century.

John Morley on Carlyle: the need for discipline

In 1870 when a new edition of Carlyle's works was published, John Morley wrote a review essay assessing the legacy of the ageing Carlyle's tenure in an important nineteenth-century cultural office – the office of 'man of letters'.[41] It appeared in the periodical *The*

Fortnightly Review. At this time *The Fortnightly* constituted a new departure in the history of the British periodical press, which was a vital Victorian cultural institution. As the title implied, *The Fortnightly* broke with the periodical conventions of the great quarterlies, *The Edinburgh Review* and *The Quarterly Review.* Politically it was radical and associated with the modernising drive of utilitarianism. Morley, a radical liberal, was its editor. Morley's essay views Carlyle's writings as archaic and inimical to modernity.

Morley was to become best known as the biographer of men of letters, so it is significant that in criticising Carlyle he should focus on *The Life of John Sterling,* and particularly the sketch of Coleridge that has already been discussed. Morley focuses on the point where Carlyle's rhetorically double-voiced prose imitates the accent of Coleridge in full Kantian flow, as he 'sung and snuffled into "om-m-ject" and "sum-m-ject" with solemn shake or quaver'.[42] What offends Morley here is stylistic parody not merely of Coleridge, but also the foundational subject/object dualism of Enlightenment philosophic and scientific enquiry which, as Foucault has argued, became central to the organisation of modern knowledge.[43] Morley is objecting to Carlyle's rejection of 'disciplined intelligence' and the sort of language that exemplifies 'the disciplined and candid exploration of intellectual problems', and in producing a commentary on the works of Carlyle, 'discipline' becomes an organising topic:

> Men who have long since moved away from the spiritual latitudes . . . can hardly help feeling as they turn over the pages of the now discarded pieces which they once used to ponder daily, that whatever later readers may have done in definitely shaping opinion, *in giving specific form to sentiment, and in subjecting impulse to rational discipline* [my italics], here was a friendly firebearer who first conveyed the Promethean spark, here the prophet who first smote the rock.[44]

Morley's commentary constructs a context in which to read Carlyle as a man of letters. Readers in the present read Carlyle against the backdrop of history. Momentarily, they can deny that history, and admire the words of the 'prophet'. Morley's reader should only have a sentimental relationship to this discourse, and ought to have moved away from 'spiritual latitudes', and this movement coincides with history which consigns theological discourse to the past. Later readers have given 'specific form to sentiment', and subjected 'impulse to rational discipline'. If this commentary thematises discipline, it also works through discipline, or to be more precise, those mechanisms identified by Foucault for regulating the distribution of discourse which I described above.

Morley's commentary seeks to enforce its judgement through an appeal to an author function; history may have intervened, other readings may have proliferated – but it is still possible to return to the origins of thought of this man of letters and recapture its primitive appeal. In turn, the invocation of author-function discourse places the commentary in a wider regime; it marks it out as part of an ongoing attempt to establish what Foucault described as a fellowship of discourse.

A fellowship of discourse is one 'whose function is to preserve or reproduce discourse, but in order that it should circulate within a closed community, according to strict regulations, without those in possession being dispossessed by this very distribution'.[45] A fellowship of discourse disciplines reading, and at this point, it is useful to compare the calculated effects of Morley's prose with that of Carlyle's in *The Life of John Sterling*; a fellowship of discourse marks out particular conditions, boundaries and limitations on the reading of texts, whereas Carlyle's heteroglot prose exposes the reader to a range of competing cultural languages and styles. It is at this point that we might consider who is being addressed, who the fellowship is bidding to inscribe in its reading community. This takes us back to the controversy over the formation of intellectuals that motivated Carlyle's biography of Sterling and its quarrel with J.C. Hare's earlier life of the same subject. For amongst the readers that Morley's essay addresses are young men studying at university, who are, according to Morley, worryingly 'Carlylite', or 'Mr Carlyle's disciples'.[46]

Morley's concern with Carlyle's impact on Cambridge under-graduates in the period bordering the last quarter of the nineteenth century has two levels to it. At one level, it was a concern with the sort of habits of language use and thought that a writer like Carlyle would inculcate in young intellectuals. This fed into a concern which resonated at a deeper level, for there was a pressing anxiety over the institutional and intellectual condition of the universities themselves. Morley's own pursuit of a varied career in journalism, publishing, writing, and ultimately party politics, was a direct consequence of his exclusion from an academic appointment. Morley had rejected orthodox religion, but in so doing he had also cut himself adrift from the Anglican Church which in the 1850s was still the central source of intellectual and organisational power in the universities. The place of the church in the universities displaced radical secularists from teaching positions, so inevitably it affected the intellectual organisation of these institutions. In the view of the group of intellectuals which the historian Christopher Harvie has called the university liberals, the curriculum of these central national institutions was outmoded and regressive. All of the later Victorian biographers in addition to Morley who will be dealt with – J.R. Seeley, Frederic Harrison, Leslie Stephen, John Nichol, James Cotter Morison – were a part of this formation and involved in university politics in the 1860s.[47]

Liberal-Comtean intellectuals and their programme

In a move which can be seen as part of a general attempt to reform and regenerate national institutions – including parliamentary democracy in the post-1867 era – the university liberals urged that there should be intellectual and structural reform of the universities. The connections between the proposals for university reform and democratic reform made by this intellectual formation comprised a political strategy: democratic reform should only be accompanied by a system of popular national education, and democracy itself should be managed by a rational, educated elite – another version of Coleridge's clerisy. Where would this elite be drawn from? From the universities, of course. The connection then was clear; democracy would be managed by an educated elite who would control the content of popular education; the universities would be the centre of culture from which the members of this elite would be drawn, so what was taught at university would have a direct bearing on the decisions made relating to popular national education, and ultimately popular national sentiment. This can be seen as an attempt to popularise elitism. But through which discourses and institutional supports was the elitism of a regenerated university culture to be popularised? This is where we can return to the question of intellectual 'discipline' as it manifests itself in Morley's essay on Carlyle; for this 'discipline' had an epistemological and institutional foundation.

In Morley's formulation of the way in which Carlyle's works should be read, 'discipline' is a development that supplements 'sentiment' and 'impulse'. There is a sense in which Morley's commentary represents, on a small scale, a positivist *telos*, with the original readers of Carlyle responding through primitive sentiment and impulse, and later readers responding in line with positivist rigour and intellectual discipline. The term 'positivist' needs to be clarified; Morley was not a positivist in the same way that Frederic Harrison was – that is to say, someone who followed the philosophical writings of Auguste Comte with an almost ritualistic sense of devotion. However, as Christopher Kent has argued, a more diffused, assimilated version of Comtean positivism was a strong current in English intellectual culture in the second half of the nineteenth century, and the universities played an important role in mediating it.[48]

Comtean positivism became a strong current because it elaborated a scientistic and historical theory of the relationship between intellectuals and the masses which could be built into existing English theories of the intelligentsia, most powerfully and influentially articulated by Coleridge through his idea of the clerisy.[49] A crucial vehicle used by the positivist intellectual for instructing the masses on the role of the clerisy or the 'savants' was the popular biography. Through a biography, an intellectual could represent exemplary lives lived by prominent figures in the past – principally men of letters and statesmen. However, in the rhetorically double-voiced discourse chosen to achieve this, the positivist intellectual could seek to establish a hegemonic relationship between this discourse and the masses. For the positivist intellectual this hegemony needed to be enduringly built around an inductive epistemology. That epistemology crucially rested on a conception of history and a theory of language (to be discussed fully in Chapter 3).

As an epistemology, Comtean positivism projected a model of knowledge in which humanity was progressively refining and perfecting its perception of the relationships between various phenomena. As the emphasis on progress suggests, the epistemology was historicist. According to this historicising epistemology, humanity would one day reach pure, inductive perception and understanding. In effect 'history' was the disciplinary guardian of the path to the final goal of humanity. As the university intellectual J.R. Seeley declared in 1863:

> It is the special work of the present age to give an historical or inductive basis, in other words a basis in fact, to moral science. And therefore in the present age *history*, considered as the possible basis of a science, begins to wear a new aspect and assume a new importance.[50]

Seeley is an important figure in relation to the present argument; he helped make the study of history into a university academic discipline. Seeley held the Regius Chair of History at Cambridge University from 1869 and was responsible for founding the History School; he delivered a number of programmatic statements on the scientific and intellectual authority commanded by history. In Seeley's view, history would be the foundational training ('an inductive basis') for those who would join the ranks of the educated elite to manage both the modern democratic state and popular education. In addition Seeley recognised that the popular reading public needed to be prepared and receptive to the authority of this knowledge; it was in this context that he recognised the value of writing and popularising the lives of statesmen through biography. As I will argue in Chapter 4, the biographical writing that Seeley produced to popularise the discipline of history was important because it assimilated the inductive, referential theory of language on which Comtean positivism was built.

To conclude with Seeley's insistence on the relationship between the discipline of history and referential language is to find a useful point of return to Raymond Williams's contention about the orders of discourse that were settled in the first decades of the nineteenth century. Many of the terms that Williams used to describe the functions of language that were organised by the rhetorical compositional discipline as opposed to the literary critical, readerly discipline, can be found in Seeley's strictures on the language of history, which was 'practical', 'external' and non-representational. I suggested at the opening of this chapter that in advancing this point, Williams identified the authoritative discourse through which history came to claim to possess knowledge about the past. The point at issue relates to when this authority was established and recognised in English cultural politics; for as we will see when we come to discuss Seeley, Seeley had to labour the point in ways that suggest that this ordering of discourse had not been settled beyond question for a lengthy period, as Williams's account suggests. I shall argue two points: first, Seeley's theory of the language of history was constructed against a spectre of 'literary' language, so Seeley's theory of the authoritative language of history can be read as a centripetal drive to discipline the contrary energies at work in language; and, second, the identification of 'literariness' as rhetorical and dangerous had implications for the complex process of institutionalising 'literature' as a form of study. In order to provide a context for both of these arguments, it will be necessary to consider first the rhetorically transgressive biographical writings of Thomas Carlyle.

2

□

Re-reading the rhetorical hero in Carlylean biography

The portable Carlyle

Thomas Carlyle's writings are being reappraised again, this time by scholars working on the emergence of the historical profession in nineteenth-century Britain. Their studies have tended to place Carlyle in a narrative in which he figures as a residual man of letters who produced 'artistic' historiography which came to be denigrated by a later generation of 'scientific' professionals. This is an undeniable context for Carlyle's writings, and one which will inform this chapter, which includes an analysis of Carlyle's historical biography, *Oliver Cromwell's Letters and Speeches*. An exclusive consideration of the 'art'/'science' debate in nineteenth-century historiography disregards another context, pointed to by Geoffrey Hartman. In his book *Criticism in the Wilderness*, Hartman (1980) suggests that Carlyle's *Sartor Resartus* 'is a genuine precursor of the philosophical critics [Benjamin, Bloom, Foucault, Derrida] of today'. For Hartman, there is an air of philosophical terrorism about Carlyle's rhetoric which makes its 'artfulness' difficult to assimilate to the nineteenth-century English literary criticism of 'belles lettres', a tradition in which Terry Eagleton was content to place Carlyle in his book *The Function of Criticism* (see Introduction).[1] This chapter will provide grounds for arguing that Carlyle's writings were complex and oppositional rhetorical acts in relation to the emergence of both 'literature' and 'history' as disciplines.

Carlyle was only assimilated to the twentieth-century version of literary studies when a branch of the latter was about to mutate into cultural studies; Carlyle was an important figure in Raymond Williams's *Culture and Society*, published in 1958. *Culture and Society* was an attempt to reappropriate a tradition from its conservative custodians, and to reorder the relationships between a series of canonical texts by the insertion of texts such as Carlyle's, which had been excluded by the tradition constructed by T.S. Eliot and F.R. Leavis. The controversial nature of Carlyle's inclusion was made clear in 1979, when Williams's interviewers for the *Politics and Letters* project challenged him to justify the space devoted to Carlyle in the broadly leftist *Culture and Society*. As an enemy of democracy, an authoritarian who advocated vicious political repression in the colonies, honoured both by Bismarck's Germany and the Germany of the National Socialists, Carlyle hardly seemed to fit. In response Williams recalled an earlier point in his intellectual career – the 1930s – when Carlyle's writings were speaking through a grim context: 'I too wrote my essay on Carlyle as a fascist when I was an undergraduate'.[2] Williams's point is that by 1958, Carlyle's writings were speaking through a different context again. What energies in Carlyle's writing engender this potential for mobility between widely divergent contexts, and how do we assess their significance in relation both to Carlyle's biographical writing, and the emergence of late nineteenth-century intellectual disciplinarity?

In order to answer these questions, I shall draw upon the work of Bakhtin. As I argued in the last chapter, the theoretical work of Bakhtin can be used to challenge the restrictive polarities that in Raymond Williams's account organised intellectual practices into distinctive disciplines in the early part of the nineteenth century – that is to say the opposition between writing/rhetoric ('externality'), which was mobilised to enclose the materials of 'history'; and reading/criticism ('internality'), which was mobilised to enclose the materials of 'literature'. Bakhtin argues that all discourse is rhetorical and calculates its effects in relation to the systems and conventions in which it has been produced and through which it will be read. Certain kinds of texts calculate their relationship to these systems and conventions in a subversive, or for Bakhtin, 'novelistic' manner. I shall argue that Carlyle's biographies are manifestly rhetorical, and generate critical images of the systems that produce them and permit them to be read. I shall also argue that, as a consequence of this, Carlyle's writings were unusually open to new contexts and readings.

I shall take as my starting point some of the early work on discourse by Bakhtin/Volosinov, and use it to read one of Carlyle's texts, *On Heroes and Hero-Worship and the Heroic in History.* This text theorised the function of a topical nineteenth-century cultural role, a role which was encountered at the end of the last chapter through looking at John Morley's assessment of Carlyle's performance in the office – the man of letters.

Discursive heroes

Carlyle theorised the role of the hero in history in *On Heroes and Hero-Worship.* It is possible to elaborate on the concept of the hero in two ways; the first is familiar, the second not so familiar. First, the hero can be analysed as the ideologically central component in the content of a quasi-mythical authoritarian politics. Second, the concept can be elaborated formally in rhetorical terms; here one can appeal to the early work on discourse by Bakhtin/Volosinov, particularly their early paper 'Discourse in life and discourse in poetry'.

In this paper, the framework of the early Bakhtin/Volosinov theory of discourse becomes apparent. For Bakhtin/Volosinov, a discursive event, or an utterance, is a complex process. It consists of three participants; a sender, a listener (the two parties to the communicative act), and the hero, this being the configuration of signs, or the topic of the utterance, which passes between the sender and the listener. The interactive and situated dimensions of this model are important; it relates discourse to its participants (its users), and its context of enunciation, either real or imagined.[3] The fact that the topic component of the utterance is described as *a hero* is very significant. For Bakhtin and Volosinov, the topic of an utterance is very like the signs that comprise a character in a narrative discourse, separate from its author, and orientated towards its listener – hence the topic as a hero. This formal, rhetorical sense of the hero is present in *On Heroes and Hero-Worship.*

On Heroes displays a remarkably reflexive strain on the technology of writing. Carlyle's heroes, even the earliest heroes with whom he is concerned, are all related to writing as a system of communication and dispersal. Thus, while we are introduced to Odin of Nordic legend through his identity as a speaking subject – 'This Odin, in his rude, semi-articulate way, had a word to speak' – Odin's speech is only effective once it has been encoded in a system of inscriptions, or runes, 'the greatest invention man has ever made, this of marking down the unseen thought that is in him by written characters'.[4] The hero is never simply a unitary individual; the hero is also an utterance, inscribed through writing, directed at complex conditions of reception and further use.

These conditions for the reception and further appropriation of heroic discourse are interrogated in the chapter on 'The hero as man of letters', which considers Samuel Johnson, Rousseau and Robert Burns. John Morley's late nineteenth-century assessment of Carlyle's performance as a man of letters has already been considered, but it is now possible to see how Morley formulated his essay as a response to Carlyle's discourse; whereas 'discipline' was the main topic of Morley's essay on Carlyle, the mobility of rhetoric is a central theme in Carlyle's theory of the man of letters:

> Certainly the Art of Writing is the most miraculous of all things man has devised. Odin's *Runes* were the first forms of the work of a Hero; *Books*, written words, are still miraculous *Runes* of the latest form! In Books lies the *Soul* of the whole Past Time; the articulate audible voice of the Past, when the body and material substance of it has altogether vanished like a dream . . . .
>
> Do not Books accomplish the *miracles*, as *Runes* were fabled to do? They persuade men. Not the wretchedest circulating library novel, which foolish girls thumb and con in remote villages, but will help to regulate the actual practical weddings and households of those foolish girls. So 'Celia' felt, so 'Clifford' acted: the foolish Theorem of Life, stamped into those young brains, comes out as a solid Practice one day . . . . What built St Paul's Cathedral? Look at the heart of the matter, it was that divine HEBREW BOOK,—! . . . With the art of Writing, of which Printing is a simple, an inevitable and comparatively insignificant corollary, the true reign of miracles for mankind commenced. It related, with a wonderous new contiguity and perpetual closeness, the Past and Distant with the Present in time and place; all times, all places with our actual Here and Now.[5]

Starting with Odin's runes, Carlyle's discourse spreads wide in a sweeping analogical movement. The hero becomes writing, but by analogy, the written message of the hero has transmuted into the expanding book culture of nineteenth-century Britain; the book functions as a hero in Bakhtin's rhetorical sense: 'Books persuade men'. Carlyle appropriates the language of religious miracles (a way of explaining astounding presence and agency) to account for what may be seen as intertextuality, or the weaving of the language of novels into the practices of everyday life. To be sure, the Carlylean critical attitude is conventionally contemptuous of domestic fiction, and patronisingly anxious about its effect on 'foolish girls' who, according to gendered ideology, feel rather than act. However, writing, rhetoric, reading and criticism are run together in a complex cultural intertext, rather than being separated out. Carlyle's analogical discourse is thus different in its discriminative practices, for it posits a connection between the effects of books in the practices of the everyday domestic sphere, and the concrete effects of the biblical text as manifested in massive architectural edifices such as St Paul's Cathedral. Finally, the heroic as text is related to the reader's historical understanding, where the present ('the Here and Now') becomes the site of convergence for a wide range of experiences of otherness. This dramatisation of a complex cultural intertext acknowledges the necessity of broadening an understanding of, first, history itself and, second, the place of diverse forms of representation and cultural practice in the formation of historical understanding. 'The hero as man of letters' might be exemplified in the individual lives of Johnson, Rousseau and Burns; but the lives of these individuals have been inscribed in writing and as discursive heroes they are entangled in the turbulent and uncertain transactions of a print culture that Carlyle's discourse attempts to dramatise.

One way in which Samuel Johnson's life became heroically inscribed was through a biography; Johnson's biography preoccupied Carlyle, as did the theory and practice of the genre's conventions. By recasting Carlyle's idea of the hero through Bakhtin/Volosinov's sense of the hero as a component in a rhetorical transaction, we are enabled, first, to refine our understanding of the implicit contract underwriting rhetorically double-voiced biography; and, second, to get a clearer sense of Carlyle's subversive inflection of the convention. All biographies are transactions founded on an implicit contract: the biographer is the sender; the biographee is the hero; a particular listener is inscribed in the hero, which in turn is inscribed with the evaluation of the sender. However, in Carlyle's biographical writing, these contractual elements are made rhetorically explicit and subject to interrogation.

The transgressive turn in Carlylean biographical writing

Carlyle's 'Count Cagliostro: Two flights' which appeared in *Fraser's Magazine* in 1833 is a good example of a biography in which the underlying contractual conventions are made both rhetorically explicit and problematic; it contrasts with Carlyle's early biographical writings, such as his life of the dramatist and aesthetician Schiller, where the rhetorical conventions are left implicit.[6] In taking on the quack alchemist Count Cagliostro as a subject, Carlyle was writing about a figure of popular curiosity who had been the subject of other biographies as a result of his exploits throughout Europe in the last decades of the eighteenth century. Cagliostro had risen from humble Sicilian origins to trans-European aristocratic grandeur; Carlyle's biography interprets the significance of this life history as though it were a mock-heroic allegory of the decay of European civilisation that culminated in the French Revolution. 'Count Cagliostro' is a sort of parody of the exemplar mode of biography. However, the mock-heroic is not the principal indicator of the transgressive turn taken by Carlyle's biography.

To begin with, the narrator of Carlyle's 'Cagliostro' explicitly enters into a dialogue with the previous biographical writings on Cagliostro. The narrator's voice is not alone in the textual frame, so it is difficult to cling on to it as a transparent authority. This becomes clear when we hear the voice of Sauerteig, a strained, theorising voice distinct from that of the narrator and the biographical hero, which grants the narrator the right to use a particular kind of discourse in telling Cagliostro's life: 'Pasquils, mere ribald libels on humanity; these too . . . are at times worth reading'; the narrator acts on the advice of this voice, preparing to write a pasquil, 'in plain words'.[7] A pasquil is a lampoon posted up in a public place; so at once, the vocabulary of the piece puts us in touch with the rhetorical public-square origins of European biography traced by Bakhtin in his account of the emergence of rhetorically double-voiced prose.[8]

In 'Cagliostro', the rhetorically double-voiced convention is dismantled: the hero, narrator, and metacommentary are different narrative components in the biography, in dialogue with one another. One subject of their conversation is the purpose of reading about a life, especially the act of reading such ludicrous 'low-life' stories as Cagliostro's. This is reflected upon in the representation of Cagliostro

– here 'Beppo' in his early life, a novice in a monastery – as one required to read improving literature to the elders over their food:

> While the monks sit at meat, the impetuous voracious Beppo is set not to eat with them, not to pick up the crumbs that fall from them, but to stand 'reading the Martyrology' for their pastime! The brave adjusts himself to the inevitable – Beppo reads the dullest Martyrology of theirs; but reads out of it not what is printed there, but what his own vivid brain on the spur of the moment devises; – instead of the names of the Saints, all heartily indifferent to him, he reads out the names of the most notable Palermo 'unfortunate-females', now beginning to interest him a little.[9]

If a Martyrology cannot control the act of reading, what might more openly transgressive texts enable? Carlyle's 'Cagliostro' is not only about transgression, it is transgressive. It can be seen as 'novelistic' in the anti-systematic sense which Bakhtin came to assign to forms of writing which argue with the limits set by systems of writing and the sort of reading they permit. In what follows, I will argue that there are connections between the Carlylean construction of writing as a heroic rhetorical utterance turned loose on the world, the Carlylean disruption of conventions for writing biography, and the broader carnivalisation of disciplines for organising writings about the human sciences. I shall examine *Sartor Resartus* in this context.

Sartor Resartus: biography in a novelistic mode

Opposing the sciences of modern 'man'

Sartor Resartus appeared in *Fraser's Magazine* between November 1833 and August 1834.[10] Ostensibly it is an attempt to translate and explain a bizarre system of philosophy by constructing a biography of the system's author, Professor Diogenes Teufelsdröckh – the attempt being juggled by an often bewildered mediating Editor. To what does Teufelsdröckh's system contribute? The Editor starts to write *Sartor Resartus* in the manner of a dissertation which triumphantly presents the advanced state of civilisation manifest in the progressive development of the natural and human sciences that characterise modernity: 'Man's whole life and environment have been laid open and elucidated; scarcely a fragment or fibre of his Soul, Body, and Possessions, but has been probed, dissected, distilled, desiccated, and scientifically decomposed' (*SR*, p. 2). The narrator introduces the reader to a view of early nineteenth-century intellectual culture which corresponds to the view of the period and its ruling episteme put forward by Michel Foucault: man is at once the subject observing the natural world, and the object of his own empirically grounded scientific philosophy. Teufelsdröckh's system constructs the philosophy of an apparently quaint and marginal aspect of human culture – clothing – so that the reader is posed with an immediate problem: how does a philosophy of clothing relate to the progress of civilisation, and how seriously is this supposed to be taken?

According to the Editor, 'man' needs to take this very seriously indeed: the absence of a clothes philosophy, 'the grand Tissue of all Tissues', prevents 'man' from evolving a totalising philosophy of himself:

> In all [previous] speculations [philosophers] have tacitly figured man as a *Clothed Animal*; whereas he is by nature a *Naked Animal*; and only in certain circumstances, by purpose and device, masks himself in Clothes. Shakespeare says, we are creatures that look before and after: the more surprising that we do not look round a little, and see what is passing under our very eyes. (*SR*, pp. 2–3)

In failing to look at clothes as contrivances or cultural devices, thinkers let something fundamental pass beneath their eyes. The philosophy of clothes picks at what Foucault has called the 'positive unconscious' of a system of thought, or that which a given system of discourses renders unthinkable for the subjects who habitually use the system.[11] So how does the clothes philosophy expose the positive unconscious of early nineteenth-century intellectual discourse to view? Like the obscure German professor who constructs the system, the clothes philosophy 'manifests a certain feeling of the Ludicrous' (*SR*, p. 38); in other words, the 'serious' philosophy of clothes will not complement the new human sciences; on the contrary it will wryly undo them from within. In this section, I will argue that *Sartor Resartus* undoes the sciences of man in the manner of a novelistic text as celebrated by Bakhtin. In *Sartor*, clothing and language become metaphorically interchangeable, so that the text can be seen to oppose an ordering of discourses in which language is no longer held to be rhetorical and a culturally constitutive energy – the positive unconscious of the early nineteenth-century ordering of discourse. Carlyle's ludicrous text is built upon a deconstruction of biographical conventions, and *Sartor* enters into a playful dialogue with the most authoritative English biographical text of the period – James Boswell's *Life of Johnson.* To begin with, it will help to situate Carlyle's *Sartor* in relation to two early nineteenth-century oppositional forces: one a counter-modern cultural institution; the other a progressively avant-garde intellectual formation – progressive but critical of the centralising disciplinary drives of modern civilisation.

As we have seen, Carlyle published both 'Cagliostro' and *Sartor Resartus* in *Fraser's Magazine. Fraser's Magazine* was a very different institution to *The Edinburgh Review*, the quarterly for which Carlyle had first been a contributor. *Fraser's* Tory politics and economics opposed the Whig politics and economics of *The Edinburgh* and the radical modernising drive of the Benthamite *Westminster Review*; in this sense, *Fraser's* could be described as defiantly counter-modern.[12] There was also a difference in organisational style. *Fraser's* projected itself as a publication managed by the fictional 'Oliver Yorke', who represented an editorial collective – this stood in contrast to the rather patrician editorial authority exercised by Francis Jeffrey at *The Edinburgh*. The kind of writing that appeared in *Fraser's* was different as well. The periodical devoted a lot of space, especially in its dealings with and commentaries upon the literati, to satire and parody; consequently, the formal presentation of much of the writing characteristically issued a challenge to the reader, sitting as it did on the precarious line between the 'real' and playful invention.[13] *Fraser's Magazine* was thus a conservative intellectual forum which supported playful and fragmentary writing.

Fragmentary and playful writing represented the common ground between this conservative formation and the more progressive, avant-garde formation upon which Carlyle's writings drew. These were the writings of a group known as the German Romantic ironists, which included Jean-Paul Richter, Schlegel and Novalis. Carlyle had acted as mediator on behalf of this group of writers and aesthetic theoreticians, who developed a body of philosophical, aesthetic and communication theory. Carlyle was amongst those who worked to introduce the writings of this group to a non-German-reading British public, writing reviews and commentaries on their work for the quarterlies and other periodicals.[14] René Wellek may well be right in arguing that Carlyle did not serve the cause of Anglo-German scholarship very accurately in performing this task.[15] However, it should be stressed that the Romantic ironists mobilised their discourses in a way that invited the transgression of scholarly boundaries.

As Kathleen M. Wheeler has argued, the Romantic ironists developed an aesthetic which challenged the classical principles of unity, decorum and authority; principles which had been common to classical theories of art.[16] For the Romantic ironists, the principle of unity had to be challenged by the montage effect of fragmentation; the work of art could no longer be seen as art merely because of its decorous adherence to the authority of convention; its artfulness emerged from the process by which it assembled itself from fragments drawn from different cultural centres, fragments which were not linked by any self-evident framework of authority. Two further challenges followed from this. First, assumptions about individual authorship and originality were challenged by the juxtaposition of fragments – in this situation, multiple authorship might be a truer expression of the nature of composition, in that authorship is shown to involve not merely the individual but previous texts, as well as contemporary writers as co-authors. Second, the reader was challenged by this fragmentary mode of assembly, in that the fragment was designed to leave room for the imagination of the reader to act. The reader had to work as a fellow labourer on the text and become a co-author, so that composition and reading were theoretically inseparable.[17]

The Romantic ironists were drawn to a new genre of writing which in their view was ideally suited to framing such challenging techniques of artistic composition. This was the novel, and their interest in the novel as a writing practice rather than a genre allows us to bring Bakhtin back into the argument. Their critical statements on this subject, as with Friedrich Schlegel's epistolary 'Letter about the novel' (1800), often draw on 'novelistic' (or new, non-canonical) forms of writing which had utilised non-artistic forms of discourse for the construction of dramatic narrative. Such a genre, in Schlegel's view, would be properly anti-generic: 'I detest the novel as far as it wants to be a separate genre'; and any theory of the novel could not be conveyed through Aristotelian categorical classicism, rather it would have to be immanent in novelness itself: 'A theory of the novel would have to be itself a novel'.[18] Jean-Paul Richter theorised the non-didactic function of the novel in a language that was itself 'novelistic':

Certainly . . . the novel should [teach], but only as a blossoming flower which through its opening and closing, and even through its fragrance announces the weather and the time of day. Its tender stem will never be cut, carpentered and confined to the wooden teacher's desk or preacher's pulpit; the wooden frame and the person standing therein do not replace the living breath of spring. And what does it mean to give lessons? Simply to give signs. But the whole world and all time are full of signs already. Yet these letters are not read; we need a dictionary and a grammar of signs.[19]

Here we might make a productive comparison with Bakhtin. For it was Bakhtin who remarked that

the birth and development of the novel takes place in the full light of the historical day . . . studying other genres is analogous to studying dead languages; studying the novel, on the other hand is like studying languages that are not only alive, but still young.[20]

Bakhtin's view of the novel finds itself on common ground with Richter's view. Bakhtin, like Richter, stresses how the novel is a form in perpetual emergence. Bakhtin opposes the study of the living novel to the study of dead languages, and this echoes Richter's striking organic metaphor of the novel as a 'tradition' ('stem') which cannot be made into a rigid system of pedagogy. Bakhtin's theory of the novel stresses how it is the genre that is most open to transformation by non-artistic discourse, and for Richter the novel acts as a grammar for *writing* and organising the *reading* of those signs. Whereas Richter's statement is organised around an anti-disciplinary metaphor, Bakhtin theorised an anti-disciplinary practice which casts light on the energies of *Sartor Resartus*.

In theorising the novel as the anti-generic avant-garde of writing, the Romantic ironists made the aesthetic the *raison d'être* of its linguistic and formal diversity. As was argued in the last chapter, for Bakhtin the aesthetic itself as an autonomous category is open to challenge by the linguistic and formal diversity of 'novelness'. And if the autonomy of 'art' is so challenged, then as a consequence the ordering of cultural discourse in which such a construction of art is maintained is challenged as well. *Sartor Resartus* can be viewed as effecting a challenge of the sort theorised by Bakhtin. In a letter to the Editor of *Sartor* – one of the many narrative delays and diversions interrupting the explication of Teufelsdröckh's clothes philosophy – a certain Hofrath Heuschrecke, an acquaintance of Teufelsdröckh and one of several voices present in the text, offers the following advice. In his letter, Heuschrecke represents the autobiographical fragments that he has collected on Teufelsdröckh as a key to the problem of his clothes philosophy, for this philosophy will not be understood 'till a Biography of him has been philosophico-poetically written, and philosophico-poetically read' (*SR*, p. 59). Heuschrecke's advice re-establishes the relationship between writing and reading, and forcefully reinstates marginalised rhetoric in the practice of criticism. Carlyle employs many of the strategies of the German Romantic ironists – fragmentariness, the questioning of authorship, involving the reader as co-author – but their effect is to challenge the ordering of early nineteenth-century disciplines described by Raymond Williams in *Marxism and Literature* and discussed in the previous chapter.

Heuschrecke's letter to the Editor also raises the question of biography as an authoritative genre of writing. The letter reaches the Editor at the point when he is confronted by Teufelsdröckh's complex and chaotic philosophical treatise, and a packet of his autobiographical fragments – the fragments having been sent from Germany by Heuschrecke. Before the Editor has received Heuschrecke's letter on the topic of biography, the Editor has already remarked that Heuschrecke seems to stand in relation to Teufelsdröckh as James Boswell stood to Samuel Johnson (*SR*, p. 20). Heuschrecke thus seems well placed to convey the truth about Teufelsdröckh's biography and thus his philosophy, because the name of James Boswell had become a byword for biographical authority, and biographical authority was a keenly debated topic in the early 1830s when *Sartor* first appeared in *Fraser's*. In the following section, I shall discuss the way in which Boswell's *Johnson* constructed biographical authority, and the way in which this authority was invoked in order to fashion relations of hegemony around the idea of the English nation. I shall then go on to discuss how *Sartor* refashions this construction.

Sartor Resartus *and Boswell's* Life of Johnson:
intertextual refashioning

Boswell's *Life of Johnson* was published in 1791 amidst a climate of anxiety brought about by the collapse of traditional political authority in France. There was intense renewed interest in the biography in the early 1830s – yet another moment of anxiety and expectation triggered by a new revolution in France (1830), which intensified reformist militancy in Britain. The new edition of *Life of Johnson* was edited and produced by John Wilson Croker, and Croker justified the new edition on the grounds that such an authoritative biography needed to be presented in a scrupulously edited, authoritative text. Because Croker was a prominent reviewer for the Tory periodical *The Quarterly Review* – and because Johnson had very strong Tory sympathies – Croker's edition of *Life of Johnson* became a keenly debated cultural event in the pages of the reviews.[21] Carlyle reviewed the edition over two issues of *Fraser's Magazine* in the April and May of 1831; but the attention that Carlyle gave to the text and the question of its authority extended beyond reviewing.

Boswell's *Life of Johnson* was an account of the life of the critic, moralist and poet Samuel Johnson, but also a record of the relationship between Johnson and Boswell. The first quarter of the narrative (from Johnson's birth in 1709 to 1763) is put together by Boswell from documents, reminiscences and readings of Johnson's own writings – both public (essays and criticism) and private (including letters and his journal). The biography changes in scope and textual organisation upon the occasion of Boswell's first meeting with Johnson; up to 1763, Boswell is not personally involved in Johnson's life. The three-quarters of the narrative that covers 1763 to 1784 (the year of Johnson's death) is organised around a series of episodes which many readers of the life remember most vividly; it comprises a series of dialogues in which Johnson engages in conversation with a variety of characters. Clearly, this form of textual organisation resembles Plato's Socratic dialogues – the arrangement of speaking parts very often makes the text read like the *Symposium* – and as such it could be said to be derived from a genre which Bakhtin has argued was a foundation upon which the subsequent history of the novel has been constructed.[22] In other words, *Life of Johnson* was characterised by heterogeneous forms of narration and dramatic dialogue.

Boswell orchestrates this heterogeneity into a unified narrative, but it takes two Boswells to do this and to prevent the text from disintegrating. One Boswell organises the outer frame, stitching the materials representing the 'life' together; the other Boswell is a character in the narrative who runs around after Johnson compiling an astonishingly detailed and energetic record of his conversations – and thereby his opinions. The Boswell of the outer frame is aware of the problems involved in representing Johnson's speech: 'His mode of speaking was very impressive; and I wish it could be preserved as musick is written'.[23] However, the Boswell character of the narrative is the guarantor of the authority of the rhetorically double-voiced act of the Boswell who mediates Johnson's opinions.

The way in which these two functions reinforce each other to create an authoritative effect is clear from an episode in which Johnson and Boswell visit the home and workplace of Strahan the printer. The episode begins with Johnson, Strahan and Boswell discussing the problem of opportunity and outlets for talent in eighteenth-century London; this gives way to Johnson's enquiry after a boy from the country whom he has recommended Strahan take on as an apprentice. Johnson gives the boy a guinea, and exhorts him to persevere and work hard at learning his trade. The discourse is socially resonant – Johnson's own lowly origin and subsequent rise to eminence are of significance here – and it prefigures the Smilesean movement in biographical writing whereby the great act as exemplars for the poor and lowly to follow; Johnson was to become a popular subject of 'improving' biography in the nineteenth century.[24] But the social significance of the event is authoritatively focused for the reader by the multiple functions of Boswell:

> I followed him into the court-yard, behind Mr. Strahan's yard; and there I had proof of what I had heard him profess, that he talked alike to all. 'Some people (said he), tell you that they let themselves down to the capacity of their hearers. I never do that. I speak uniformly, in as intelligible manner as I can.'[25]

The two Boswells are at work here: the Boswell who is a character in the narrative, following Johnson, recording his voice; and the Boswell who coheres the outer frame of the text, mediating Johnson's view of his own speech – we should note that Johnson is clearly marked in the text as a speaking subject. Together, they create the conditions for legitimating, through the effect of concrete, empirical observation, Johnson's view of his own speech – that he talks in the same way to all people. Sequentially, this prepares the reader for the episode with the apprentice boy. But Boswell's rhetorically double-voiced prose has more profound implications for the reader. If we think of rhetorical double-voicedness as an ideological discursive event – that is to say, an act in writing which seeks to organise and resolve the reader's relationship to key questions of value and belonging – then the view of Johnson's speech which is mediated by Boswell is subtly hegemonic in aim. This becomes more apparent if it is thought through in terms of Bakhtin/Volosinov's theory of communicative activity: Boswell as a textual function sends Johnson, the hero of both the biography and the communicative act, to an assumed addressee. The addressee is assumed and positioned in a particular way by means of the values that are inscribed in the hero. Those values ask the reader to accept that Johnson's speech is speech that transcends class. The corollory of this is that readers should be able to reach a consensus based around Johnson's voiced opinions. Whether or not this consensus can be achieved is of course a different question; Boswell records that the spectacle of Johnson conversing with the apprentice boy gives rise to 'ludicrous emotions' – a complex response which resists crude or simple summary, and suggests that the text glimpses the difficulty of enforcing a monologic significance on the meaning of the episode. However, a monologic settlement is desired by the text at crucial framing moments – as when, in the 'Advertisement to the second edition' (1793), Boswell uses the language of nationhood in claiming to have '*Johnsonised* the land'. The language of nationhood which is embedded in this claim of pedagogic success is given a more urgent ring by references to the revolution in France, and its '*Philosophy* . . . employed against the peace, good order, and happiness of society'.[26] *Life of Johnson* at least makes the assumption that it authoritatively addresses a common community sharing the same empirical frame of reference and social prejudice that constitute Englishness. Such values and prejudices were contested by *Sartor Resartus*.

Sartor Resartus is subtitled *The life and opinions of Herr Teufelsdröckh* and would seem to promise a biography following in the tradition of *Life of Johnson*. But Teufelsdröckh is a resistant biographee: 'from the archives and memories of the best-informed classes, no biography of Teufelsdröckh was to be gathered . . . besides, in his sly way, he had ever some quaint turn, not without its satirical edge, wherewith to divert such intrusions' (*SR*, p. 12). Accordingly, Heuschrecke soon proves to be a false Boswell; the Editor, after quoting Heuschrecke's letter on biography, reports a suspicion that this Boswell has purloined the language of Teufelsdröckh without acknowledgement (*SR*, p. 60). However, Heuschrecke is conspicuously not a false prophet; his imperative on the need henceforth to write and read biography 'philosophico-poetically' invites us to read *Sartor* as a deconstructive interrogation of Boswellian biographical conventions.

Sartor signals this by wrenching apart the frames which the various Boswellian functions contrive to make coherent. The boundaries of rhetorically double-voiced discourse are fluid and unstable in *Sartor*. Attention is drawn to the functional nature of the organiser of the outer frame; the Editor declares that 'Who or what such Editor may be, must remain conjectural, and even insignificant: it is a voice publishing tidings of the Philosophy of Clothes' (*SR*, p. 9). The 'voice' of the Editor is publishing, or reproducing in text, 'tidings of the Philosophy of Clothes' – it does not lament the passing of the real presence of Teufelsdröckh's voice in the way that Boswell laments the passing of Johnson's. The voice does, however, make gestures which invite a form of identification; for it

> is animated with a true though perhaps feeble attachment to the Institutions of our Ancestors; and minded to defend these, according to all hazards; nay, it was partly with a view to such a defence that he engaged in this undertaking. (*SR*, p. 9)

The voice of the Editor is thus hesitantly English. The language of nationhood which is explicit in Boswell's framing statement is implicit here, and so invites us to reconstruct the sort of reader to whom it was addressed.

An English middle-class reader of 1831 was likely to have been prejudicial to the French Revolution of 1830, and anxious about the intense social agitation in Britain which was leading up to the Reform Act of 1832. Such prejudices and anxieties are played upon, and *Sartor* does nothing to allay them. When the Editor quotes seemingly impenetrable extracts from the clothes philosophy, the Editor challenges the reader: 'what, for example, are we to make of such sentences?' (*SR*, p. 33). The Editor's discourse is resistant and apparently attached to the common-sense English empiricism of Boswell and Johnson. However, when the Editor of *Sartor* disseminates both the discourse of the hero and the hero as a formal component of a discursive event to the reader, both the inability to reach understanding and the potential of the hero to provoke hostility are stressed. Unlike Boswell's view of Johnson's speech which invites assent to the values it purveys, the Editor simply cannot assert the hegemonic potential of Teufelsdröckh's un-English, anti-empirical philosophising.

The boundary confusions relating to the source of an authoritative voice and the collapse of confidence in empiricism produces a problem that eats at the heart of the Editor's project in *Sartor* – narrating an empirically grounded history of the life and opinions of Teufelsdröckh becomes impossible because there is no authoritative source of observation. This was an impossibility produced by a new set of conditions. History as an epistemological practice was transformed by the new human sciences in which 'man' became both subject and object of philosophical and scientific investigation. That is to say history represented itself as a practice of empirical observation, recording and reportage, and a relationship to documentary and archival sources. Boswell's *Life of Johnson* is in this respect a paradigmatic text; it illustrates the extent to which this new historiography became important to the internal validation procedures of the truth of biographical writing. In *Sartor* the boundary confusions over voice spill into other boundary confusions, which in turn challenge the central place of empirically grounded historicist epistemology in the field of the human sciences by asserting the primacy of rhetoric.

The place of rhetoric in Sartor: *undressing historicism*

The Editor reports that the clothes philosophy displays 'a well-nigh boundless extent of field; at least, the boundaries too often lie quite beyond our horizon' (*SR*, p. 28). The Editor declares that:

> Herr Teufelsdröckh has one scarcely pardonable fault, doubtless his worst: an almost total want of arrangement . . . . Apart from its multifarious sections and subdivisions, the Work naturally falls into two Parts; a Historical-Descriptive, and a Philosophical-Speculative: but falls, unhappily, by no firm line of demarcation; in that labyrinthic combination, each Part overlaps, and indents, and indeed runs quite through the other. (*SR*, p. 27)

As an author, Teufelsdröckh refuses to work within the discrete areas of knowledge demarcated by disciplinary boundaries. The textual rendition of the clothes philosophy should fall, according to the Editor, 'naturally' into two parts: a Philosophical-Speculative, and a

Historical-Descriptive. As the Editor implies, the Historical-Descriptive should be the grounding upon which the Philosophical-Speculative is built. Here we have to take account of the Foucauldian view of the primacy of historicism in the discourses of the human sciences.[27] If the speculative philosophy of clothes is to achieve the foundational status that it promises to deliver to the incomplete order of the human sciences, then the philosopher-subject needs to be able to delimit a field of enquiry, and then to describe, adopting the role of historian-subject, the development over time of a particular object – in this instance, clothing and its place in the progressive development of human culture. The problem is that the textual rendition of the clothes philosophy does not represent this intellectual practice in action. Historicism loses its sovereign position as the two orders of enquiry keep running into one another, transgressing boundaries and producing a 'labyrinthic combination'.

To think in a labyrinth is to admit that thinking can fold back on itself, an entangled state of affairs that finds blind spots. But this process of entangling is precisely what gives Teufelsdröckh's clothes philosophy its radical edge. For the philosophy of clothes is a metaphor for a practice of rhetoric and its subversive talent for exposing the restrictiveness of an ordering of discourse that sought to assign to language a categorical object status with limited powers:

> Language is called the Garment of Thought: however, it should rather be, Language is the Flesh-Garment, the Body of Thought. I said that Imagination wove this Flesh-Garment; and does not she? Metaphors are her stuff: examine Language; what, if you except some few primitive elements (of natural sound), what is it all but Metaphors, recognised as such, or no longer recognised; still fluid and florid, or now solid-grown and colourless? If those same primitive elements are the osseous fixtures in the Flesh-Garment, Language, – then are Metaphors its muscles and tissues and living integuments. An unmetaphorical style you shall in vain seek for. (*SR*, pp. 57–8)

Here the discourse on clothing ('Garments') metamorphoses into a discourse on language ('Metaphors'). Teufelsdröckh uses the language of clothing to challenge the content/form opposition that follows from the subject/object model of Enlightenment perception and thought: that is, when the subject apprehends an object and its relations to other objects through time, the language that is used to represent the objective content of the act of thought is merely form or dressing. Teufelsdröckh challenges the grounds on which this scheme of thinking is based; far from being just form, language is a material force, a rhetorical body ('muscles and tissues and living integuments') which as an agent organises and constitutes a field.

Carlyle's writing can be seen as being steeped in German idealism, yearning after a universe of ideal essences that lies behind a world of sham, cant and appearance. Aspects of the writing manifest this; but other aspects – as with this framed utterance of Teufelsdröckh's – manifest a strain of genealogical materialism that has come to be associated with Nietzsche, and later Foucault. Although Teufelsdröckh has implicitly rejected one mode of historicism, he has not abandoned historicity. Like Nietzsche, Teufelsdröckh advances the view that all language is metaphorical and a bid for power, but that history has rendered some forms of language apparently more 'metaphorical' (or 'literary') than others.[28] Teufelsdröckh is advancing both a theory of rhetoric, and a view of the historicity of interpretive convention; fields of 'knowledge' are constituted by rhetoric, but institutionalised interpretive practices can organise – and crucially obscure – an understanding of rhetoric and its powers. This discourse provides a perspective on the novelistic radicalism of *Sartor Resartus*, in that it re-establishes the relationship between rhetoric and reading.

The significance of this reinstatement of rhetoric to the politics of *Sartor* can be overlooked if we concentrate too heavily on a reading of the text as the ironically displaced 'spiritual autobiography' of Carlyle. Clearly it borders on spiritual autobiography – but it borders on so many other genres too. We need to bear in mind that Teufelsdröckh is not only a tortured soul in search of spiritual awakening, but also a radical critic of society and a defender of the poor and oppressed:

> Lifting his huge tumbler of *Guguk* . . . he stood up in full coffeehouse . . . and proposed this toast: *Die Sache der Armen in Gottes und Teufels Namen* (The Cause of the Poor, in Heaven's name and ——'s)! . . . one day he would probably be hanged for his democratic sentiments.' (*SR*, p. 11).

The Editor refers to an understanding of the clothes philosophy as 'the new promised country' (*SR*, p. 213), and *Weissnichtwo*, the university city where Teufelsdröckh teaches can be translated as 'Know-not-where'. *Sartor Resartus* has a utopian dimension inscribed in it.

Like More's *Utopia* of 1516, where the reader's understanding of codes and conventions is turned upside-down, *Sartor* defamiliarises the common-sensical basis underpinning the institutions of Englishness – 'Magna Charta . . . the Pomp and Authority of Law, the sacredness of Majesty . . . all inferior Worships (Worthships) . . . the Thirty-nine Articles' (*SR*, p. 215). But *Sartor* goes further than More's *Utopia*, in that it presents common sense as so much woven cloth, or powerful metaphoric devices. Their very grounding in convention is exposed rhetorically by inviting a reassessment of the conventions through which they are written and read. Thus the final chapters interweave apparently discrete systems of rhetoric and writing: they offer a portrait of the social system enforced by the British union, wherein class difference is drawn through the rhetoric of religious organisation and observance; 'such are the two Sects ["the Dandies" and "the poor-slaves"] which, at this moment, divide the more unsettled portion of the British People' (*SR*, p. 227). Central to this ludicrous portrait is an account of the 'Sacred Books' of the middle-class 'Dandaical Body' – the sacred book being none other than the fashionable novel. Thus the 'novel' as a cultural phenomenon, treated as a reified 'fiction' by an emergent criticism centred on the act of reading circumscribed by aesthetics, is metaphorically made strange while being restored to its real status as a generative, ideological repository of middle-class speech and ritualistic practice. Such is one aspect of the playful 'novelistic' effect of *Sartor*.

This 'novelistic' effect transgresses borders of discourse, and in doing so strives to alter the status of reading – 'that tough faculty of reading' as Teufelsdröckh calls it (*SR*, p. 221). *Sartor* seeks to position the reader as co-author, and this practice is embodied in the figure of the Tailor; simultaneously social functionary, textual function, and metaphor – *Sartor Resartus* means 'the Tailor re-patched'. If clothing and language are metaphorically equivalent systems, then the function of clothes maker must be the model for all practitioners of inscription and interpretation, for 'what too are all Poets and moral Teachers, but a species of Metaphorical Tailors?' (*SR*, p. 231). Significantly then, the model of intellectual vigilance elaborated by the discourse of *Sartor Resartus* finds its parallel in the guise of a complex process of labour; like the Tailor, moral teachers and readers jointly labour in a labyrinth of textual cloth. Teufelsdröckh is a radical tailor and interpreter; the reader is invited to become a radical tailor and interpreter in accompaniment.

The utopia on offer in *Sartor* places the transformation of reading and interpretation prior to the transformation of society – but it is not a substitute for it, as the chapter (book III, chapter VII) on 'Organic filaments' suggests. Because *Sartor* stresses the active interpretation of inscription so forcefully, it is all too easy to convert it into a Barthesian engine for killing the authority of authorship and celebrating the utopian image of the 'birth of the reader'.[29] Whereas Barthes is simply inverting a binary opposition and reinscribing the privileged position with the repressed term, *Sartor* is exploring the border country that structures the opposition in the first place – and this makes it closer to Bakhtin's practice. As Graham Pechey has argued, Bakhtinian concepts are always migrating between borders.[30] And as Gillian Beer has argued, the generative metaphoric powers of Carlylean discourse mobilise and unfix the apparently fixed categories and positions like 'writer' and 'reader'.[31] Indeed, in unfixing the positions that strive to secure writing to *a* context Carlyle's writing is prone to become unfixed and mobile between multiple contexts that it could not foresee. The implications of this mobility will be discussed in the final section of this chapter. In the next section, I shall explore the way in which Carlyle's challenge to the ordering of early nineteenth-century cultural discourse was extended through what has been perceived as his 'literary' intervention in English historical biography, *Oliver Cromwell's Letters and Speeches*. This will help to reassess Carlyle's 'literariness' in the light of a concern with the mobility of his discourse.

Carlyle's *Cromwell*: literariness in history

Teufelsdröckh, vibrating everywhere between the highest and lowest levels, comes into contact with public History itself. For example, those conversations and relations with illustrious Persons, as Sultan Mahmoud, the Emperor Napoleon, and others, are they not as yet rather of a diplomatic character than of a biographic? The Editor, appreciating the sacredness of crowned heads, nay perhaps expecting the trickeries of a Clothes-Philosopher, will eschew this province for the present; a new time may bring new insight and a different duty. (*SR*, p. 125)

We have seen how *Sartor* exposed a discursive positive unconscious which occluded the culturally constitutive power of rhetoric. The discipline of historiography – the representation of historical events in

written narrative – was a paradigmatic contributor to this positive unconscious in that it claimed to evade rhetorical forms of representation when showing the events of public history. From the above we can see that the Editor of *Sartor* recognises how the study of 'public History itself' as a delimited body of knowledge granted legitimacy to 'illustrious Persons' as agents in the domains of high politics and the state. *Sartor's* Editor evades confronting this source of power-knowledge at this point, but the Editor imagines that a different 'duty' might arise in the future. When Carlyle came to construct an historical biography in the 1840s, it addressed a period in British history when the 'sacredness of crowned heads' was repudiated; *Oliver Cromwell's Letters and Speeches* covered the period of the Civil War and Cromwellian Commonwealth.[32] As I will show in this section, the 'literariness' of Carlyle's *Cromwell* repudiated the practices of his-toriographical writing as well as the crowned heads. To begin with, it will be helpful to account briefly for the reviled status of representation in the early nineteenth-century theory of historiography before discussing, first, English reactions against it in the 1840s and, second, the particular subversiveness of Carlyle's 'literary' historical biography.

Historical writing: representation and 'literariness' in Macaulay and Carlyle

Raymond Williams has argued that while history is dependent for communication on narrative form, its 'objectivity' and authority came to be built on the occlusion of this dependence: 'the narrator or even the fact of the narrative is occluded in the form'.[33] Stephen Bann has looked for the originating moment of this occlusion, and finds it in Leopold von Ranke's programmatic dictum on the objectivity of the historian – that history 'wants to show only what actually happened (*wie es eigentlich gewesen*)' (1824). Ranke borrowed this, with modifications, from an earlier statement by Wilhelm von Humboldt (1821). As Bann argues, Ranke modifies Humboldt's assertion – that 'the historian's task is to *present* [my italics] what actually happened' – in such a way as to bring about 'the effective elision of the question of representation'.[34] This can be seen in the context of both Foucault's and Williams's arguments about the elision of rhetorical awareness brought about by the systematic reorganisation of cultural discourse that occurred in the late eighteenth and early nineteenth centuries. It should not be assumed, however, that Ranke's theory met no resistance, because in

England in the 1840s the 'literariness' of historical representation was being elided neither by Lord (Thomas Babington) Macaulay nor Carlyle.

An important question still needs to be posed: did 'literariness', or representational foregrounding, serve the same cultural-political ends in Macaulay's and Carlyle's respective historiographical writings? Macaulay's historical writing owed a great deal to the field of fiction writing; the intersection of the domestic and the national-political in Macaulay is a consequence of this. By contrast, Carlyle's *Cromwell* insists on its epic status – it is a 'Cromwelliad' echoing Homer. By constructing the difference between Macaulay and Carlyle in these terms we return to Bakhtinian generic categories for assessing 'literariness' – specifically the genres of novel and epic. Macaulay's 'literariness', given its debt to fiction, might be thought of as novelistic and innovative. In being epic in the manner of the great poems of the monoglot classical cultures, Carlyle's 'literariness' in *Cromwell* would seem to have reversed away from the innovative counter-modernism of *Sartor*. But as we saw in Chapter 1, Bakhtin's concepts invite us to avoid constructing such simple oppositions to account for stylistic differences between texts, and we need to explore the similarities and differences between Macaulay and Carlyle further.

Macaulay's *History of England* – the first volume appeared in 1849–1861 – utilised conventions of novel fiction which were acknowledged by its reviewers,[35] but its discourse also comprised characteristics which we might define as epic. Macaulay's text was resonant with the language of romantic fiction; thus Charles II 'had patiently endured the termagent passions of Barbara Palmer and the pert vivacity of Eleanor Gwynn';[36] while in the case of the Duke of Monmouth 'Henrietta had reclaimed him from a life of vice. . . . He loved her to the last, and he could not die without giving utterance to his feelings'.[37] As well as using this language Macaulay's narrative history drew on the subject matter of the popular novel, in the sense that it embraced such matters as travel and domestic detail, and used as sources 'private' diaries and letters.[38] The 'literariness' of Macaulay's *History of England* is crucially framed and distanced from the present by the technique of distanciation which is a feature of the very important framing chapter (ch. III), in which 1685 and 1848 are shown to be radically distinct by dint of the progress that had intervened and decisively separated them. Macaulay's history is marked by the distance that it uncovers between past and present:

A hundred and sixty years ago a person who came up to the capital from a remote county generally required twelve or fifteen meals, and lodging for five or six nights by the way. . . . At present we fly from York or Exeter to London by the light of a single winter's day.[39]

In *The History of England*, the presence of a distanciating frame renders the world of 1685 a distant world; though as I will argue in Chapter 5, not all of Macaulay's 'literary' historical writing was fitted with this 'safety-catch' of a distanciating frame. It is appropriate to call upon Bakhtin's definition of epic here, for epic, according to Bakhtin, is constituted in part by the sense of distance it creates between its subject matter and its readers.

Carlyle's *Cromwell* shares this Bakhtinian epic characteristic, with the narrator frequently commenting on how distant and inaccessible Cromwell has become to contemporary understanding; moreover, *Cromwell* is about a hero and the national past – a crucial component in Bakhtin's definition. Bakhtin's definition also situates epic in a rhetorical frame by raising the question of address: 'in its style, tone and manner, epic discourse is infinitely far removed from discourse of a contemporary about a contemporary addressed to contemporaries'.[40] Clearly Macaulay's *History* and Carlyle's *Cromwell* are about past issues and persons rather than contemporary ones. However, their respective styles of addressing sources conveying the past to readers reveal different perceptions as to their relationships with their contemporaries. In *The History of England*, the narrator's discourse simply reports on where sources containing traces of the distant past may be found; the address to the reader assumes that the sources 'contain' the past and will thus 'show' the same thing to every reader.[41] By contrast, the editor of *Cromwell* makes it clear that fundamentally different accounts have been constructed from the sources mediating his hero to the present – these sources being Cromwell's letters and speeches. The hero's utterances have been rhetorically textualised; Cromwell is a 'hero' in the sense that he is an inscribed utterance, circulating in a print culture and in need of interpretation; interpretation is presented as a political battle that is conducted in the present. Carlyle's *Cromwell* is an epic, but its 'literariness' can be seen as radically novelistic in that it argues with the frames that govern the production and reception of utterances that count as historical.

Cromwell *as discursive hero*

The opening chapter of *Cromwell*, 'Anti-Dryasdust', in which competing voices struggle to interpret the essence of the seventeenth century from unyielding sources, is rhetorically stylised and dramatic. 'A well-known writer' is introduced on the first page who articulates a virulent contempt for the institutions and interpreters who mediate seventeenth-century sources to the reading public. The voice of the 'well-known writer' represents the British Museum – archives of the King's Library Civil War pamphlet collection – as heaps of rubbish from which no sense can be gleaned, and in which the investigator might become lost: 'to the English mind at this hour, the past History of England is little other than a dull dismal labyrinth, in which the English mind, if candid, will confess that it has found . . . next to nothing' (*OCLS*, vol. I, p. 6). Thus, access to the labyrinthine archive in which English history of the seventeenth century has been customarily located will not help the 'ingenuous reader' (*OCLS*, vol. I, p. 12) to make sense of history. In short, the voice declares that popular needs will be served elsewhere; the 'ingenuous reader' will discover the essence of the seventeenth century in a biographical text that collects and traces the utterances of Cromwell, inspired as these utterances are with the right way of seeing. The point that the editor makes continually is that Cromwell's collected letters and speeches are sufficient in themselves for understanding the seventeenth century. To this end Carlyle's project addressed itself to 'the popular English mind' (*OCLS*, vol. I, p. 16) though the 'popular' is constructed as a constituency almost beyond reach. Whereas Boswell's biography of Johnson claimed to be able to speak for popular English values and prejudices, Carlyle's *Cromwell* contends that 'the popular' has been rendered inarticulate by the knowledge-producing techniques of elite culture.

'Anti-Dryasdust' declares itself to be an act of contestation in defence of the 'popular'. Moreover, the sources which comprise the chronological life are presented as acts and events:

I called these letters good, — but withal only good of their kind. No eloquence, elegance, not always even clearness of expression is to be looked for in them. They are written with far other than literary aims; written, most of them, in the very flame and conflagration of a revolutionary struggle, and with an eye to the despatch of indispensable pressing business alone. . . . There is in these Letters . . . a *silence* still more significant of Oliver to us than any speech they have. Dimly we discover features of an Intelligence, and Soul of a Man, greater than any speech. The Intelligence that can, with full satisfaction to itself, come out in eloquent speaking, in musical singing, is, after all, a small Intelligence. He that works and *does* some Poem, not he that merely *says* one is worthy of the name of Poet. Cromwell, emblem of the dumb English, is interesting to me by the very inadequacy of his speech. (*OCLS*, vol. I, p. 78)

The editor's 'elucidations' overturn a number of assumptions that might have been made about the nature of the sources that 'show', in Rankean terms, 'what actually happened'. First, the editor uses a discourse of judgement and evaluation associated with the critical discourses of art and aesthetics. But the normative categories that guarantee 'good literary aims' are then refused; the letters are not examples of conventional eloquence and are to be valued – paradoxically – for the quality of silence, or inarticulacy. Cromwell's inarticulacy is an emblem of 'the dumb English' – another attempt to construct an image of 'the popular English mind' – and in the same stroke the parameters of aesthetic discourse are challenged by the recall of an archaic definition of poetry. Inarticulacy is the sign of a subject who works or does some poem, rather than of one who simply says one. A poem is then defined as an act of work rather than *an* autonomous work; a productive act and an event rather than just linguistic artifice. If Cromwell's life as inscribed in the letters is a great poem or heroic epic, then it is not an epic in Bakhtin's closed monologic sense. Rather than just being epic 'literary' history, the editor's elucidations challenge the discourses which construct the line of demarcation between the 'literary' and the 'historical'.

Despite this challenge, Carlyle's biography still manifests a strong desire to project Cromwell's speech as monologic truth. Carlyle saw Cromwell as the embodiment of Puritanism, and Puritanism as the transparently moral driving force of the English Revolution – a dictatorship of the elect. This view had to fight against the historiography of Clarendon and Hume which presented Puritanism, and especially Cromwell, as hypocritical. Thus the editor's rhetorically double-voiced prose attempts to close any perceptible gap between Cromwell's words and deeds; in apprehending Cromwell as a speaking subject, the reader is invited to see 'a man whose word represents a thing . . . what this man speaks out of him comes to pass as a fact; speech with this man is accurately prophetic of deed' (*OCLS*, vol. II, p. 54).

However, this statement welds together two potentially opposed paradigms for explaining the relationship between words, things and deeds. The first – 'a man whose word represents a thing' – is premised on a nominalist view of language in which one word names one thing in an utterance or inscription that is self-contained: Ranke's view of historiography as virtually non-representational owes something to this. The second – concerning the relationship between speech and deed that 'comes to pass' as 'prophecy' – is in touch with Foucault's rhetorical notion of prophetic discourse in time 'weaving itself in to the fabric of fate'.[42] Because Cromwell draws his prophetic speech from 'Divine Handwriting abroad . . . on the sky', the seventeenth-century culture that Carlyle's *Cromwell* represents is not one in which words relate unproblematically to things; rather, it is a culture in which individuals and groups struggle to prophesy and possess the future by interpreting dense patterns of signs. Although there is a desire to project Cromwell as the privileged reader of signs and the speaker of monologic truth, the editor reports Cromwell as saying that his utterances are 'metaphorically and allegorically' grounded (*OCLS*, vol. III, p. 276), displaying 'figurative ingenuity' (*OCLS*, vol. IV, p. 149). In order to interpret Cromwell's utterances, readers – no matter where they are situated – have to transport signs, discourses and narratives from elsewhere. Interpretive conflict is woven into the form and content of Carlyle's biography of *Cromwell* and this perhaps explains the editor's interest in the individuals and groups who contested Cromwell's authoritative reading of the signs of the times.

The editor is fascinated with popular signs and their relations to the symbols of authority: to give an instance, the meaning of the imposition of episcopalian hierarchy on Scotland in 1617 is sought through the popular name attached to the bishops, '*Tulchan* Bishops' (*OCLS*, vol. I, p. 43), which forces an analogy between a 'tulchan' – a calf-skin stuffed to give the false appearance of a calf – and the falseness of the episcopacy. In focusing on this detail, the editor has found an instance of the mode of producing meaning 'discovered' in *Sartor*, or the way in which the layers of linguistic 'cloth' that patch, construct and conceal the world can be penetrated by a convention-breaking metaphor or substitution. Furthermore, the editor's elucidation points to this shared popular sign as having a discernible effect on the course of public history.

The fascination with popular resistance is, however, ambivalent. A concern with the interpretations that ground communal solidarity arises again in respect of the Levellers who, through the work of twentieth-century Marxist historians like Christopher Hill, have come to be seen as an important radical grouping in the English Revolution, buried by the condescension of public, constitutional history. The editor credits the Levellers with an acute capacity for demystifying symbols of power by reading the real relations behind them through the interpretive framework of clothes metaphors, and they should be seen accordingly as 'a class of men dreadfully in earnest; – to whom a King's cloak is no impenetrable screen' (*OCLS*, vol. I, p. 291). Yet it would be misplaced to claim that Carlyle's *Cromwell* shares the perception of Christopher Hill, for at other points in the narrative, the editorial voice is uncompromising in its intolerance towards 'impractical' Levelling, castigating 'Dryasdust' historians for futile gestures of fair-mindedness in the face of its programme (*OCLS*, vol. II, p. 33). The editorial voice struggles to hold two contradictory perspectives in tension.

This ambivalence is manifest elsewhere in the editorial 'elucidations' in a metaphor projecting the English mind as being divided like two different forms of tree growth. On the one hand, it is like the schematically cultivated Dutch-dragon tree, disciplined to grow in a uniform way. On the other hand, 'a deeper portion of the English mind inclines decisively in the forest-tree way', and thus rejects this discipline in order to emerge spontaneously (*OCLS*, vol. I, p. 259). By means of this metaphor, the text dramatises a tension between a dominant authority and powerful residual forms of popular dissent. These perspectives are represented by competing voices; on the one hand is the disciplinary voice of Presbyterian London crying 'Apply the shears!', and on the other, the oppositional voice of the New Model Army advocating a tolerant attitude to dissent by answering 'Apply them *gently*; cut off nothing that is sound!' (*OCLS*, vol. I, p. 259). These competing voices are present-tense constructions, and they are framed in a stretch of present-tense explication; the editor rhetorically addresses readers, inviting them to 'read this Extract from a work still in Manuscript, and not very sure of ever getting printed' (*OCLS*, vol. I, p. 258).

Both the foregrounding of the act of writing – not to mention the technology of printing through which writing is reproduced for circulation – and the 'presentness' of the construction are important. First, historiography is demonstrably representation rather than a Rankean elision of representation. And, second, the present-tense explication invites the reader to cancel the epic distance between the reading context of the present and the past that is being represented.

If Carlyle's *Cromwell* needs to be seen in the context of a general turn to the 'literary' in the construction of English historiography in the 1840s, Carlyle's 'literariness' still needs to be distinguished from the 'literariness' that Macaulay wove into *The History of England*. Macaulay's literariness involved employing fictional conventions to represent a distant past, whereas *Cromwell* can be seen as novelistic, in so far as it displayed a determination to go beyond the thresholds and limits set by fields of discourse – a determination which characterised *Sartor*. In epic style Carlyle's *Cromwell* attempts to project the power of a heroic individual, but at the same time that individual is part of a culture which collectively struggled over the interpretation of signs in an attempt to settle a new social and political order. Moreover, *Cromwell* collapsed the epic distance between past and present, so that the dramatisation of that seventeenth-century struggle was rhetorically mobilised in the present of the nineteenth-century reader. In the final section of this chapter, I shall discuss the consequences of the mobility of Carlylean rhetoric.

The mobility of Carlylean rhetoric

To conceptualise the mobility of Carlylean rhetoric, we need first to think about audience, but then to develop this thinking so that we arrive at a position which enables us to situate Carlyle's texts in relation to a multiplicity of audiences – with different political interests and positioned at different points in time. In my reading of *Sartor Resartus*, I pointed out how the Editor's discourse could be read as a rather provocative address to a conservative middle-class audience of 1831, fearful for the security of the political and social order that supported it. The editor of *Cromwell* similarly challenges a conservative middle-class audience – the threat in the middle of the 1840s being Chartism. This can be seen in the editor's representation of an episode from 1647 when the New Model Army 'agitated' for Cromwell to move the

Civil War in a more radical direction. Indeed, in focusing on this, the editor directly addresses and attempts to transform dominant encodings of the sign 'agitititor'; for the term 'agitator', used to describe elected agents representing army grievances, is, as defined by the editor, a misspelling of 'Adjutator'. In the editor's lexicon, adjutators are legitimate functionaries who sought to secure what was 'strictly their just right' (*OCLS*, vol. I, pp. 268 and 266). The editor's discourse displays an awareness of the way in which a conservative middle-class audience would encode the word 'agitator': it would resonate with the readings of Chartist 'agitation' derived from contemporary accounts fearful for middle-class property and privilege.

Having identified a target of the address, it is tempting to rest the analysis there. It is beyond reasonable doubt that conservative middle-class people existed in significant numbers in the 1830s and 1840s, so the audience focused on was a dominant one. However, it is less certain that this way of proceeding comes to terms with the complex construction of a text; for this complexity might provide a variety of positions for a multiplicity of audiences. Carlyle's biographical collation of Cromwell's letters and speeches wove together a variety of ideological discourses; the letters and speeches themselves consist of a mix of political injunction and spiritual, confessional and prophetic discourse; and of course the 'elucidatory' editorial commentary opened up a range of contradictory positions to complicate this further. The rhetorical energy and diversity of Carlylean texts would have opened up different positions for a multiplicity of social, political and theological interests to align with and argue over. Tony Bennett has accounted for the multiplicity of possible modes of identification in texts in his theory of 'reading formations'. Reading formations are socially formed and motivated practices of reading which prioritise particular discursive configurations in texts.[43] Bennett's idea of the reading formation is a radical one, in that it does not assume any inherent hierarchy of discourses in a text; texts are 'productively activated' by reading formations – that is to say, different hierarchies of signification are produced by different interest groups situated at different historical moments. While this is a process to which any and every text is subject, some texts are more open to it than others.

Carlyle's novelistic biographies were of this open order. *Sartor* is an unsettled and unsettling heroic utterance because it cannot wholly imagine which communities it is addressing – or will come to address. This might shed a rather different light on the utopian dimension of

Sartor – at least if we adopt that definition of utopia which takes its original meaning to heart – utopia as nowhere. Or, as *Sartor* has it, 'know-not-where' (*Weissnichtwo*). For *Sartor* knows not where it will come to rest. Indeed, *Sartor* articulates a view of the text in relation to the unknown superaddressee (see Introduction). Its mode of address will have an effect on an immediate addressee in an immediate context, but this is

> [t]o say nothing of those pregnant considerations, ethical, political, symbolical, which crowd on the Clothes-Philosopher from the very threshold of his science; nothing even of those 'architectural ideas', which as we have seen, lurk at the bottom of all modes, and will one day, better unfolding themselves, lead to important revolutions. (*SR*, p. 216)

The text gestures towards a future in which its ideas might circulate and initiate 'important revolutions'. Revolutions lead from a tantalisingly incomplete 'analysis' – more the promise of an analysis – which weaves together politics and science, connotations both of base ('lurk') and superstructure ('architectural ideas'). Assuming a mobility between addressees situated at different points in time, it is possible to see the commensurability between this rhetoric and a socialist form of analysis; especially when we consider that in response to the revolutions of 1848–51 Marx found that he needed a clothes philosophy (ideology) to show how a society can hide from itself through the cultural conventions in which it shrouds itself. In Marx's 'Eighteenth Brumaire of Louis Bonaparte', Marx draws upon clothing metaphors in order to analyse events in France of 1848–51 which in turn would lead to an understanding of the complex relationship of determination between the economic base, class, ideological superstructures and political parties.[44]

A revolutionary socialist reading formation might also have been able to activate productively an exemplary relationship between economics and politics in the editor's narrative about the 'adjutators' in *Cromwell*. The editor explains that in agitating (adjutating) for 'just rights' by means of setting up soldier parliaments, the army are initially concerned with grievances relating to matters of back-pay and conditions of service, which surface early in 1647, and reach a head in May and June at Saffron Walden. These grievances, however, are symptomatic of a much broader debate, concerning the voice of the army in national affairs, and the direction – either towards monarchy or republicanism – towards which those affairs themselves should tend.

The act precipitating the fusion between the immediate short-term concern and the broader political issue, which involves taking King Charles I into the custody of the army against the will of the civil parliament, is performed by 'Cornet Joyce, – once a London tailor, they say, evidently a very handy active man' (*OCLS*, vol. I, p. 270). The editor goes on:

> The Controversy, at this point, has risen from Economical into Political: Army Parliament in the Eastern Counties against Civil Parliament in Westminster; and 'How the Nation shall be settled' between them; whether its growth shall be in the forest-tree fashion, or in the clipt Dutch-dragon fashion?—(*OCLS*, vol. I, p. 271)

The reader is asked to participate in living, unfolding dilemmas. A socialist reading formation might find a position in this narrative commensurate with its own analytical discourse, by attaching considerable significance to the way in which Cornet Joyce is an agent who enables others to see the underlying connection between an economic crisis and the potential for radical action in the political order.

The argument is not that Carlyle 'anticipates' socialism born of Marxism. Instead, the argument is that those who in the later part of the nineteenth century came to read, write and act from a position that was committed to the socialist transformation of society, were able selectively to appropriate and mobilise discourse from Carlyle's contradictory rhetoric.[45] It was precisely the threat of this which prompted the activities of a generation of liberal academics and writers, like J.R. Seeley and John Morley, who were opposed to the emergence of a socialist society – in their view an irrational society. As we shall see, these writers attempted to discipline the conditions leading to the appropriation and use of cultural discourse. In the 1860s these academics and writers confronted a political scene in which Carlylean rhetoric had already been mobilised for a project which defined itself as socialist. The Christian Socialist intellectual formation began to appropriate Carlylean rhetoric in the 1840s and 1850s. The Christian Socialists were conservative socialists and they feared the modernising drives of capitalism that led to class conflict – of which Chartism, in their analysis, was a symptom. Their solution to class conflict was education for working people which would enhance mutual understanding between classes. The key figure connecting Christian Socialism to Carlyle was Charles Kingsley.

Like Carlyle, Kingsley gained access to *Fraser's Magazine* as an enabling cultural institution when he published *Yeast: A problem* in 1851; the self-consciousness of the narrative organisation of *Yeast* was well served by the experimental, playful but socially and politically (Tory) committed writing that *Fraser's* supported. But the exemplary text here is Kingsley's *Alton Locke* of 1850.[46] Carlyle – appropriately – is doubled up by the text. He is cited in person by Alton Locke, the narrator-autobiographer (*AL*, p. 36), but he also appears in the guise of the Scottish bookseller Sandy Mackaye (*AL*, pp. 45–6), who introduces the narrator to a tradition of protestant and non-conformist English writing. Alton Locke is a tailor, and he is radicalised by being introduced to the nature of his trade through a version of the clothes philosophy which connects exploitative government contracts to a much broader system of impoverishment (*AL*, pp. 112–13). He is also 'an unwarranted hero as Thomas Carlyle has it' (*AL*, p. 76).

The character makes other crucial discursive connections between aspects of Carlyle's heroic life of Cromwell, Christian Socialist ideology and the struggle to understand and interpret Chartism. For Alton Locke is both a descendant of the Cromwellian Independents and a Chartist whose autobiographical narrative is about learning to read and write a way into a culture. Kingsley's text attempted to speak for and represent a sizeable group of autodidacts, for whom the practice of literacy inevitably led to writing. As the work of Brian Maidment has shown, pedagogic discourses on reading and writing produced by both Kingsley and Carlyle were persistently important and popular throughout the nineteenth century.[47]

Alton Locke was a text where questions of 'literariness', reading, writing and historical identity were meshed together. It can certainly be argued that Carlylean discourse provided it with some of its rhetorical building materials. At one point Alton Locke connects the topic of agitation articulated by the editor of Cromwell's letters and speeches to a utopian, visionary impulse: 'they must either dream or agitate; perhaps they are now learning how to do both to some purpose' (p. 92). In the view of a later generation of biographer-intellectuals – J.R. Seeley, John Morley, Frederic Harrison and Leslie Stephen – rhetorical flourishes of this kind were suspect, precisely because of the possibility of appropriation by some irrational political interest. Such rhetoric needed to be framed by disciplinary protocols – protocols

which, as we have seen in this chapter, Carlyle's writings actively
disregard. 'History' was to be restored to a position of authority in a
reordering of discourse. In the next chapter, I will offer an account of
this ordering of discourse, and the role that a liberal intellectual
formation played in constructing it. These intellectuals were formed
primarily in the institutional environment of Oxford and Cambridge;
so I will start by discussing why Charles Kingsley eventually became
unacceptable as the Professor of Modern History at the University of
Cambridge.

3

□

The Comtean ordering of discourse

In 1860, Charles Kingsley was appointed to the Regius Chair of Modern History at Cambridge University. This chapter will begin to consider the way in which intellectuals used the authority of the universities in an attempt to address and influence a wider community – a theme which will be developed further in the next chapter. As I argued earlier, while there is an inextricable relationship between the categories of the intellectual and institutional, the relationship is mediated by intellectual formations which work through institutions, formulating cultural strategies from positions situated between a number of institutions. In illustrating this point, the chapter will focus on the emergence of a liberal intellectual formation for whom the writings of the French philosopher and sociologist Auguste Comte were centrally important. In introducing Comte, I will argue that his philosophy provided this intellectual formation with two things: first, a sense of the pedagogic potential of the subject of history; and second, a theory of language which underpinned attempts to institute a disciplined ordering of discourse.

Charles Kingsley at Cambridge: professing 'opinion' in Modern History

Charles Kingsley's appointment to the Chair of Modern History at Cambridge was followed by the inclusion of a framing statement to *Alton Locke*. This 'Preface' was addressed 'To the undergraduates of

Cambridge'. This appeared in addition to the framing statement that Kingsley added in 1854, which was 'Addressed to the working men of Great Britain', and which claimed extensive, first-hand knowledge of the social, political and economic improvement in the condition of the working class in the era after the Chartist agitation of the 1830s and 1840s. In fact, we can plot a relationship between the addresses to these two socially distinct addressees, and then come to an understanding of the educational function that Kingsley expected Modern History to perform.

Kingsley explains that his address to the undergraduates is a placatory response to the hostility that *Alton Locke* provoked in Cambridge when it first appeared. The first edition of *Alton Locke* disseminated an unflattering picture of Cambridge University, representing it as a bastion of privilege which ignored and excluded working-class autodidacts like the tailor-poet. Kingsley explains that he has 're-written all that relates to Cambridge life', which had been 'drawn from my own recollections of 1838–1842' (*AL*, p. 1). Kingsley's address explains that the rewriting has been necessitated by the improvement of attitudes amongst undergraduates, who now display a humility and seriousness in their understanding of the relationships between the classes. This improvement has gone hand in hand with the broad ameliorative tendencies celebrated in the address to the working men of 1854.

It is in this sense that Kingsley conceives the pedagogic function that Modern History will come to have. In his address to the undergraduates, Kingsley styles himself as a teacher of Modern History. As Professor, or an authoritative representative of the university, what did this give him the authority to profess? In the Cambridge of the 1860s, Kingsley professed a subject which had little prestige attached to it: in an honours curriculum that was dominated by the 'hard' disciplines of classics and mathematics, Modern History did not enjoy high status. It was taught as a part of the Moral Sciences Tripos, introduced in 1851, which was distinct from the classics school and designed for teaching students who were believed to be less able.[1] Kingsley was expected to lecture to and tutor these students, so the post was not simply a sinecure, and Kingsley took his duties seriously.[2] Even so, in spite of Modern History carrying a university post established by the sovereign and appointed by the Crown, the institution did not take Modern History very seriously.

However, the status of Modern History was beginning to change, and outside Cambridge things were different. In Oxford, the importance of Modern History in the moral sciences had been recognised since 1841–42, when Thomas Arnold had held the Regius chair.[3] It was also valued in key popular educational movements – or rather middle-class initiatives which attempted to organise the popular. In 1854 the Christian Socialist formation founded the Working Men's College in London. This institution was designed to provide a framework in which working men could embark on an improving programme of education. It was conceived as an institution which would promote better understanding between the classes. As such, F.D. Maurice, its principal founder, eschewed the teaching of vocational subjects, and emphasised the teaching of the humanities. Literature was thus a popular subject – one of the first places in which 'English Literature' took shape – so too was history.[4]

The discourse that Kingsley constructs suggests the non-professional status attached to the subject of Modern History within Cambridge; it is worth quoting the first paragraph of his address in full:

> I have addressed this preface to the young gentlemen of the University, first, because it is my duty to teach such of them as will hear me, Modern History; and I know no more important part of Modern History than the condition and the opinions of our own fellow-countrymen, some of which are set forth in this book. (*AL*, p. 1)

First, Kingsley does not assume to speak from an authoritative position that can command hearers; he assumes to speak to 'such of them as will hear me'. Second, Kingsley's view of what Modern History actually consists of is arresting from the point of view of what the study of history became. Far from being premised on the idea that History consists of the study of sources, the marshalling of evidence and the construction of disinterested and verifiable arguments about the past, Kingsley states that he 'knows no more important part of Modern History than the conditions and opinions of our fellow-countrymen'. In other words, Modern History should be unashamedly 'present-centred'.[5] It is concerned on the one hand with exploring the conditions of life experienced by people living under the social and cultural relations of the present; and on the other hand Modern History is concerned with the 'opinions' of these people. I will look more closely at the problems posed by the term 'opinion' for another generation and grouping of intellectuals in a moment, but 'opinion' needs to be seen as a problem in the context of the final claim that Kingsley makes: that the conditions and opinions of his fellow-countrymen are represented in *Alton Locke*, the text that his address frames.

The authority claimed for *Alton Locke* is, as a consequence of this framing address, quite considerable. In being a narrative constructed out of opinions circulating in the 1830s, 1840s and 1850s, *Alton Locke* is presented to readers as a rhetorical intervention in the unfolding process of Modern History. Kingsley's framing discourse does not construct Modern History as a unilinear process of amelioration; *Alton Locke* might be about the 1830s and 1840s, but Kingsley warns that the text might also function as a prophecy:

> I have now to tell those of them who read this book that it is not altogether out of date . . . fresh outbursts . . . [of agitation] are always possible in a free country, wherever there is any considerable accumulation of neglects and wrongs. (*AL*, p. 7)

Alton Locke's radical opinions could be exhortations to action. Furthermore, like the Carlylean texts on which Kingsley's writings build, *Alton Locke* is a mix of discourses, a repository of often contradictory 'opinions', which could be dispersed throughout the culture of print, and open to appropriation by protest groups.

The 'field' of Modern History and its relation to political opinions became a contested area – or to put it more precisely, 'Modern History' had to be organised as an authoritative 'field' of knowledge from which the anarchy of 'opinion' was to be eliminated. It is in this context that I will offer, in the next chapter, an account of the significance of the biographical writing of J.R. Seeley, Kingsley's successor to the position of Regius Professor of Modern History. Although an academic with status conferred by the institution of Cambridge University, Seeley's work on the field of Modern History can be traced to his affiliations to a dispersed formation of intellectuals, for whom the philosophical and sociological system of Auguste Comte was a common reference point. It is to this system, and the use that was made of it by this formation, that I shall now turn.

The Comtean system

Auguste Comte's writings constructed an epistemological, historical and sociological account of human development. Comte identified three major epochs of human history, each of which was characterised by a dominant method of ordering perceived phenomena and claiming knowledge of the significance of those phenomena; these he called the theological, the metaphysical and the positive. According to Comte, while the theological and metaphysical epochs were necessary stages in the progress of human civilisation, they were premised on error leading from the way they perceived the relations between phenomena, and the conclusions (theological and metaphysical) that they drew from their perceptions. Under the promised regime of the positive epoch, phenomena would at last be perceived in terms of their real, verifiable relations of causation and succession. For Comte, the time in which he wrote – the early decades of the nineteenth century – saw the industrial civilisations of the West poised on the epochal threshold of the positive stage.

Yet this epochal transformation could not be grasped without a struggle, and Comte's system embraced a sociology of knowledge which attempted to explain the resistance. For Comte, historically specific but regressive epistemologies became embodied in concrete social institutions, such as the church and universities, which were loath to relinquish constituted authority despite the dawn of a new epistemological age. Through a synthetic and systematic methodology, Comte's writings attempted to elaborate a theory of social statics and dynamics. This theory could be used to explain and reorganise the epistemological basis on which the social and institutional crisis of industrial civilisation was built.

The positions and selective traditions developed for explaining our academic culture might lead us to believe that Auguste Comte made a negligible contribution to its formation. Students of English literature and English history – who are familiar with the role that such proudly unsystematic thinkers as Matthew Arnold and F.R. Leavis, or William Stubbs and Herbert Butterfield, played in developing the practices and values that they use in studying authors or periods – might be unable to recognise a place for Comte, a system builder and theorist. Yet as Christopher Kent's view of Comte suggests, French theory arrived on English shores well before the late 1960s. For Kent, Comtism 'was not the exotic aberration of a coterie of eccentrics but rather a comprehensive ideology remarkably harmonious with certain established English currents of thought and remarkably well suited to the the needs of a middle class intellectual élite'.[6] Kent is reacting to a view of Comte as a marginal social theorist with whom only John Stuart Mill amongst 'serious' English intellectuals dallied, before he became alarmed by Comte's secular ritualism – a ritualism that seduced a later minority of 'cranks' like Frederic Harrison who came too late and too liberal for the Oxford Movement. But as Mill himself suggested, Comtism permeated British intellectual culture more thoroughly than in France.[7] Given this assertion, and Mill's own selective use of Comte's system, it is important to try to understand Comtism as a discourse which intellectuals in specific class and intellectual formations were able selectively to mobilise and use in the service of institutional politics. This is apparent if we first look at the place of 'opinion' in Comtean discourse, and then examine the way it was appropriated by Frederic Harrison, a member of the younger generation of English liberal-Comtean intellectuals.

'Opinion' in the regime of the scientific positive polity

In 1819, Comte wrote an essay entitled 'Separation of opinions from aspirations'. Comte argues that in the modern polity, these two categories need to be distinguished both at the level of analysis and in practice:

> It is reasonable, natural and necessary that every citizen should have political aspirations, since all have an interest in the conduct of social affairs. . . . But a political opinion expresses more than desires. It includes a judgement, for the most part decided and absolute, that these can only be satisfied by particular measures and by no others. Now on this head it is ridiculous and unreasonable to pronounce without special study. . . . Thus, many people, who sincerely desire liberty and peace, have, nevertheless, notions as to the means of securing . . . [their desires] so erroneous that if put into practice, they must lead to disorder and arbitrary power.[8]

Analytically, a political opinion should be distinguished from a political desire because it contains a judgement; in practice, opinions which are really no more than unreasoned desires will lead to the exercise of erroneous judgements in directing society, and social and political anarchy will follow. The confusion of opinion with desire is a feature of the politics of the first phase of human development, when politics were 'vague, mysterious, devoid of principle, in a word, theological'. Vagueness and the multiplication of desires and principles leads to the anarchic multiplication of different opinions and corresponding protest movements. The stage of development at which opinion and aspiration will be separated is the positive stage when politics will be 'transformed into a positive science', so that politics becomes a question of induction and observation of phenomena in the manner of astronomy or medicine.[9]

Comte's selection of medicine as an exemplary practice is significant, in that it marks his project out very clearly as a further elaboration of the early nineteenth-century sciences of 'man', to which Foucault's writings have critically addressed themselves. According to Alan Sheridan, medicine is awarded the status of the paradigmatic human science in Foucault's writing; 'the founding science of all the sciences of man'.[10] Comte's attempt to bring politics into the same 'positive' regime of observation and verification as medicine has important implications for the enunciator of political opinion. For, as Foucault has argued in connection with the birth of the clinic, the doctor became

> not only the privileged, but virtually also the exclusive, enunciator of this discourse, in the form of institutional relation that the doctor may have with the hospitalised patient . . . [and] in the modalities of teaching and diffusion that are prescribed or authorized for this knowledge.[11]

From this it follows that for Comte, the ideal enunciator of political opinion should henceforward be a specialist with authority to disqualify 'lay' speakers.

One might ask, what is new here? In practice, traditional Western polities had always created exclusive spaces for privileged enunciators of political discourse. These 'statesmen' were granted access to civil and military instruments for operating on the body politic. The difference is that Comtean discourse makes the qualification for enunciation rest on a foundational epistemology rather than, as was the traditional condition, birth and aristocratic connection. And this construction of politics as an epistemology needs to be linked to Foucault's analogous point about the doctor's exclusive control of the teaching and diffusion of medical discourse, for this adds a new dimension to restrictions placed on the circulation and distribution of political 'knowledge'. Political knowledge was to be articulated by specialists through a discourse generated and overseen by institutions of education. How was Frederic Harrison guided by Comte's strictures on 'opinion' in his attempt to further the debate on the ordering of English cultural discourse?

Frederic Harrison: 'opinion' and history

Focusing on Frederic Harrison enables us to reconnect the question of political 'opinion' to the question of Modern History and educational institutions in an English context – a set of connections first examined through Charles Kingsley's framing 'Preface' to *Alton Locke*. Frederic Harrison became a disciple to Comte, but discipleship was mediated through complex networks of pedagogy and friendship. These networks were generated by the key English cultural institutions of public school and university. For instance, Harrison had imbibed Comtean theory through the teaching of Richard Congreve, a former pupil of Thomas Arnold's Rugby, and tutor to Harrison at Wadham College, Oxford.[12] Harrison was part of a generation of under-graduates who studied at Oxford and Cambridge in the 1850s and early 1860s; many of them had been active in the politics of university reform, before the 1867 Reform of the franchise was to provide them with a focus for a broader public mission. They were motivated by a desire to create an alliance between themselves as an upper-middle-class intelligentsia and the working class. This alliance would be based on a popular democratic cultural movement.[13] They were the very model undergraduates to whom Charles Kingsley addressed his second 'Preface' to *Alton Locke*; except that they were not inclined to be directed by Kingsley's discourse – though they attempted to diffuse Comtism through the educational institutions with which Kingsley was associated.

In the 1860s, Frederic Harrison gave a series of lectures on the broad topic of historicism, which were published together, only much later (1894), in a collection of essays entitled *The Meaning of History*. On leaving Oxford and his immediate network of Comtist associates,

Harrison went to London to teach at F.D. Maurice's Working Men's College. In lecturing on history, Harrison attempted to bring the Kingsley-style history teaching offered by the educational institution of the Christian Socialists into line with Comtist thinking. Maurice saw this as a sectarian intrusion, and opposed Harrison's approach. Harrison hired his own secularist hall and delivered the lectures from there instead.[14] I will focus on one of these lectures, entitled 'The use of history'.

Harrison's approach is not overtly didactic; the lecture begins by urging the reader or listener to try to imagine successfully undertaking a range of practices and activities conducted without the implicit understanding of history upon which they so clearly depend. History is then formulated as the very stuff of common sense. To this extent at least, Harrison's conception of history is like Kingsley's: it is living in the culture of the present moment. However, Harrison's conception of the historicity of the present is more selective than Kingsley's. Whereas Kingsley claimed that the 'opinions' – note the plural, which implies difference and possible contradiction – of his fellow-countrymen were one of the most important sources in assessing the nature of Modern History, Harrison alludes to 'opinion' in a much more restrictive sense, even though at first he appears to strike populist chords:

> All this [historical knowledge] may be very useful for statesmen, or philosophers, or politicians; but what use is this to the bulk of the people? The bulk of the people, if they are seeking to live the lives of rational and useful citizens, if they only wish to do their duty by their neighbours, are really and truly politicians. They are solving political problems, and are affecting society very deeply. . . . A man, provided he lives like an honest, thoughtful, truth-speaking citizen, is a power in the state. He is helping to form that which rules the state, which rules statesmen, and is above kings, parliaments, or ministers. He is forming *public opinion*. It is on this, a public opinion, wise, thoughtful, and consistent, that the destinies of our country rest, and not on acts of parliament, or movements, or institutions.[15]

The idea that through public opinion the common person can have a more powerful impact on the direction of the history of the polity than the statesman is indeed populist. But it is a restricted populism. A subject or citizen is only a power in the state, contributing to the formation of a 'consistent' public opinion if he (and not she) is rational, useful, honest, true-speaking and thoughtful. The implication here is that there is only one form of public opinion that legitimately directs Modern History, and it is defined by formal ethical categories pertaining to the individual. Harrison seems not to want to admit the possibility that two individuals might both be honest, thoughtful and true-speaking while accentuating these markers of an ethos with contrary world-views.

In fact, Harrison's discourse is resistant to admitting difference, and where it is admitted it appears in terms that threaten cataclysmic consequences for the people:

> Had they the wisest teachers or the highest social or moral purposes, they would all be lost and wasted in an interminable strife, and continual difference; for family, town, property, society, nay, language itself, would be things which each would create for himself, and each would create in a different manner. It would realise, indeed, the old fable of the Tower of Babel.[16]

As the allusion to the Tower of Babel suggests, language figures prominently in this catastrophic scenario of difference. Indeed, in referring to 'language itself', there is a suggestion that language is recognised as culturally constitutive. In fact, Comte's system did hold that language was one of the central constitutive energies that comprised social and cultural practices. But it also recognised that language comprised contrary energies that required the imposition of discipline.

Comte on language

Precisely how did language fit into Comte's system? Comte formulated a theory of language in his *Système de politique positive*, first published in four volumes in French between 1851 and 1854. It was translated into English in the 1870s when it appeared as *The System of Positive Polity*. Frederic Harrison was the translator responsible for the second volume of the philosophic system, entitled *Social Statics*, in which a theory of language as a social static was elaborated. Before looking at this in detail, it will be helpful to begin by focusing on the first volume of Comte's system, the *General View of Positivism and Introductory*

Principles. In this volume, Comte examines what he sees as the sometimes threatening influence that intellectual formations have brought to bear on the development of 'public opinion' in the modern period, and this helps to put his theory of language into a reactive context.

As we have seen, Comte's system embraces a sociology of knowledge which tries to explain resistance to the inevitable triumph of positive knowledge and the positive polity. For Comte this resistance takes the form of regressive epistemologies which become embodied in social institutions. As we shall see, Comte defines language as a major social institution, and language is the means by which writers communicate with the public. According to Comte, the writings of particular groups can embody regressive and threatening epistemologies. When Comte considers the intellectual formations that have been influential in developing the conflicting strains of public opinion since the middle of the eighteenth century in Europe, he finds that they consist very largely of 'artists, and especially poets'. In Comte's view, the adulation with which the public showered them propelled them to offices for which they were not qualified: 'stimulated by the applause which they received from the uninstructed audience, [they] fell into the error of seeking political influence'.[17] It is significant that Comte calls the audience 'uninstructed', for this implies that the audience – the people – were being led in ways which were contrary to their natural tendencies. These intellectual formations of artists and poets have increasingly responded to public applause by striving to reach the command points of the polity. In effect, they have transformed themselves from intellectual formations into the leaders of fully fledged political movements.

In Comte's view, the most damaging historical example of misplaced political leadership by poets and artists was the rule of the Ideologists during the second phase of the French Revolution; they were 'incapable either morally or intellectually of directing the second phase of the revolution, which they were hardly able to distinguish from the first phase'.[18] For Comte, legitimate *political* direction is dependent on an ability to make proper distinctions, and this is a corollary of using the signs that constitute language in a way that observes their correct order and relationships. The main contrast between the intellectual formations attempting to mould public opinion and direct the Modern History of Europe and the people is in their use of language. The people might be an uninstructed audience, but they use language 'reliably' in a way that romantic 'communists and socialists' do not.[19] It is here that we need to turn to Comte's explicitly articulated theory of language.

In *Social Statics* language and property are theorised as the two great conservative institutions binding the social fabric together. According to Comte's theorisation, the material powers of these institutions are distributed through the social fabric in different ways. Property is owned by individuals on an unequal basis, prompting legitimate competition and progress. By contrast, language cannot be owned by an individual; it is held by the collective, and is thus 'a kind of wealth which all can make use of at once'.[20]

We need to remember that language is theorised as a social static rather than a dynamic aspect of society, so the theory of common ownership that is advanced is a conservative one. Indeed, language is characterised by its capacity to fix the social order rather than to indulge it through visions of radical change, for language itself is fixed by an independent and necessary order: 'order is profoundly impressed upon the actual structure of our signs; for their value depends entirely on their fixity'.[21] Comte claims that this 'law' is concretely recognised in social practice by 'the people' who recognise this fixity and preserve it; for 'the people' are the conservative custodians of language. This way of constructing 'the people' connects with Harrison's ideal citizen in 'The uses of history'. For in being 'truth-speaking', the citizen is one who respects and conserves the structures of language.

For a developmental theory Comtism is clearly on difficult ground when it conceptualises language in such a static, conservative manner. Language, like every other aspect of the Comtean system, has developed over time. And this diachronic development implies that the relationship between the order of signs and the order of the non-discursive is in flux rather than being fixed. In fact, Comte has to recognise mutability in language. But Comte's theory of this dynamic in language has the effect of restraining insights into a Foucauldian view of rhetoric as 'the aberrant dimension of language', whereby rhetoric opens up the dimension of contestation in which thought can ceaselessly transcribe, compare and analogise the various objects of its investigation.[22] This is precisely the sort of insight and space of contestation that Carlyle's writing opens up, enabling a challenge to conventional orders of discourse. I say that Comte's theory of language can only 'restrain' these insights because the energetic contrariness of the rhetorical dimension in language cannot be eliminated from the explanation. Like Volosinov/Bakhtin in the 1920s, Comte has to come to terms with the rhetorical dimension of language which is intimately related to the multi-accented nature of the sign:

> The very ambiguities of language, which academic pride attributes to the slender vocabularies of the people, bear witness to the often profound analogies, not seldom happily seized by the common instinct of mankind many centuries before the learning of philosophers has been able to perceive them. In my work on positive philosophy, I have already pointed out the most striking instances, the two senses of the word *necessary*, the double meaning of which had never been explained until the positive philosophy has been able to do so. . . . I might also illustrate this remark by many other phrases of double meaning: such as 'just', 'order', 'property', 'humanity', 'people'. The sense of the word *Positive*, which I have already traced, will enable the reader to continue this thought for himself.[23]

Comte's attempt to negotiate the plurality of the sign is populist: 'the people' developed a shrewder understanding of what is latent in double meaning before the philosophers and intellectuals (until Comte, that is). Unlike Volosinov/Bakhtin, who understood double meaning to be one more effect of the heteroglossic tendencies in language – different ideological communities within the same sign community inflecting a common 'word' with different significances – Comte's populist understanding of double meaning is monoglossic. For 'the people's' grasp of 'profound analogies' always prefigures a process of unifying meanings which the positive philosophy will complete. Comtism clearly emerges here as one of those centripetal cultural drives of the sort identified by Bakhtin, which attempts to discipline the centrifugal energies of language.

If Comte's system recognises the problem of the centrifugal energies of language, it incorporates certain disciplinary strategies in an effort to overcome them. These strategies are characteristic of those developed for regulating the possession and distribution of discourse in modern societies, as discussed by Foucault in his essay 'The order of discourse'. Comte's theory gave rise to two distinct kinds of strategy: first, the discipline, and second, the fellowship of discourse.

Disciplinary strategies

Comte's views on the necessity of creating a unitary public opinion, founded on an authoritative epistemology and policed by an intellectual elite, can be seen as the discursive base on which the discipline of Modern History was elaborated in 'English' cultural politics. I write about 'English' – meaning a hegemonic term attempting to organise a fluid, contested grid of social, cultural and political relations – deliberately, in that the 'English Nation-State' was one of the objects that the disciplinary discourse of Modern History sought to create and legitimate. I am also writing about a discipline in a quite specific, Foucauldian way: the discipline of history was elaborated as a framework for generating authoritative statements about the past which would facilitate the framing of authoritative statements about the direction of public opinion. I will discuss this break with the practice of writing history developed by intellectuals like Carlyle, Macaulay and Kingsley in my next chapter, by locating it in the context of the politics of institutional reform in the universities in the 1860s, and the attempt by one wing of the liberal intellectual formation to use history to organise the public opinion of 'English' civil society.

Comte's centripetal theory of language had broad implications for attempts to organise the activities of reading and interpretation. If it was possible to instruct readers in the language of history, then it followed that the theory articulated assumptions about what could not be included within this domain, a type of discourse which was its Other. Comte developed a framework for dealing with the aberrant, rhetorical dimension of language.

To explain this, it is necessary to go back to Comte's starting point in theorising language: the point at which language and property are presented as the two great conservative institutions of society. Although Comte begins by distinguishing these two systems on the basis of the way in which they are distributed, he concludes by plotting a relationship between them. The conservative guarantees offered by property and language can be undermined because both property and language are open to abuse 'due in both cases to the wish to enjoy without producing'.[24] Thus, property is abused when it is 'enjoyed' without the concomitant effort necessary to produce it; and language is abused when artefacts constructed from it are merely enjoyed rather than produced. Of course, Comte could be taken as saying that all 'the people' should turn to writing, and be active producers of the texts which help to mould and shape public opinion and taste; and in principle, Comte admitted the importance of the popular production of 'people's' art.[25] Given its centripetal inclinations, however, the Comtean system displays a defensiveness about the status of language as common property. In prioritising linguistic production, the authority of authorship is stressed by the theory, and there is a telling distinction made between the intentions of the producers of 'original works' and the deviant pleasures of enjoyment exercised by their 'mere interpreters'. Who were these 'mere interpreters'? They should be seen simultaneously as 'the people' and intellectual formations of romantic artists and philosophers of the modern period who resisted the progress of positivism. Comte's faith in the conservative instincts of 'the people' had its limits, especially where the subversive activities of a romantic-socialist intelligentsia were deemed to have intervened and upset 'the people's' conservative instincts.[26] Thus, the language of a nation as written by conservative custodians of its expressive relationship to the 'fixed' order could be enjoyed; but in practice, the number of authoritative producers of this original work would be small, and the 'mere interpreters' would have to recognise that restrictions would be placed on their activities. As such, Comte's theory of language can be seen as the discursive base on which a 'fellowship of discourse' of the kind identified by Foucault in 'The order of discourse' could be constructed. According to Foucault, it is the function of a fellowship of discourse 'to preserve or reproduce discourse, but in order that it should circulate in a closed community, according to strict regulations, without those in possession being dispossessed by this very distribution. . . . The roles of speaking and listening were not interchangeable.'[27]

Where does late Victorian biographical writing fit into this attempt at ordering discourse? This is the question that I will explore in the final two chapters of this book, but some preliminary pointers can be established here. In a lecture given to the New Schools at Oxford University on the subject of authoritative reading material for reaching an understanding of the 'use of history', Frederic Harrison told his audience that 'what we need to know are the leading lines of this mighty biography, the moral and social links that bind us to the series of our ancestors in the Past'.[28] For Harrison, the master-narrative of the past was a great biography, so influential individual lives could be written as biographical microcosms of this great story. This clearly serves as a reminder of the central importance of biography to the Comteans. Comte himself produced a biographical calendar of positivist 'saints', and the English positivists, led by Harrison, mounted a similar publishing venture in the 1890s, entitled *The New Calendar of Great Men*. The function of these biographies was clear: they were issued to commemorate those figures from the history of civilisation who had advanced the necessary movement away from the theological and metaphysical stages, and towards the realisation of the positive stage. These biographies also need to be seen as replies to other biographies written by earlier intellectuals. In the view of positivist intellectuals, biographers like Carlyle failed to present their subjects in an appropriate linguistic relationship to the emergence of the positive stage. My next chapter will be concerned with J.R. Seeley and John Morley who, as contributors to a broader intellectual project, wrote biographies in an attempt to inscribe readers in the discipline of history.

4

☐

Biographies of statesmen and the epistemology of positive political history

In 1869, Charles Kingsley stepped down from the Regius Chair of Modern History at Cambridge University. He was replaced by John Robert Seeley, who has come to be recognised as a distinctive contributor to the construction of history as an academic discipline in the universities.[1] This chapter will explore what it meant for history to become an institutionalised discipline under Seeley.

Because Seeley's first major contribution to the field of Modern History was set out in the form of a biography of a nineteenth-century European statesman, entitled *The Life and Times of Stein*, this chapter will also re-examine the role that biography played in the emergence of the discipline of history in nineteenth-century cultural politics. Christopher Parker has posed this question and provided an answer that views biography as a paradigm; paradigms being, in the Khunian framework that Parker employs, puzzle-solving devices deployed in constructing historical explanations.[2] For Parker the emergence of history as a discipline can be explained in terms of a paradigm shift; there was a waning of influence away from explanations that drew on an amateurish exemplar paradigm, and an increased tendency to construct explanations derived from a more methodologically rigorous developmental paradigm. The old exemplar paradigm solved historical problems with recourse to biography, the agency of an individual subject being the device used for explaining historical events; while the new developmental mode of explanation, which shared epistemological ground with Comtism, attempted to discover progressive continuity in an historically variable object, be it a social structure, ruling idea or institution. Even so, Parker sees that the shift from an amateurish biographical paradigm to the scientist and professional developmental paradigm was uneven and there was overlap between them.[3] This is evidenced by the fact that when Seeley attempted to construct Modern History as a disciplined field, he used biography as a medium.

I shall argue that the endurance of biography in disciplined history is not only attributable to uneven development in the emergence of a dominant paradigm, but was also a function of the status that biography possessed as a disseminator of disciplinary initiatives. Seeley's use of biography tells us about the late nineteenth-century university intellectual's desire to discipline the circulation of opinion in a wider society. In fact this political desire was widespread, and the 'biography of the statesman' became the strategic tool of an intellectual formation which was committed to the reconstruction of public opinion through history as a discipline. As this chapter will demonstrate, an analysis of the disciplinary discourse that constructed such biographical texts enables us to connect disciplinary strategies validated by the authority of the university to the work of intellectuals positioned in and between other institutions of cultural production.

This shared disciplinary discourse was founded on a fear of rhetoric, and along with narrative, rhetoric is a dimension of language use that has preoccupied perhaps the best-known contemporary commentator on the textuality of historiography. In recent years significant deposits of rhetoric have been excavated from supposedly hard-fact historiographical prose by Hayden White. The rhetorical systems identified by Northrop Frye for the analysis of 'literary' texts have provided White with a comprehensive framework for demonstrating the way in which the classics of nineteenth-century European historiography produced their meanings by figurative techniques of persuasion. Like Michel Foucault and Raymond Williams, White is concerned to historicise and politicise the discourses which occluded the presence of rhetoric from nineteenth-century historiography. Accordingly, White has argued that the revolutionary upheaval in Europe in the early part of the nineteenth century helped to shape a defensive historiographical practice which was founded on an alliance between an ostensibly 'plain' prose and an anti-revolutionary politics.[4] This chapter will argue that Seeley's contribution to the construction of history as a discipline needs to be seen as a late nineteenth-century

English inflection of this defensive alliance. Seeley's biographical construction of the statesman as the authoritative speaking and knowing subject directing the historical process manifests a fear of 'literary' rhetoricians whom Seeley characterises as 'metapoliticians' – a name coined after Comte's metaphysical stage, because they represented an unruly residual force to Seeley and his fellow-intellectuals.

J.R. Seeley

Before being appointed Professor of Modern History at Cambridge, Seeley had held the Chair of Latin at University College London since 1863. In common with so many other liberal intellectuals who were prominent in the universities, the law and journalism around the period of the 1867 Reforms, Seeley came from an Evangelical family whose business was publishing, reformist advocacy and campaigning.[5] In London during the 1850s and 1860s, Seeley was in a similar position to Frederic Harrison in that he placed himself in contact with both the Christian Socialist and positivist intellectual groupings.[6] Unlike Harrison, who was a clearly committed positivist looking for converts amongst the Christian Socialists, Seeley was on the fringes of both formations, not clearly defined by either. Apparently undogmatic with regard to anything that would be flagrantly controversial, but well known for strong and radical views on curricular reform at University College London, Seeley was put forward as a candidate for the Regius Chair of Modern History at Cambridge. Seeley was approached simultaneously by Gladstone, who wanted to know his views on Christ and revealed religion, and Kingsley, who was hostile to Comte and wanted to know Seeley's views on his system. Seeley was able to satisfy his enquirers on both counts while managing to remain tactfully evasive.[7] Although he was not Gladstone's first choice, Seeley was appointed.[8] Even though Kingsley's questions about Comte were directed towards an assessment of Seeley's position on Comte's importance to the teaching of Modern History, little attention was paid to the scholarship which Seeley had produced in the field. That he had not produced any did not provoke disquiet.

This was due to the fact that a 'field' of Modern History was barely constituted. Seeley's occupation of the Regius Chair at Cambridge is important because, as Professor, he drew together a number of discourses, the combined effects of which sought to make Modern History into a discipline, or as Foucault defines a discipline, a 'system of control in the production of discourse'.[9] As I argued in the last chapter, in the middle of the nineteenth century the idea of Modern History was closely tied to anxieties about the way in which people read in the light of their social experience, and came to reformulate their readings as reactive and contrary strands of public opinion. As such, a discipline which set in place an epistemologically grounded system for regulating the production of statements relating to Modern History was simultaneously a system which sought to regulate the production of new statements relating to the formation and direction of public opinion. Seeley's Inaugural Lecture as Professor of Modern History at Cambridge is a discourse on this theme. Although it was addressed internally to the institution, it had important implications for the long-standing debate about liberal education, and this was a debate about the academy's authority in a broader structure of social relations. Accordingly, I will situate the lecture in the context of positions taken up around this debate. Seeley's Inaugural seems to weld two of these positions together in a contradictory way. I will suggest that his use of a popularising biographical form is an attempt to go beyond these positions.

The scholar-statesman and the problem of liberal education

Seeley's Inaugural was about the effects of history teaching, though like Kingsley's discourse before him, this was explicitly linked to questions of public opinion and politics – it was entitled 'The teaching of politics'. In the course of this lecture, Seeley declared his intention to develop the newly founded History School at Cambridge into a 'school for statesmanship'.[10] In other words, Modern History at Cambridge would produce professional 'practical' politicians who would be rigorously taught by professional methods. This implied two things: first, that the graduates of Modern History would be equipped with specialist knowledge which would better enable them to manage the state; and, second, that Modern History itself would have to become professionalised as a specialist body of knowledge. Seeley's tenure at Cambridge would seem then to mark the point when authority was being wrested away from amateurs like Kingsley.

Moreover, Seeley seemed to propose that an authoritative and instrumental form of knowledge should be taken within the walls of the academy and shared only with the elite. This had ramifications with regard to the politics of university reform. In this sense, Seeley's view of a training in Modern History apparently made a break with the emergent consensus on liberal education, which was against fixing students into a specialised role. In fact Seeley's Inaugural seemed to cling on to a residual practice of pedagogy.

These emergent and residual positions have been described by Ben Knights in his account of the debate over liberal education which was conducted inside and outside the universities.[11] Knights argues that, from the middle of the nineteenth century, a debate about university teaching was initiated which was conditioned by a new and pressing awareness of the social implications of pedagogy. Under the old tutorial system of teaching, students were coached individually in classical languages or mathematics by the dons or tutors of their college. These tutors had mastered the texts and paradigms which assured success in examinations. Their function was to pass the key to this success to undergraduates. For most graduates, a degree was a rite of passage to some influential position in the state or civil society. A minority of graduates – some not very distinguished – either obtained official positions at the university as tutors, or made a living for themselves as unofficial coaches, a career made possible by the inadequacy of many of the official tutors. The function of the pedagogue was to coach new generations of undergraduates for exams and a career. There was an instrumental, class-based elitism associated with this which prompted Kingsley's anger in the first edition of *Alton Locke* (see Chapter 3). The social perspective which informed that anger also propelled the cultivation of an ideology of liberal education which sought to reform the old system.

As Knights points out, this ideology was developed most cogently by Mark Pattison at Oxford. It aimed to upgrade the professorial system. Professors would lead designated schools of study which would be responsible for the teaching of undergraduates. Professors would be appointed to their position on the basis of their ability to conduct original scholarship and research. This was necessarily specialised work, but the ethical framework which supervised its conduct was the key to its liberal nature. In Pattison's view, research had to be disinterested, that is to say, embarked upon for its own purpose and value. As such, a complex process of questioning and evaluation went into the framing of research topics and the dissemination of their findings. This complex process of questioning and evaluation would constitute the regime governing the symposia-like discussions which professors would conduct with undergraduates. The university was first and foremost a community of scholars, but a community of scholars which would be linked to the broader community by organic filaments. Instead of being endowed with the narrow ability to pass examinations, university graduates would be schooled in an ethos which would grant them a legitimate right to pose disinterested questions about a problem or controversy relating to the particular profession or social role to which they found themselves 'called'. They would be specialists in the art of legitimation itself.

Seeley's discourse in the Inaugural Lecture appeared to weld together aspects of both the residual and emergent systems of pedagogy in a rather contradictory blend. Following the residual system, Seeley's discourse outlines an instrumental understanding of education which would narrowly prepare an elite for a predetermined role – that of statesman. But following the emergent system, the Inaugural is enunciated from a professorial position by a researcher who teaches undergraduates about the protocols governing the disinterested pursuit of truth in Modern History. Two different and potentially contradictory relationships of authority to wider society are implied in Seeley's discourse. Both are elitist, but only one apparently recognises the need to obtain consent. On the one hand the schoolmaster of future statesmen does not seek the consent of broader society; he assumes a right to govern based on the restricted transmission of specialised knowledge, and would impose a ruling elite. However, the professorial address assumes that wider society will recognise the governing elite that the School of History passes on to them because of the disinterested habit of mind with which the university has furnished the elite. In so far as it is an advocate of elite expertise at all, the professorial liberal educator is first and foremost an expert in the practice of legitimation itself.

Seeley attempted to reconcile the contradictory discourses at play in his 1869 Inaugural through his later biographical historiography, but this solution needs to be seen in the context of 1867 and the emergence of democratic institutions and increasing opportunities for the publication and circulation of popular materials: the contradictory positions at play in Seeley's Inaugural and his subsequent turn to biographical historiography are recognitions that elitism had to be popularised. On the question of the significance of the institutionalising of history as an academic discipline, I agree with Rosemary Jann's view that 'the withdrawal of historians into the academy did not signify so much a break with wider society as a different mode of influencing it'.[12] When we examine Seeley's practice as a biographer, we shall see that there is no contradiction between the university school's perception of itself as the instrumental producer of an elite which would be imposed on wider society, and an ideology of liberal education that seeks consent for its practices through the demonstration of refinement and discrimination. Biography came to be perceived by Seeley as the vehicle through which both specialist knowledge and expertise in legitimation could be demonstrated to a popular audience. It is in this sense that I will explore Seeley's use of biography to disseminate the discipline of Modern History.

Seeley and the uses of biography

In 1879 Seeley wrote an introduction to the translated autobiography of a minor German poet by the name of Ernst Moritz Arndt, entitled *The Life and Adventures of E. M. Arndt*. Arndt had been writing during the wars and revolutions of the early nineteenth century when Central Europe was subject to the Napoleonic system. Arndt had been an associate of the Prussian statesman Stein, and it was principally this connection that led Seeley to translate and publish an account of his life. In the same year, Seeley pursued this venture further and published a massive biography, *The Life and Times of Stein*.[13] As Deborah Wormell has argued, the biography of Stein was Seeley's bid to be recognised as a genuine scholar of Modern History, and it was published under the authoritative stamp of the University Press at Cambridge.[14] The biography of Stein is concerned with a career, spanning the late eighteenth century and the early nineteenth, which was devoted to serving the Prussian state. His activities on behalf of Prussia coincided with a period of acute crisis for both state and civil society. Seeley claimed that Stein fully understood, organised and spoke for the German version of 'The Anti-Napoleonic Revolution' that had its antecedents in the Peninsular resistance. 'The Anti-Napoleonic Revolution' was, according to Seeley's claim, a revolution that brought into existence the unified nation-state (*S*, vol. II, p. 41). Clearly, such a claim had important implications for a popular English

audience that Seeley sought to discipline; the political science of the
nation-state was, for Seeley, the principal object of investigation for
the Modern Historian, and Seeley wrote in the dedication of *Stein* to
the German scholar Reinhold Pauli, 'I only hope to teach my own
countrymen, and do not dream of instructing the Germans' (*S*, vol. I,
p. vi).

It was also important that Seeley chose to tell of the foundation of a
nation-state through a biography, and in his work on Arndt, Seeley
articulates a theory of biography. Seeley's theory of a biographical
approach to the dissemination of historical discipline stresses its
potential to exploit the popular, so it attempted to colonise the same
popular constituency for which Carlyle's *Oliver Cromwell's Letters and
Speeches* had claimed to speak in the 1840s. In fact Seeley's biographies
can be seen as disciplinary correctives to Carlyle's writings –
particularly in the way that Seeley's construction of his biographee
Stein warns against the dangerous energies of rhetoric.

Seeley justifies both his biography of Arndt and biography in general
thus:

> It is one question how history ought to be written for the purposes of
> science, and another by what means some useful knowledge of it may be
> generally diffused. The mass of mankind, those who will have little
> leisure for reading, and no motive for it but amusement, will not read
> any more about states and governments than can be presented to them
> in the biographies of famous men.[15]

The use of biography is linked to the need to popularise historical
knowledge. This situates Seeley's discourse; it is suspended uneasily
between the academy with scientistic ambitions where it originates,
and popular pedagogic networks which might mediate between the
academy and popular reading formations. Seeley appropriates the
language of the Society for the Diffusion of Useful Knowledge which,
as we saw in Chapter 1, was active in the 1820s and 1830s, using
biographical writing extensively in its mission to educate. In ap-
propriating the discourse of the Society for the Diffusion of Useful
Knowledge – a formation which in 1879 was defunct – Seeley was
simply drawing attention to an uncertainty regarding the agencies
which might mediate between the academy and popular audiences.
Also it indicates that Seeley's programme could not extricate itself
from the biographical projects of the 1830s and 1840s, the years of the

Chartist agitation. In addressing this tradition, Seeley's writing has to negotiate Carlyle's legacy. When reading about the 'Age of Napoleon' from the vantage point of Arndt's text, the reader

> will watch it in the main from Germany, but not, as he has so often done before, through the eyes of some mere philosopher or recluse poet, of Goethe, or Schiller or Jean-Paul, but through the eyes of one who has felt intensely the pressure of his time, who himself joined and suffered in the struggle of his country against Napoleon. In this biography therefore, the reader can, without trouble, and not without pleasure, make himself acquainted with the Napoleonic age.[16]

Seeley stresses that reading Arndt's biography will be a 'pleasurable' activity, but it is also important to note that this 'pleasure' involves displacing the perspective of a formation of Romantic writers and poets: Goethe, Schiller and Jean-Paul Richter. In Chapter 2, I argued that the German Romantic ironists were important in shaping Carlyle's textual practice, so Seeley's objection is not confined to this group and their perspective on the Napoleonic period, but extends to the way in which their textual strategies had proliferated via Carlyle into the discussion of history, politics and statecraft. The point about style is made more forcefully by Seeley in his biography of Stein:

> When in the biography of a person belonging to this period the narrative reaches the French Revolution, the reader instinctively prepares himself for a complete change of both matter and style. He expects a sudden breach of continuity, a disappearance of all that has hitherto occupied the scene, and in its place a crowd of new personages and new ideas. He expects first a discussion of the first principles of politics, the rights of man and the social contract, and afterwards an Iliad of war and battles. . . . But in Stein's life the French Revolution is no such important date, and for many years after the outbreak of it his occupations and thoughts continued to be . . . what they would have been had it never taken place. (*S*, vol. I, p. 74)

The rhetorical energy of Carlyle's *French Revolution*, published in 1837, is the target of this particular corrective. Principally though, it is Carlyle's disruptive treatment of the rhetorically double-voiced biographical convention that has to be negotiated by Seeley in his biography of Stein. Whereas Carlyle's life of Cromwell opened with an internally dialogic clash of voices warring over the memory of the Protector, Seeley's biography of Stein notably opens by stating that there will be no confusion of voices in his text, that the reader will always be aware of who is speaking authoritatively of the biographical subject (*S*, vol. I, p. xi).

To what ends does the biographer exercise this authority? Frequently, the biographer pauses the narrative to pose questions concerning the selection of biographical material. Such acts permit the biography to make explicit the rules and exclusions that constitute history as a disciplinary mode of writing; so that when referring to one of Stein's regular bouts of retirement from the service of the Prussian state, the biographer remarks that 'during this vacant interval, he ceases to have a biography' (*S*, vol. I, p. 52). Biographical knowledge of Stein can only be articulated through codes appropriate to the discussion of politics and the state. Following Rankean prescription, Seeley claims that the biography of Stein is uncontaminated by the touch of narrative and rhetoric: 'I shall have little narrative to offer. No enthusiastic public meetings were held, no dramatic debates took place; I can tell of no crushing replies, no perorations delivered at sunrise, no apt classical quotations' (*S*, vol. II, p. 234). It is at this point that we can begin to consider Seeley's construction of the discipline of history in terms of a fear of rhetoric.

Biography against 'metapolitics': the production of the true past and the path to the true future

The biographer's discussion of the disciplined selection of biographically relevant material connects to the broader project that Seeley's *Stein* represents; that is, an attempt to discipline the language in which statements about history and politics should be cast. It is in this sense that the biographer represents his subject uttering 'shockingly plain words' (*S*, vol. I, p. 17). The nature and 'object' of these 'shockingly plain words' becomes apparent in Seeley's commentary on his biographee's own account of his education:

> Stein is almost silent about the great philosophical movement of his life time [Goethe, Schiller and the Romantic ironists are here implied] as if no such movement had been going on; the only effect it produces on him is to excite a keen feeling of alarm lest it should, in any way, extend

to practical politics, and lest the management of affairs should in any degree pass into the hands of those whom he calls, with strong contempt, *metapoliticians*, that is of course those who stood in the same relation to problems political as metaphysicians to the students of nature. . . . Poetry was to him, as in fact it is to most men, only a more impressive kind of rhetoric. . . . His object at Gottingen was not literature but political science. (*S*, vol. I, pp. 31–2)

Seeley's double-voiced prose makes a distinction between 'practical' referential language and rhetoric – the latter is constructed as the mere stuff of literary decoration. The Comtean theory that I analysed in the last chapter is organising this distinction. The very term that Stein coins for describing the formation of artists and intellectuals comprising the German Romantic movement – 'metapoliticians' – can be related to Comte's term for the stage prior to the ascendancy of positive philosophy, the metaphysical stage. Metapolitics is only ever a form of rhetoric; fears about the unguarded powers of language – what Foucault has described in 'The order of discourse' as 'logophobia'[17] – are aroused when such poetic utterances, devoid of 'substance', are acted upon or used to form public opinion. Stein's use of language is, by contrast, disciplined and positive in that his language is a transparent mediator of empirical observations, which refer to objects in themselves, or the relations between objects. Out of this distinction comes a discipline, a domain of objects grounded in an epistemology: 'political science' is Stein's 'object'.

Because of his empirically disciplined seeing and speaking relationship to this domain of objects, Stein is credited with the capacity to speak authoritatively on the identity (identity here meaning similarity, or the presence of common properties) of political problems as objects recurring in the comparative histories of states. As such, Stein is credited with the powers of diagnosis and prognosis in the manner of medical discourse – as we saw in the last chapter, for Foucault medicine was the paradigmatic discourse of the modern human sciences. It is in this functional light that Seeley frames Stein's document, 'A representation of the faulty organisation of the cabinet'. This document, like others framed by Seeley's rhetorically double-voiced prose, is practical and external in its bearings: 'Scarcely ever in his life, indeed, did [Stein] write anything without an immediate practical object' (*S*, vol. II, pp. 285–6); we need to recall here that in accounting for the separation of 'historical' from 'imaginative' writing that occurred in the early nineteenth century, Williams pointed to the way in which 'historical' writing was designated as an 'external', practical, non-representational form.[18]

The document is a critique of the Prussian political machine, and it asserts relations of identity amongst a number of historical objects – states – to which it refers to demonstrate its authority; so that 'he who reads with attention the history of the dissolution of Venice, [and] of the French and Sardinian monarchy, will find in these occurrences grounds to justify the most dismal anticipations' (*S*, vol. I, p. 273). Notably, this statement on the relationships of identity between objects concludes by entering into the language of anticipation, so that it becomes a prognosis of the future. Future-orientated discourse is intertextual ground that Seeley's discipline has to seize from Carlyle's construction of 'prophecy', and this can be seen in his direct appropriation of a line from Carlyle's *Cromwell*, where the soldier-hero transforms into a prophet-hero. Seeley claims the same honour for Stein: 'in him, as it was said of Cromwell, hope shone like a fiery pillar when it had gone out everywhere else' (*S*, vol. II, p. 484, and *OCLS*, vol. III, p. 229). In alluding to Carlyle's text so directly, Seeley's text seeks to reconcile the theological discourse of prophecy and faith to its own disciplinary mission. In the biographical narrative, this allows Seeley to endow this source with the value of vindicated prediction at the point where the Prussian state is beset with crisis, so that 'the old fault was committed, which Stein had so recently pointed out . . . a few months later, the King was . . . humbling himself before Stein . . . history [gave] its verdict entirely against the King' (*S*, vol. I, pp. 284 and 291). Strikingly, history is here invoked as a court whose jurisdiction is the delivery of final, definitive 'verdicts'; verdicts which can only be issued in the affirmative when the appeal is articulated through the proper disciplinary words of history, which in their turn delineate 'practical' political objects. I shall return to the connection between history and juridical discourse in the next chapter.

In Seeley's biography of Stein the failure of a culture to study collectively such a 'practical' domain of objects becomes the basis for an historical explanation for why Prussia collapsed before the invading armies of Napoleon in 1806:

> In the most military of all states, literature, because it sprang from a
> class which enjoyed exemption from military service, and as a

consequence the tone of public feeling which is determined by literature, was in especial degree wanting in the military spirit . . . and this fact goes some way to explain the phenomenon of a military state fighting exceptionally ill which we have had so long before us. (*S*, vol. I, p. 439)

Seeley constructs 'literature' as the material product of a particular class, or more accurately, intellectual formation. This 'literature' had considerable institutional status as a moulder of 'public feeling'. In other words, Seeley recognises literature as a form of rhetorical power that shapes subjects in their imaginary relations to the conditions in which they live. Indeed Seeley's statement claims that 'literature' was more powerful than the military discipline set in place by Frederick the Great's military state. Seeley draws upon Comte's negative assessment of the functions of a literary intelligentsia. In Seeley's view the Romantic literary intelligentsia of Prussia and Central Europe misled the public who applauded them; 'the people', here represented by 'public feeling', were diverted from their 'natural' conservative relations to language by 'metapoliticians'.

In constructing 'literature' as a dangerous form of rhetoric, Seeley's biography of Stein produces an explanatory statement about the past. The statement also issues a warning about the effects of the unrestricted proliferation of discourse. Like other statements about the historical past, it would resonate in the present moment of its release. For Seeley this could only be desirable if it provided 'public opinion' with the intellectual equipment to resist those forces of 'metapolitical' manipulation which were asserting themselves in Europe in the later decades of the nineteenth century; Seeley wrote in an unpublished lecture about 'that political formation which is so rife on the continent, the Red Spectre, [which] is nothing but public opinion dominated by bad method. Socialism, communism, everything of that kind are [*sic*] simply a bastard political science divorced from history.' As such, Stein's mastery of the conservative language of political science needed to be demonstrated to 'the people' whose conservative instincts were, in Comte's construction of 'the people', receptive to it. Furthermore, it needed to be demonstrated before the 'metapolitical' discourse of the 'Red Spectre' took hold; we should recall that the opening words of *The Manifesto of the Communist Party*, written by Marx and Engels in 1848, were: 'A spectre is haunting Europe – the spectre of Communism.'[19] Seeley's attempt to slay his version of this spectre involved aiming Stein's powers of diagnosis and prediction at the heart of the present – and this is how the biography of Stein closes.

The present-centred significance of the closure of *The Life and Times of Stein* resides in a debate that Seeley records between the Roman historian Niebuhr and Stein, the elder statesman at the end of his career, over the problem of the European revolutions of 1830 – the moment, we should remember, when *Sartor Resartus* was published. Niebuhr's reaction is one of shock and pessimism; prior to the outbreak of revolution, an attachment to historicism and a belief in progress had convinced him of its impossibility. As a response, he searched the archive for an explanatory analogy. Seeing no relationship of identity between the revolution of 1830 and the English Revolution of 1688, he concluded that politics as traditionally constituted were not the driving force of 1830. Consequently he abandoned the search for an analogy in the modern period, and looked to the ancients. As we shall see in the next chapter, Niebuhr developed an historical account of the foundations of ancient Roman society which stressed the formative role of ballads and poems of protest. Niebuhr trawled this period once more and looked again at the history of the Roman Gracchi. In the struggles around the Gracchi, Niebuhr saw factors that marked out a relationship of identity between Roman history and the history being made in 1830. The point of identity was the emergence of the social question into politics, the social being a complex system of pressures and rhetorics that develop an awareness of class, property relations and material inequalities. Looking again at the nineteenth century Niebuhr located the mature crisis point for the social question in England; England in the nineteenth century was a repetition of the problems confronting the Gracchi of ancient Rome. Reluctantly adopting the function of a prophet, Niebuhr declared that the crisis could only intensify.

We need to remember that in his unpublished harangue against the 'Red Spectre', Seeley conceived of a politics that premised itself on questions of the social rather than questions of nationhood and state development to be founded on bad method. Accordingly, Stein figures in Seeley's biographical prose as a spokesman for history as a disciplinary corrective to Niebuhr's faulty 'metapolitical' method. This method fails to find a proper 'object' of study, articulates the problem rhetorically and, for the purposes of public opinion, dangerously.

Writing in 1879, Seeley makes the validity of Niebuhr's prophecy the issue of contention and turns Stein's diagnostic power upon it. The biographer records that Stein likewise reads pessimistically the signs of the times in the Europe of 1830. But he stops short at concurring with Niebuhr over his discovery of identity between the Rome of the Gracchi and nineteenth-century England. Stein, who reads the relations between signs past and present from a disciplined perspective, can see nothing but difference. And according to his biographer's directive, the authority underwriting this assertion of difference can be read in its 'present' status as an empirically verified prediction and not false prophecy:

> Without boasting much of what has been accomplished in England since that time, we may still feel that here Niebuhr's 'Burden of England' has not proved a true prophecy, and that he himself would retract it if he could come again amongst us. (*S*, vol. III, p. 523)

Overall, Seeley's construction of Stein as a possessor of specialist knowledge is an assertion of the right of the unelected but exclusively educated statesman to govern. Viewed in the context of Seeley's drive to make the History School at Cambridge 'a School of Statesmanship', *The Life and Times of Stein* could be read as an attempt to exclude public opinion from the process of political decision-making. However, Seeley was also writing in the context of a popular democratic polity. The solution that Seeley crafts is one based only in part on reserved specialist knowledge. In practice, the knowledge is not reserved at all, but designed to be circulated. For this reason, the disciplinary discourse through which it is generated is on display through the biography. The biographer becomes an expert in legitimation, placed between the academy and the multifarious communities that lie beyond its immediate control.

Seeley's fashioning of history as a university discipline with a social mission was based on a fantasy: the academic teaching of history would be founded on epistemological discipline which regulated the production of statements about the 'truth' of the nation's past – the nation was the principal object of study; it was hoped that the communities which were beyond the control of the academy would bow to its authority and use its discipline to construct new statements about a common national political future. Seeley's project – in so far as it was embodied in popular biography – never got beyond the fantasy stage because the biography he wrote hardly lent itself to popular circulation. His biography of Stein was prolix and unsure as to which community it wanted to impress most, the academy or a popular audience. In the event, it satisfied neither. Seeley also wrote about a German biographical subject and a topic in Modern German History. As I have argued, the spectre of Carlyle has to be defeated on the way to defeating the 'Red Spectre', and this pressures Seeley into writing not only about Germany, but through and against the textual traces left by a Romantic intellectual formation introduced into English by Carlyle. Like Edward Gibbon before him, it was as though Seeley backed away from a head-on confrontation with figures and events in the Modern History of England: 'I should shrink in terror from the modern history of England, where every character is a problem and every reader a friend or enemy'.[20] None the less, from his Chair in Cambridge Seeley fashioned an authoritative and influential discourse for writing about history and politics. As we shall see later in this chapter, this was appropriated by other liberal intellectuals who, by virtue of the positions they occupied in other institutions of cultural production, saw themselves as better placed to reach a popular audience through the biographical dissemination of the discipline of history.

John Morley

The focal point of this intellectual formation was John Morley, who had seen for himself the potential for using the popular biography of English subjects from the recent past to circulate anti-socialist political and economic ideologies. Morley's *The Life of Richard Cobden* was published in 1878, the year before Seeley published *The Life and Times of Stein*. The biography commemorated the political career of Cobden, chief architect of the Anti-Corn Law League. While Seeley's *Stein* concluded by focusing on 'The burden of England' in the 1830s, Morley's *Cobden* constructed an account of the way in which the political questions of the 1840s came to be settled. The 1840s had been a decade in which two movements battled over the question of how to lighten the social 'burden of England' – these two organisations being Chartism and the Anti-Corn Law League. Morley's rhetorically double-voiced prose conveys powerful images of Cobden winning consent through his speaking skills:

> The thoughtful among them recognised the rare tone of reality, and the note of a man dealing with things and not words. He produced that

singular and profound effect which is perceived in English deliberative assemblies when a speaker leaves party recriminations, abstract arguments, and common places of argument to inform his hearers of telling facts in the condition of the nation.[21]

In this representation of Cobden's first speech to Parliament the reader is told that Cobden has a sure grasp of political 'reality', which is opposed to 'abstract argument' and the divisions of party, faction and the multiplication of 'opinions' which this Other produces. This grasp enables Cobden to deliver telling diagnostic facts to his hearers about 'the condition of the nation'. Notably, only the 'thoughtful' few would have recognised this, so the reader is asked to remember that the thoughtless many would have been deaf to it. There is a populist elitism inscribed in this; the reader is invited to become one of the few who would have recognised Cobden's diagnostic skills – skills guaranteed by the biographer's representation of Cobden's speech, which refers to objects or 'things', and not merely other 'words'. As such, the voice of the biographer draws upon a discourse that we have seen before in our dealings with Seeley. It is a discourse premised on a Comtean theory of the relations between language, political action and legitimate historical agency. So in what sense was John Morley a positivist, and how did his position in late nineteenth-century intellectual culture enable him to build upon the disciplinary project initiated by Seeley?

Like Seeley, Morley was loosely associated with the English positivists; by playing disciple first to James Cotter Morison of Lincoln College, Oxford, and later to John Stuart Mill – the former a strict adherent of Comte, the latter more of a fellow-traveller – Morley became well acquainted with Comtean theory. Along with figures like Seeley and Frederic Harrison, Morley held that it was the function of a liberal intellectual elite to set about infusing public opinion with positive discipline. But Morley's life-course followed a different path to Seeley's, and he was prevented from pursuing this goal from within an academic institution.[22] Morley had been sent to Oxford by his socially ambitious father, a surgeon in Blackburn who had converted to the Church of England from Methodism. While at Oxford, Morley lost his faith, found inductive method, rebelled and then refused to take Anglican orders. This estrangement from the ecclesiastical basis of Oxbridge culture was common amongst a generation of liberal intellectuals; I shall say more about its effects on perceptions of intellectual fellowship in the next chapter. In Morley's case, it terminated his academic career; for Morley's father the taking of Anglican orders, which would have raised the social standing of the family still further, was the only possible reason for his son's attendance at Oxford. Morley was deprived of all further financial assistance, left Oxford early with a pass degree and had to seek employment.

He found it in a number of spheres – first journalism, then publishing, and later, party politics. Around the time when Morley left Oxford, new journalistic opportunities were opening up. A new order of reviewing or opinion-moulding was emerging to challenge the dominance of the old Tory and Whig quarterlies and monthlies. One of the new organs, *The Saturday Review*, employed Morley as an occasional journalist, later a staff writer. In 1867 – the year of the second franchise reform – James Cotter Morison and John Stuart Mill advocated that Morley should be made editor of *The Fortnightly Review*, the leading new radical liberal journal founded in 1865. It was also in the mid-1860s when Morley became associated with Macmillan the publishers, acting for the firm as a reader. In 1868, Morley made his first attempt to enter Parliament; he was unsuccessful, but he was eventually returned for Newcastle upon Tyne in 1883. Thus by 1878, when *The Life of Richard Cobden* was published, John Morley was actively working through two key institutions of cultural production – journalism and publishing. In addition, Morley was close to being installed in the post-1867 party political system. And through his intellectual connections with figures like Morison at Oxford, Henry Sidgwick at Cambridge and John Nichol at Edinburgh, Morley was still closely associated with the university system. In other words, Morley was perhaps the key member of the late nineteenth-century liberal intellectual formation, forging links between a range of institutional sites and practices, and coordinating the activities of fellow-intellectuals.

We should not assume that Seeley and Morley were fellow-intellectuals who were in agreement in all respects. Morley came to be at odds with J.R. Seeley when the latter emerged as the chief historian and apologist for British imperialism. Morley argued publicly with Seeley over the question of where the history of the English state had been made, and where it should continue to be made; Seeley's *Expansion of England* argued that it was made in the colonies, while Morley's review of that text asserted the centrality of eighteenth-century domestic politics.[23] This disagreement marked out opposed positions which ultimately came into conflict over the Home Rule Crisis of 1886, the consequences of which caused deep divisions between liberal intellectuals.[24]

None the less, Morley agreed with Seeley's image of the statesman and the assumptions about agency that were associated with it. Morley's biography of Oliver Cromwell, published in 1900, was framed by the proposition that

> universal history has been truly said to make a large part of every national history. The lamp that lights the path of a single nation receives its kindling flame from a central line of beacon-fires that mark the onward journey of the race.[25]

The fact that this is delivered through the frame of a biography indicates that Morley shared Seeley's view of the efficacy of biography for disseminating widely the discipline of history. In addition, Morley's proposition implies the existence of universal history as described by Comte, within which there could be discerned a specific master-narrative of English political history. Pre-eminent in this master-narrative were the activities of a few gifted statesmen who, in line with universal history, gave a legitimate sense of direction to the development of the nation-state. Morley initiated a project which attempted to realise this master-narrative through a canon of biographical portraits. His unique position, intersecting between a range of cultural institutions, enabled him to coordinate the activities of a number of intellectuals who were asked to popularise Seeley's version of historical discipline through a series of small and affordable biographies of English statesmen.

'Twelve English Statesmen'

Morley was general editor of the series entitled 'Twelve English Statesmen'. The publishers were Macmillan, the firm with which Morley was closely associated. Many of the twelve small volumes were timed to appear in 1888, the bicentenary of the so-called 'glorious revolution of 1688'. This sense of timing indicates that the publishers and Morley wanted the texts to make a definitive contribution to the popular understanding of British political history.

In fact, there was a popular demand for historical education. The later decades of the nineteenth century saw expanding educational opportunities; we have already seen how the old universities like Oxford and Cambridge became aware of the possibilities of developing Modern History as a disciplined field, and in the extension lecture movement that was organised by these universities – an attempt to satisfy the educational aspirations of working people and women – history was a popular subject.[26] To service this demand, Macmillan were responsible for producing student handbooks and primers. 'Twelve English Statesmen' was a series produced for this purpose, as was the more famous 'English Men of Letters' series which Morley also coordinated and edited. I will discuss both the extension lecture movement and 'English Men of Letters' in the final chapter. Indeed, the following discussion of 'Twelve English Statesmen' will conclude by suggesting that the biographies comprising 'English Men of Letters' were a necessary complement to the regime of reading presupposed by the liberal-Comtean ordering of discourse.

Chronologically, the master-narrative of English political history told through the lives of 'Twelve English Statesmen' opens with E.A. Freeman's life of William the Conqueror and concludes with J.R. Thursfield's account of the life of Sir Robert Peel. The writers of these biographies were for the most part contemporaries of Morley's at Oxford and Cambridge who, when commissioned to write, were positioned in different institutions of civil authority and cultural production.[27] I have already accounted for the position of Morley, who wrote a biography of Robert Walpole (1889). Frederic Harrison, biographer of Oliver Cromwell (1888) and Chatham (1905) moved on from lecturing at the Working Men's College to be appointed to a position on the Statute Law Commission (where trade union legislation was on the agenda),[28] and to write for the new periodicals. There were others who worked in this sphere of the so-called 'Higher Journalism'.[29] Among these were H.D. Traill, biographer of William III (1888) and contributor to *The Saturday Review* and *The Pall Mall Gazette* (edited by Morley from 1880); and J.R. Thursfield, biographer of Sir Robert Peel (1891) and leader writer for *The Times*, and later the first editor of *The Times Literary Supplement*. Lord Rosebery, who wrote on Pitt the Younger (1891), was a major parliamentary figure in the Liberal Party.

Others who wrote biographies for the series were professional historians, academic appointments to the new history schools in both the old and new universities. T.F. Tout, the biographer of Edward I (1893), was appointed to the Chair of History at the new Victoria University, Manchester, in 1890. Bishop Mandell Creighton, biographer of Cardinal Wolsey (1888), was Professor of Ecclesiastical History at the University of Cambridge. Although E.A. Freeman, biographer of William the Conqueror (1888) was from an earlier generation (b. 1823), his enthusiasm for that socio-historical methodology known as 'the Comparative Method' links him to the younger intellectuals like Seeley.[30] In seeking to make disciplined comparative history primarily about politics, Seeley was building upon Freeman's earlier dictum concerning the focus and subject matter of history – that 'History is past politics and politics is present History'.[31] It was precisely the potential for comparison and analogy that resided in statements about the past that led Morley's biographers to be bound by the disciplinary rules of positive epistemology and language theory in writing their biographies. This was necessary, because the sort of statements produced by the biographers of these figures were to serve readers as a basis for generating new statements about the politics of their own present.

The statesman-like voice and the history of the present in popular biographies of statesmen

Following Seeley, statesman-like speech in the 'Twelve English Statesmen' biographies is the specific property of certain privileged and authoritative speakers who boast a command of 'practical' or 'objective', 'external' language. Like Seeley's *Stein*, these biographies often make clear distinctions between qualified and unqualified speakers in the political domain. In Lord Rosebery's *Pitt*, the subject's 'large and statesmanlike' position is at least in part defined by its being opposite in nature to the speech of Fox and Shelburne, neither of whom use 'plain words', and Shelburne's utterances being represented as 'a mere labyrinth of stilted ambiguities'.[32] Ambiguous utterances open up an aberrant dimension of language use which, as we will see, comes to be commonly and negatively identified as rhetoric or 'literariness'.

The statesman-like voice 'reflects' the 'inherent Englishness' both of the legitimate political action that has been historically exercised and the place where it occurred. The opening of the biography of William III, written by H.D. Traill, is in this respect exemplary:

> It is significant of the peaceful and, so to speak, constitutional character of our English Revolution that by far its most momentous scenes were enacted within the four walls of the meeting-places of deliberative assemblies, and find their chronicle in the dry record quotes and resolutions. We have no 'days' in the French sense of the word . . . to commemorate. The gradual accomplishment of the political work of 1688–89 is not marked and expressed like that of 1789–92 at every stage by some outdoor event of the picturesque.[33]

The difference between England and France turns on an inside/outside opposition. The French Revolution was 'marked and expressed at every stage by some outdoor event'; the domain of French politics is dispersed into the street. By contrast, the domain of English politics and history is centred and concentrated on the enclosed space of Parliament. Moreover, in the case of England, these interiorised events 'find their chronicle' – note that they naturally correspond to the predetermined shape of a story and do not have to be interpreted – through 'dry record quotes and resolutions'; whereas French politics of the street is 'marked and expressed' in terms of the 'picturesque'. The exterior/interior opposition is supplemented by another opposition; that of the representational/non-representational. The term 'picturesque', which has clear associations with the literary, suggests artifice; French politics of the street are 'expressed' in language that has slipped away from externalities and practicalities. Implicitly, the opposite is the case in regard to the 'dryness' of the English historical record, safely sheltered between four walls.

None the less, violent revolutionary activity had been a feature of the British experience during the period of the Civil War, the Commonwealth and the Protectorate. Cromwell was consequently a figure who needed to be carefully drawn by a variety of different members of the liberal intellectual formation at different times – a process beginning with Goldwin Smith's inclusion of Cromwell in his lectures on English statesmen delivered at Oxford in 1867.[34] Frederic Harrison wrote the biography of Cromwell for 'Twelve English Statesmen' and I shall discuss Harrison's negotiation of these difficulties in due course. For the moment though, I shall concentrate on John Morley's biography of Cromwell, published by Macmillan in 1900. This was not, strictly speaking, a contribution to 'Twelve English Statesmen', but it followed the tracks laid down by the series that Morley coordinated. It can also be read, like Seeley's *Stein*, as an act of intertextual 'reply' to Carlyle's *Cromwell* which, as we saw in Chapter 2, posed a threat to the stable ordering of discourse.

Part of Morley's explanation of the social and political upheaval of the earlier seventeenth century is derived from his characterisation of the 'un-English' Charles I:

> Charles was not an Englishman by birth, training, or temper, but he showed himself at the outset as much a legalist in method and argument as Coke, Selden, St John, or any Englishman among them. It was in its worst sense that he thus from first to last played the formalist, and if to be a pedant is to insist on applying a stiff theory to fluid fact, no man ever deserved the name better.[35]

Charles is not an 'Englishman' by birth, but worse than that, neither is he an 'Englishman' by training or temper. In attempting to be a legalist he ends up by being a 'formalist'. The term that Morley chooses is significant, especially in the way it is invoked as the negation of inductive method: in being a formalist, Charles applies stiff theories to fluid facts which cry out for a referential language of empirical observation. As such, Charles is 'un-English' because he is a metapolitician. If Charles ignores the grounding epistemology of practical politics and leads the nation into civil war and revolutionary violence, Cromwell is on hand to pick up the pieces: 'As Ranke put it, Cromwell viewed his own ideals, not from the point of view of subjective satisfaction, but of objective necessity; and this is one of the marks of the true statesman.'[36] With the reader asked to view Charles as the practical Cromwell's Other, Charles's 'formalism' also becomes a subjectivism – a term which by the end of the nineteenth century, as Ian Small has pointed out, had become negatively associated with Paterian aesthetics and its disregard for authority.[37] By contrast, Cromwell's statesmanship is guaranteed by his 'objectivity'.

In drawing attention to Cromwell's 'objectivity' the biographer invokes the authority of the founder of objective empirical history, Ranke, who was crucial in effecting the apparent elision of the fact of representation from historiographical prose narrative. As such, an important chain of authority is established: the practical objectivity of Cromwell is recognised by the methodological objectivity of Ranke, and both are recognised by Morley the biographer. This chain of authority has important implications with regard to legitimating the objectivity of Morley's discourse in relation to its 'present', a theme which preoccupies the statement that frames Morley's biography of Cromwell:

> The thirst after broad classification works havoc with the truth; and to insist upon long series of unqualified clinchers in history and biography only ends in confusing questions that are separate, in distorting perspective, in exaggerating proportions, and in falsifying the past for some spurious edification of the present.[38]

Unlike Charles I, the biographer will be no formalist; instead, he will empirically assess the life of Cromwell in relation to the crisis of the past, and in so doing assess the proper comparative relations of similarity and difference between past and present. When the biographer has to deal with the discontent in the New Model Army at Saffron Walden in 1647, the statement is clearly an attempt to 'objectivise' the relations between past and present:

> The whole scene and its tone vividly recall the proceedings of a modern trade union in the reasonable stages of a strike. In temper, habit of mind, plain sense, and even in the words and form of speech, the English soldier of the New Model Army two centuries and a half ago must have been very like the sober and respectable miner, plowman or carter of today. But the violence of war had hardened the fibre, had made them tough under contradiction, and peppered them both for bold thoughts and bolder acts.[39]

Morley is here rewriting an event addressed by Carlyle's *Oliver Cromwell's Letters and Speeches*, and before the political implications of Morley's 'objective' statement of the comparative relation between past and present can be appreciated, Morley's stylistic 'answer' to Carlyle's textual practice needs to be considered. To begin with, Morley's discourse claims to relate a unified 'scene . . . and tone'. By contrast, Carlyle's representation of 1647 and its aftermath oscillates between diegetic narrative and extensive direct quotation from writings by the Army 'Adjutators'. Although Morley's discourse stands in a diegetic relationship to its object, the effects it seeks are mimetic. It refers to human traits ('temper, habit of mind', etc.), which reside metonymically in individual types (nouns like 'soldier', 'miner', 'plowman') and this referential effect stands as a guarantee of its objectivity. Carlyle's diegesis, on the other hand, openly proclaims itself as apart from, and a *representational* paraphrase of, events and tendencies which is not limited to one world of discourse; this is exemplified by the way in which the disturbances of 1647 are articulated through the Dutch-Dragon tree/forest-tree metaphoric opposition (*OCLS*, vol. I, p. 259; see also Chapter 2).

How is Morley's 'answer' to Carlyle's representation of this episode to be read as an ideological act in the political contest over the ordering of cultural discourse? Carlyle's account is not dependent on one context; the potential for mobility is written into the many worlds of discourse from which Carlylean rhetoric is built; by contrast, Morley's account creates an effect of referentiality which delimits and closes a domain of 'objects'. By conceding a similarity between working men in the present and agitators in the New Model Army of the past, Morley's statement recognises the impulse to read forms of discontent (working-class struggles with capital) and their institutionalisation (trade unions) in the present against forms of discontent from the past. This impulse invites discipline, for according to Morley, perceptions of similarity are based on error; workers in 1900 live under conditions which guarantee their respectability, whereas Englishmen in the seventeenth century living through a civil war did not. 'Contradiction' is a condition of the past, whereas 'respectability' is a universal condition of the present, regulating the possible range of statements that can be made about the connections between social and economic relations and forms of political agency.

Reading the mobile signs of the times

Morley's *Cromwell* fears an outbreak of reading which might forge a connection between the sources of unrest in the seventeenth century and similar sources in the late nineteenth century; it attempts to resist this by formulating a disciplined style which aims to restrict the mobility of discourses of protest between contexts. Indeed many of these liberal intellectual biographers uneasily confront the fact that the discipline of history which they are striving to set in place might still at any moment be undermined by oppositional acts of reading. As E.A. Freeman admits in his biography of William the Conqueror for

'Twelve English Statesmen', although disciplined statements about the past might be generated for demonstrating the development of liberal democratic propriety, a dissident method of reading is always present in the signs from which they are constructed:

> We never can be as if the Norman had never come among us. We ever bear about us the signs of his presence. But that those signs of his presence hold the place which they do hold in our mixed political being, that badges of conquest as they are, no one feels them to be badges of conquest – all this comes from the fact that if the Norman came as conqueror, he came as a conqueror of a special, perhaps almost of a unique kind.[40]

Freeman is entrusted with the task of writing the biography that celebrates the 'unique' (monological) origins of English statesmanship; but 'Englishness' actually comprises a multi-accented collection of signs which could be read in more than one way – as the play in Freeman's discourse admits – to emphasise origins in conquest and political usurpation. 'Englishness' might not be a stable source of political identity; on the contrary, it could be a fiction covering the contradictions of a 'mixed political being'.

Indeed, Freeman's biography of the Conqueror raises a difficulty with regard to the status of 'fictions'; for it is precisely those 'legal fictions and euphemisms' instituted by his subject for the spoliation of Saxon lands that have had such momentous material consequences.[41] The prospect that the Conqueror's duplicitous fictions can generate such effects begs the question: how is the student of history to be assured of the legitimacy of the statesman-like speech of the powerful agents in history? This question goes to the heart of the problem posed to liberal intellectuals by the apparent gap between Cromwell's words and actions, and the legacy of Carlyle's *Cromwell* as a frame for opening up the Protector's letters and speeches to popular reading and interpretation. As I argued in Chapter 2, Carlyle's directives on the speech of his subject are as ambiguous as the utterances themselves, and the novelistic 'elucidatory' prose transgresses the conventional relationship between the orders of 'aesthetic' and 'political' discourse. Frederic Harrison's biography of Cromwell for 'Twelve English Statesmen' negotiates this problem. This is the biographer's commentary on Cromwell's first recorded speech to Parliament:

Such was the first speech of Cromwell's which has come down to us, where he appears as a statesman, impressing his policy on Parliament and the nation. Both in form and in substance it is in the highest sense characteristic. There is the strong personality, the rough mother wit, the vivid and racy phrase, as of a man in authority taking counsel with his familiars, not as of the orator addressing the senate. There is the directness of purpose with laborious care to avoid precision in detail, any needless opposition, and all personal offence. The form is conciliatory, almost allusive; even the specific measure recommended is left to be inferred or subsequently defined. Yet the general purpose how clear! The will behind the words how strenuous![42]

Harrison's rhetorically double-voiced prose admits certain problems with Cromwell's speech viewed as the language of politics. It is imprecise, invites inference, and is even allusive. Yet it is, as the biographer's discourse seeks to assure us, the speech of a statesman. The reader is assured of this because the biographer's discourse works to limit the proliferation of the effects of Cromwell's speech: 'The general purpose how clear! The will behind the words how strenuous!' To be sure, Harrison admits that Cromwell's speech is rhetorical, but the rhetoric has presence – 'strong personality' – and its potential for proliferation is limited by an account of the relationship between addresser and addressees – 'a man in authority taking counsel with his familiars'. Both of these factors made it legitimate for Cromwell to 'impress his policy on Parliament and the nation', and for Parliament and the nation to be persuaded by statesman-like eloquence.

In his biography *Chatham* for 'Twelve English Statesmen', Harrison puts this limited defence of rhetoric more systematically. This systematic statement needs to be seen in the context of a problem on which the biographer elaborates: many of the sources recording Chatham's speeches were bound up in textual networks not of Chatham's making; Samuel Johnson, for instance, was one of the parliamentary reporters of Chatham's speeches. Accordingly, the biographer has to discriminate between 'statesman-like' speech and forms of expression which are passed off as 'rank Johnsonese', or 'fictions' of true speech.[43] How is this to be done?

An age which values itself on being nothing if not practical, commonplace, free-and-easy, and sceptical, is wont to sneer at the value of eloquence, and to despise it as literary artifice. But eloquence is of two kinds. There is the verbose advocacy of Cicero before the Praetor;

there is the heroic appeal of Demosthenes to his fellow-citizens. The first is literature; the second is statesmanship.[44]

Like Cromwell's rhetoric, which is aimed at and appreciated by Parliament and the nation, the eloquence of Demosthenes is aimed at and appreciated by particular addressees – his fellow-citizens. Contained in both of these constructions are notions of a common language community. As such, the Comtean view of language as a shared, conservative institution is in play. The eloquence of Demosthenes, Cromwell and Chatham is legitimate rhetoric because it respects the conservative rules of reference to the fixed order which is imposed on the signs of language. On the other hand, Ciceronian rhetoric is an illegitimate form of 'political' speech; it is 'verbose', and in this condition, the listener is in danger of being indulged by its aberrant conditions of existence. Harrison explicitly labels this latter kind of rhetoric 'literature'.

A similar understanding of 'literature' figured in an attempt to stabilise the frames and orders of discourse which were transgressed by Carlyle's elucidatory prose in *Oliver Cromwell's Letters and Speeches*. In 1904, a new edition of Carlyle's text was edited by S.C. Lomas. The edition was introduced by C.H. Firth, the new Regius Professor of Modern History at Oxford University, who was strongly committed to the idea of history as a field of scientific research. The introductory and scholarly apparatuses added to the 1904 edition of Carlyle's text serve to impose the authority of the new discipline upon Carlylean 'deviations', which Firth describes as 'imagination run riot',[45] thus assigning the biography to 'the domain of literature [rather] than to the domain of history'.[46]

As we have seen from the consideration of J.R. Seeley and the work of a group of associated biographer-intellectuals, this view of 'literature' as 'imagination run riot' arose from the disciplinary discourse of history that they shared and disseminated from a variety of institutional sites; 'literature' was a sort of aberrant linguistic supplement, history's Other. This understanding of 'literature' was also very important to the version of literary criticism that I want to explore in my final chapter. As I suggested earlier, recent accounts of the emergence of literature as an educational tool in the nineteenth century, like Eagleton's, have claimed that 'literature' stood for a placatory humanistic ideology. However, the view of literature that was advanced by liberal-Comtean intellectuals was far more complex than this, even though they conceived a place for literature teaching which would service the construction of a homogeneous public opinion. It was complex because these intellectuals recognised the plurality of the sign which in turn pointed to the dissident power of the heterogeneous cultural activity of reading itself – a power which could misread or challenge claims that might be made about politics and the direction in which the nation should move. It was in this sense that a more general attempt to organise reading was mounted; in practice, this can be seen in operation in Harrison's biographical commentary on Cromwell's speech, and Firth's commentary on Carlyle's prose. The discipline of history is the discourse in dominance within an ordering of discourse, but the biographer's voice also invokes other techniques of limitation to produce the effect of a publicly and politically acceptable form of rhetoric. These techniques of limitation ask readers to recognise certain forms of language which are external, practical and productively rhetorical in a controllable way. Implicitly, there also has to be an attempt to deal with the linguistic supplement which evades this discipline, and which has to be policed as 'literature', or a form of language which is effective but only in an 'imaginative' or aesthetic sense. In the final chapter, I shall examine the other series of biographies edited by John Morley – 'English Men of Letters' – and will argue that this series constituted the fellowship of discourse that carried out this policing.

5

□

Limiting the literary: biography and the construction of a fellowship of discourse

This final chapter will examine the way in which late nineteenth-century liberal-Comtean intellectuals perceived the energies released by 'literariness', and how they attempted to limit the threatening effects of these energies on the act of reading. As the foregoing analysis concluded, popular biographies which were produced in an attempt to circulate the 'rules' of the discipline of history continued to articulate an anxiety about the diversity and subversiveness of the reading practices that they might have to overcome. This problematic informed a simultaneously launched attempt to organise the act of reading through another series of popular biographies entitled 'English Men of Letters'. This series of biographies sought to establish the relations of authority supervising reading. Subversive reading was conceived as the activation of a certain kind of textual rhetoric; a kind perceived to be shadowed by a supplementarity that could not be contained by the project of discursive regulation embodied in the discipline of history. An instance of this mode of threatening textual rhetoric was Macaulay's popular imitation of ballads from ancient Roman culture – *The Lays of Ancient Rome*, a text widely circulated and read during the nineteenth century, and the second half of this chapter will consist of a reading of the political dynamics of James Cotter Morison's commentary on this hybrid 'literary-historical' text, contained in Morison's biography of Macaulay for 'English Men of Letters'. In order to explain the political dynamics of Morison's commentary, the first half of this chapter will account for the ordering of discourse that 'English Men of Letters' sought to institute. This account will draw on Foucault's theories of fellowships of discourse and author-function discourse. I will begin by establishing the parameters of intellectual fellowship that bound figures like John Morley and Leslie Stephen, and the ways in which these parameters of fellowship were simultaneously confirmed and frustrated by the institutional settings – public schools and universities – which defined them. I will go on to show how these intellectuals attempted to establish this fellowship as a form of public pedagogy which was designed to supervise popular reading relations. The fellowship was reproduced and authoritatively inscribed in the biographical commentaries comprising 'English Men of Letters' in an attempt to ensure wide, influential circulation. Monological reading was to be supervised by that technique of limitation described by Foucault as the author function, and the chapter will focus on the way in which John Morley constructed an author-function discourse which would assist the advance of liberal-Comtean cultural politics. The containing effects of this author-function discourse on possible ways of reading the aberrant dimension of Carlyle will be discussed, and this will lead to the concluding discussion of Macaulay and *The Lays of Ancient Rome*.

Along the way I shall rethink many of Terry Eagleton's points about the practice of late nineteenth-century literary criticism which have come to be influential, such as the assertion that literature was constructed as a simple substitute religion, that Matthew Arnold was the key figure in the development of criticism, and that 'literature' emerged as the central object of study in an 'English' ideological cultural programme. My argument will make three main points: first, Morley and Stephen's attitude to religion was founded on anxiety and hostility necessitating complex acts of intellectual contestation; second, there were versions of criticism competing with Matthew Arnold's; and third, for the formation of intellectuals with which I am concerned, literature was not the principal object of study in their cultural-political project. Instead their principal object was history. The effects of literature – perceived as a slightly untrustworthy, often aberrant rhetorical practice – were constantly being measured against the sovereign thresholds of historical discourse. When found wanting, this inferior discourse was attributed to an author and delimited as 'literary', the discourse being 'modified in its efforts' as Foucault observes, 'by the fact that it is recognised as literary'.[1] One other theme will be traced: fellowships are arrangments which depend on constructions of masculinity, and as a consequence the gender-based assumptions about the threat posed by 'literariness' will also be explored. It is to the masculine construction of intellectual fellowship in nineteenth-century public schools and universities that I shall first turn.

All fellows together?

"He calls us *fellows*," was the astonished expression of the boys when, soon after his first coming, they heard him speak of them by the familiar name in use amongst themselves.'[2] This is A.P. Stanley in his hagiographical biography of his old headmaster Thomas Arnold. We have already encountered Thomas Arnold as Professor of Modern History at the University of Oxford, and Arnold's sense of the importance of history to a modern education was an inheritance bestowed on a generation who were touched by the pedagogic ethos and system of Rugby. In the quotation above the biographer records the surprise registered by some pupils at Rugby when the Doctor, not well known for his geniality – 'As for rioting, the old Roman way of dealing with that is always the right one; flog the rank and file, and fling the ringleaders from the Tarpeian Rock'[3] – appeared to loosen up a little. Their surprise might have been due to an inability to reconcile this familiarity with other aspects of the Doctor's behaviour. As Stanley recounts, many of Arnold's pupils were repelled by his 'sternness', and an aloof distaste for 'wasting words on trivial occasions'.

A chosen few 'fellows' came to recognise this as 'manliness and straightforwardness'.[4] They saw no contradiction between inclusiveness of address and stern, austere discipline, and saw in Dr Arnold's demeanour an invitation into a privileged and gendered sense of belonging, which in the context of Arnold's Rugby was an offer of entry into a male elite bonded by a scheme of values centred on rigorous intellectual discipline – no wasted words – and a serious, broadly Christian, social consciousness. A.P. Stanley's biography of Arnold celebrated a public-school ethos which was keen to stress a masculine code that grounded its hegemonic aspirations through an eschewal of differences of religious doctrine and social background. Its Coleridgean ideology was important to the formation of the Christian Socialists; Thomas Hughes's *Tom Brown's Schooldays* (1857) is the best-known popular celebration of the connection between Arnold's Rugby and Christian Socialism. But it also produced a more cerebral generation of 'fellows', such as Richard Congreve, who focused their activities on the study of history.[5] While at Oxford, Congreve reached Comtean historicism via a reading of Book VI ('On the logic of the moral sciences') of Mill's *A System of Logic*, and this commitment to an historical method was passed on to a younger group of Comtist disciples, 'fellows' like Harrison and Morley.

These 'fellows' became convinced of the centrality of history through a system of pedagogy which was elitist and hierarchical. While the Arnoldian system was Socratic, the master/disciple relationship was never in doubt; to all at Rugby, Arnold was either a 'master' or 'instructor',[6] and with regard to his theological teaching, his biographer records the 'frequent topic of censure that his pupils were led to take up his opinions before their minds were duly prepared for them'.[7] As we have seen Foucault claim in developing the concept of the fellowship of discourse, fellowships distribute speaking roles unequally, and Arnold's pedagogical system carried with it certain rights and obligations with regard to the speaking roles that were possible; the master was instructor and questioner, and only after a certain rite of passage could these be safely reversed – once at university, Arnold's former pupils 'now felt the privilege of being able to ask him questions on the many points which his school teaching had suggested without fully developing'.[8]

University, however, brought ambiguous rewards, and students could find themselves excluded from the 'fellowship' of the universities, despite the display of considerable intellectual talent. Teaching fellowships were positions appointed by colleges; emoluments were attached, so they provided economic security. They were also controlled largely by the Church of England. Right up to the 1870s,[9] the established Anglican Church was an important controlling power in the affairs of Oxford and Cambridge. Dissenters were not allowed to matriculate at Oxford, matriculation being conditional upon subscription to the Thirty-Nine Articles of the Church of England; dissenters were allowed to study for degrees at Cambridge but they were not permitted to graduate. It followed that pronounced agnostics and atheists were similarly excluded from teaching fellowships. In 1854, Leslie Stephen was appointed to a Goodbehere Fellowship and made a Don of Trinity Hall, Cambridge – though it was conditional on Stephen taking Anglican orders within a year. When Stephen could not in conscience do this, he was required to leave the university. As we saw in the last chapter, Morley's potential teaching career as a university intellectual was terminated by his refusal to enter the Church.[10] Thus men whose ethos was modelled on the Arnoldian intellectual and moral (if not Christian) fellowship were excluded from the fellowship of an important national institution.

Although in the 1850s the liberal-Comtean intellectual project had been frustrated by the Anglican power structure of the universities, by 1903 its disciplinary content was authoritatively institutionalised in the British Academy. As we have seen already, Seeley's fashioning of the discipline of history at Cambridge gave positivism a place in the curriculum, and the British Academy drew Fellows from the reformed universities. The Academy also recognised the role of those intellectuals who had fought for university reform in the 1850s and, since their exclusion from the universities, had pursued a programme of intellectual work from outside the academy; Leslie Stephen was one of the original Fellows of the British Academy. The corporate purpose of the Academy – to discover the principles which regulate the progress of human society, and to advance the discovery of positive truth – was to be executed throughout a range of intellectual disciplines, managed by four sectional committees: History and Archaeology, Philology and its various departments, Philosophy, and Jurisprudence and Economics. Significantly, 'literature' was not managed by a separate disciplinary committee; in so far as it was a formalised mode of study for the British Academy, it was a department of Philology, which is to say that the interpretation of 'literature' for this body was always subordinate to a scientific, comparative-historical epistemology.[11] In fact, the positivist historicism espoused by the Academy meant that history was the foundational discipline, which kept the methodologies exercised by the other sectional committees on the epistemological royal road to positive truth. Lord Reay in his presidential address put it thus:

The task of the historian is very similar to that of the explorer of Nature's laws. Our colleague, Professor [J.B.] Bury, has . . . eloquently emphasised the application of strict scientific methods to the study of History, as the study of 'all manifestations of human activity.' Historical research with a view to obtain facts will be entitled to claim our most cordial support.

When Reay asserts that the discovery and collation of historical 'facts' will command 'our most cordial support', he is speaking within and for a positivist ordering of discourse. While scientific history is sovereign, Reay adds that although

> this strict scientific attitude voices the very aim of the Academy . . . if the facts of History are placed on record in an artistic, literary form, we shall not fail to appreciate such presentiment, as long as historical truth is not sacrificed.[12]

As such, there was a place for 'literature' in the Academy's fellowship of discourse, but its place was conditional. Words deployed in the service of historical explanation would be welcomed. Words wasted on trivial occasions would have to be dealt with by a fellowship of discourse.

How was this fellowship constituted, and how was its authority reproduced in popular forms? The Arnoldian project at Rugby envisaged an educated elite moving out from the school, thence to a university, and from there to a profession, providing a platform from which to play a privileged role in the direction of civil society. However, the whole relationship between elite-producing cultural institutions and civil society was open to transformation by the democratic reforms of the 1860s. Elitism had to be popularised. It is in this context that we can read John Morley's essay on 'The study of literature' for it outlined a framework which sought to inscribe its listeners formally in a fellowship of discourse that was at once Arnoldian and Comtean. Morley's essay also needs to be seen in the light of a popular textual realisation of this fellowship of discourse – the series of biographies that he edited entitled 'English Men of Letters'.

'English Men of Letters': reading and writing in a fellowship of discourse

'English Men of Letters' was designed to act as a series of guides to the lives of significant authors who had written in English. To qualify, these writers had to be neither English – Robert Burns, Nathaniel Hawthorne – nor men – Fanny Burney, Maria Edgeworth, George Eliot. I will say more about the construction of such categories of inclusion and exclusion shortly – for the category of the 'author' is itself, as Foucault has shown, not a self-evident, ahistorical given, but a discursively produced principle for generating and prohibiting relationships between texts.

In addition to being biographies, volumes in the 'English Men of Letters' series offered substantial commentaries on the writings produced by their biographee. As such, they were study-guides addressed to those who, having received an elementary education from the provisions of the Forster 1870 Education Act, were spurred on to undertake the formal study of English writing at a higher level:

> An immense class is growing up, and must every year increase, whose education will have made them alive to the importance of the masters of our literature, and capable of intelligent curiosity as to their performances. This Series is intended to give the means of nourishing this curiosity, to an extent that shall be profitable for knowledge and life, and yet be brief enough to serve those whose leisure is scanty.[13]

The university extension movement had been founded by Canon Barnett of Toynbee Hall in order to provide educational opportunities for those excluded from traditional higher education – the lower-middle and working classes, and women from all classes – but it was eventually taken over and organised by Oxford and Cambridge. It was seen as an opportunity to diffuse the fruits of elite culture with missionary zeal.[14] In 1887, the Vice-Chancellor of Oxford University described the 'mission' of the extension lecturers thus:

> The lecturers whom we send through the country are a kind of missionary; wherever they go they carry on their foreheads the name of the university they represent. To a great majority of these persons with whom they come into contact it is the only opportunity afforded of learning what Oxford means and what is meant by the powers of an Oxford education.[15]

In the same year John Morley addressed the students of the London Society for the Extension of University Teaching (Mansion House, London) on 'The study of literature'. The students whom Morley addressed may well have incorporated volumes from 'English Men of Letters' into their study; as Chris Baldick has suggested in his study of the social mission of English criticism, the lectures delivered on these courses were normally organised around a biographical paradigm.[16] Morley's address is a justification for studying 'literature', but as with justifications developed by others since then – like F.R. Leavis – 'literature' is seen as a form of resistance to cultural disintegration. For the address contains an assessment of the energetic centrifugal forces at work in language that Bakhtin would describe as heteroglossic, and which Morley anxiously accounts for as anarchy pressing from without *the* language: 'Domestic slang, scientific slang, pseudo-aesthetic affectations, hideous importations from American newspapers, all bear down with horrible force upon the glorious fabric which the genius of our race has reared'.[17] Morley asks his listeners/readers to accept that although the language is a 'fabric' which can be coloured by many alien dyes – a fear of popular forms of speech ('slang') and the effects of the productive forces of American culture are singled out – in reality, the English language is a homogeneous development.

Morley claims that it has been made homogeneous by the 'genius of our race'. This phrase carries Comtean assumptions about the developmental relationship between language, the people and an elite band of cultural producers. As we have seen (Chapter 3), Comte's theory of language held that nature has fixed its essential order on the signs that structure this conservative institution, an intuitive understanding of which is transmitted and developed through 'our race' which is assigned the quality of 'genius'. Although 'genius' would seem here to be an attribute of the collective, we need to bear in mind that Morley is instructing his audience on 'The study of literature', and 'literature' was being constructed as the writings and thoughts of particular geniuses – Shakespeare, Milton, Dryden and Pope being the principal exemplars. Morley's idea of the 'genius of our race' implicitly prioritises elite written production over common 'appreciation', and this was one of the constructions of 'literature' that organised the 'English Men of Letters' series of biographies. While the collective might be able to enter into and appreciate 'genius' at work, it was particular geniuses who laboured and produced writing which stabilised the signs of language in relation to the order of nature. This implied another, much more suspicious, understanding of the effects of 'literariness' perpetrated by the writings of rhetoricians.

Morley's discourse is in touch with Comte's anxiety about the practices of 'mere interpreters', or those who enjoy language without the effort that goes into the production of a writing based on the disciplined practice of relating language to nature. And like Comte,

Morley is not simply citing lax students as 'mere interpreters'; rather, he has in his sights a particular formation of writers and intellectuals, exemplified by Carlyle, Macaulay and John Ruskin – all of these figures are interpreters rather than producers because they have unleashed a rhetoric which is insufficiently disciplined. While Morley styles Carlyle as a reckless interpreter, the fact remained that Carlyle's 'interpretations' were texts in popular circulation which needed to be anchored to a view of the writer as owner, or author, because of the danger of dissident acts of appropriation. This is the problematic which frames John Nichol's biography of Thomas Carlyle for 'English Men of Letters'.

John Nichol had been a contemporary of Morley's at Oxford and, at the time of writing the life of Carlyle, held the position of Professor of English Literature at Edinburgh University. His *Carlyle* (1892) included a commentary which sought to stabilise those 'self-contradictions which, even when scattered further apart, perplex his readers and render it impossible to credit his philosophy with more than a few strains of consistent thought'.[18] Nichol's reading is in agreement with our earlier account of Carlyle's novelistic prose. However, Nichol is deeply worried about the consequences that will follow from Carlyle's contradictions, which Nichol renders as Carlyle 'taking liberties with his readers' (C, pp. 190–1). There is of course another way of looking at this, which is to say that Carlyle's inconsistencies open a space enabling readers to take the liberties, and from this angle Nichol's biography seeks to place limits on any potential interpretive liberties mobilised by Carlylean contradictions. The biographer observes:

> It is the misfortune of original thought that it is hardly ever put in practice by the original thinker. When his rank as a teacher is recognised, his words have already lost half their value by repetition. His manner is aped by those who find an easy path to notoriety in imitation; the belief he held near his heart is worn as a creed like a badge; the truth he promulgated is distorted in a room of mirrors, half of it a truism, the other half a falsism. . . . There is an ambiguity in most general maxims, and a seed of error which assumes preponderance over the truth when the interpreters are men easily led by formulae. (C, pp. 197–8)

To counter the threat posed by deviant 'interpreters', Carlyle's *œuvre* is given the status of thought rather than writing. In so far as this prelinguistic thought can be imperfectly exteriorised in words, the words only retain their 'value' when they are close to their origin; distance from their origin in the form of repetition immediately debases them. And following from this, the Carlylean *œuvre* is only pure when its interiorised status as 'belief' (the earnest thoughts from the 'heart') is protected from an exteriorised transmutation into a public 'creed' (which is compared to a 'badge'). Finally, once exteriorised, the author's private 'beliefs' are fatally distorted by a process of accumulating supplementarity strikingly compared to a room of mirrors, so that a commitment to the retention of their interiority is the only possible way to preserve their perception of 'truth'. But this is necessarily a defensive affirmation of 'truth'. 'Practical' writing – the 'exteriorised' language of statesmanship and history – authoritatively shadows this account as discourse which can have legitimate effects in the world of politics and public opinion. Carlyle's writing is, by contrast, cast as 'subjective' and only true to itself when interiorised. Carlyle's writing has been aestheticised by the rhetorically double-voiced prose of Nichol's biography. It has been moved across a threshold in order to be contained as 'literature' which should be read, or interiorised. The implications of these strategies also figure in Morley's address to the extension movement's students of 'literature'.

Morley warns the student of literature that to attempt to write and imitate the style of loose interpreter-writers like Carlyle, Macaulay and Ruskin would be damaging, and might even exacerbate the heteroglossic 'anarchy' which is the main source of Morley's anxiety. Instead, students of literature need to confine their studies to the practice of reading, primarily those writers who produce an exemplary understanding of the relationship between language and nature.[19] The students addressed are inscribed within a Comtean framework, in so far as the community of English language users is divided between consumers (the majority) and active producers (the elite). This fellowship – like Dr Arnold's teaching methods – assigns roles which grant unequal access to discourse.

Morley addresses his audience as readers; or more precisely, as members of a fellowship whose activities are regulated by the formal restraints designed to limit the circulation of discourse. To gather more precise guidelines about how reading should be practised, we should look back to Nichol's closing assertion in the extract from *Carlyle* quoted above. Nichol's warning – that men are too easily led by formulae – implies that the ideal reading is an empirical reading which is conducted through a language of observation and description. The closing insight into the dialogic energy in language (which is reduced to a question of truth and error), suggests that this empirical reading should be a monological reading. This coincides with an important proposition put forward by Graham Pechey in his discussion of difficulties surrounding the concept of dialogism in Bakhtin: that there are, strictly speaking, no monological texts, only monological readings.[20] The authorial figure of the English man of letters was a key to the attempt to get monological reading strategies observed in this fellowship of discourse.

What is an author? What is an 'English Man of Letters'?

In 1969, Michel Foucault wrote an essay asking the question 'What is an author?'; slightly less than a century earlier (1878) in his biography of Diderot, John Morley asked the question 'what is an English Man of Letters?' Both questions impinged on the relationship between modes of ordering cultural discourse and the direction of intellectual culture at crucial social and political junctures. For Foucault 'the author' functions negatively as a principle for limiting the social circulation of discourse. In posing the question 'what is an English Man of Letters?', Morley was attempting to settle the very function of authorship as the monologic supervision of reading relations which Foucault has recently attempted to dismantle.

Foucault's essay 'What is an author?' is in part about the problem of reading the works of Karl Marx and Sigmund Freud, and can be related specifically to the acts of political and cultural contestation which have become synonymous with '1968'. Marx especially was an author whose works were used as guides to praxis – a reading of these works according to authorial sanctions certainly informed the French Communist Party's understanding of the events that unfolded, and based on this reading, the Party insisted that the events of May 1968 did not constitute a revolutionary situation.[21] Foucault's claim that both Marx and Freud should be seen as 'founders of discursivity', or scriptors who have established 'an endless possibility of discourse' enables a very different mode of reading their texts.[22] This mode of reading presupposes the dismantling of those limiting technologies which have been constructed for producing readings based on a discourse of monological authorial ownership. It is these technologies that Foucault analyses in asking the question 'What is an author?' Foucault's essay is an attempt to analyse what he coins as 'author-function discourse'. The author function is in part designated by a proper name, but it is a proper name in a system, for:

> Such a name permits one to group together a certain number of texts, define them, differentiate them from and contrast them to others. The author's name serves to characterise a certain mode of being of discourse: the fact that the discourse has an author's name . . . shows that this discourse is not ordinary everyday speech that merely comes and goes, not something that is immediately consumable. On the contrary, it is a speech that must be received in a certain mode and that, in a given culture, must receive a certain status.[23]

At one level, the author function individualises discourse. Foucault argues that the historical emergence of the author function was bound up with the capitalistic commodification of writing, and the construction of strict rules of ownership, defining the author's rights, author–publisher relations and rights of reproduction.[24] John Nichol's biography of Carlyle for 'English Men of Letters' clearly deploys an elaborate inflection of these practices when Carlylean rhetoric is designated as its author's 'thought', or an object that he individually owns. Foucault's critique of the author function is aimed at some of the positions positively affirmed by Comte. Foucault's critical view of this mode of enclosing active rhetoric is a reaction to Comte's dictum, that the communal pleasures of language should not be enjoyed without deference to the productive genius that makes art and ideas. Comte's privileging of producers of linguistic artefacts seeks to limit the proliferation of discourse in practice, which Foucault also identifies as one of the key effects of the author function: 'the author is the ideological figure by which one marks the manner in which we fear the proliferation of meaning'.[25]

If at the level of false impressions the author function individualises discourse, at the level of functions and effects it is classificatory, and it is this system of classification that bestows 'authorial' status on acts of discourse. Classification individualises a unit of discourse or text only by assessing its individuality in relation to other acts of discourse. An extended network of discourses and texts managed by disciplinary limits and thresholds are implied by its use. Foucault admits that the author function is a complex principle of limitation when situated at the level of a single book or series of books carrying one signature; it becomes more complex again when used in relation to groups of works or entire disciplines.[26] John Morley wrestled with this complexity when he asked the question 'what is an English Man of Letters?' If Foucault's essay 'What is an author?' was a critical intervention in the politics of pedagogy in the late 1960s, then Morley's negotiation of the author function through biography was an intervention in the politics of popular pedagogy in late nineteenth-century Britain.

John Morley's men of letters: authorial discourses and the 'historic idea'

'English Men of Letters' looks like a testimony to the catholicity that prevailed over the study of writing in English in the later part of the nineteenth century. Philosophers and political theorists – Locke (Thomas Fowler), Hume (T.H. Huxley), Adam Smith (Francis W. Hirst), Hobbes (Leslie Stephen), and Burke (John Morley) – were included; so too were historians – Gibbon and Macaulay (James Cotter Morison) – alongside the poets that latter-day students of English studies might expect to find there – Spenser (Dean Church), Milton (Mark Pattison), Dryden (George Saintsbury), Pope (Leslie Stephen) and Wordsworth (F.W.H. Myers). And long before Ian Watt's *Rise of the Novel* had apparently broken new ground in literary history by charting the rise of the novel (1957), 'English Men of Letters' devoted biographies to Defoe (William Minto), Richardson and Fielding (Austin Dobson). However, as we shall see, this apparent catholicity was carefully supervised by author-function discourses which differentiated between worth and value of these men of letters.

In earlier chapters we have seen how the function of the man of letters was itself a topic in nineteenth-century cultural debate, and when Macmillan appointed Morley as commissioning editor for what became 'English Men of Letters', he attempted to reorientate this debate. This is evident in his deliberations over the title for the series; was it to be 'Short Books on English Authors' or 'English Men of Letters'?[27] Morley had difficulties with the implications of the title that he eventually chose: 'I am more and more averse to Men of Letters. To call Bunyan and Burns . . . by that title is certainly not good'.[28] We should recall that Burns was one of Carlyle's men of letters in *On*

Heroes and Hero-Worship, but there is more to Morley's objection than this. For Morley's difficulty with the title 'English Men of Letters' articulates the problem of devising author-function discourses for these diverse figures which would ensure that their writings were read and used appropriately, according to the historicist protocols of the liberal-Comtean fellowship of discourse. Morley attempted to find a French solution to an English problem through his biography of Diderot, published in 1878.[29]

In this biography Morley's rhetorically double-voiced prose makes Diderot's traceless 'talk' the essence of his power; 'Diderot was endowed with the gifts of the talker rather than the writer' (*D*, vol. I, p. 38). This way of constructing Diderot is marked by a distrust of Diderot's writing, which is represented as 'declamatory, ill-computed, broken by frequent apostrophe, ungainly, dislocated and rambling' (*D*, vol. I, p. 38). This leads to the judgement that 'his genius was spacious and original, but it was too dispersive, too facile of diversion, too little disciplined' (*D*, vol. I, p. 37). We need to bear this judgement in mind when considering Morley's use of Diderot in defining the function of the 'man of letters':

> Unlike the Jesuit father whom he replaced, he has no organic doctrine, no historic tradition, no effective discipline, and no definite, comprehensive, far reaching, concentrated aim. The characteristic of his activity is dispersiveness. Its distinction is to popularise such detached ideas as society is in a condition to assimilate; to interest men in these ideas by dressing them up in varied forms of the literary art; to guide men through them by judging empirically and unconnectedly, each case of conduct, of policy, or of new opinion as it arises. (*D*, vol. I, p. 18)

In his consideration of the short biographies comprising 'English Men of Letters', Ira Bruce Nadel has used Morley's definition to explain the rationale behind the project.[30] This is a reasonable argument; as his letter to Macmillan in November 1877 suggests, Morley would have been occupied in the writing of *Diderot* simultaneously to commissioning biographies for 'English Men of Letters'. But Nadel tends to take this to be an essential Comtean definition of the function of the man of letters. It is doubtful whether the discourse works in quite this way, for it is a comment on Diderot's position, function and shortcomings at a specific moment of historical transition, and is concerned with powers that Diderot lacked as well as those he possessed.

The statement ends by describing the productive function of the man of letters in Enlightenment France, which involves 'dispersing' or circulating writings which guide, shape and reform 'thought' in a period of transition. These writings are dispersed for pleasurable consumption. However, it is important that these discourses be seen as 'empirical' observations that are merely 'dressed' in this 'literary' form, for they will at some point need to be subjected to a disciplined practice of reading which can discriminate between the trivial and the important and lasting – remembering that other view of Diderot's writings, which judged them to be 'dispersive' and unreliable.

This is where we need to consider the significance of the opening of the above statement, or what Diderot found himself without, namely the 'discipline', or 'historic tradition', of the Church, embodied by the figure of the Jesuit Father. As we have seen, Morley was a non-believer whose career path had been blocked by the institutionalised power of the Church, and the control that it continued to exercise over the organisation of higher education. While the control exercised by the Church of England over the universities had been broken by the beginning of the 1870s, the new national system of elementary education was seen by Morley and other liberal intellectuals as instituting a new competition between the Church of England and the dissentient religious communities.[31] Morley is difficult to reconcile with Eagleton's view of late nineteenth-century literary critics as set out in *Literary Theory*, mourning the passing of organised religion and seeking for a substitute. The statement on Diderot suggests Morley was attracted to the Church, but this was largely to do with the power of its disciplinary technologies – in this instance the author function that it had historically used in the construction of disciplinary traditions.

As Foucault has argued in 'What is an author?', the canons of exegesis instituted by the Fathers of the early Church (particularly Saint Jerome (*c*. 331–420) exercised a lasting influence on the construction of the author function.[32] The author function became a powerful source of arbitration for determining authoritative narratives, and so those texts and discourses upon which the 'tradition' of the Christian Church had been built. This is precisely the strategy that Morley appropriates. As the biographer of Diderot, Morley's goal is to construct an adequate author function which will enable readers to discriminate between his subject's 'dispersive' written utterances.

Diderot's significant writings can then be situated in a tradition which has been progressively advanced by similarly orientated discourses by other men of letters.

But on what principles did Morley's biographical text construct this author function, and what tradition was it seeking to build? To answer this, we need to appreciate that Morley's biography of Diderot included estimates of other writers and writings contemporary to Diderot. In this sense, Morley's construction of an author function is a complex process of classification – it is situated at the intersection of a diverse body of writers and texts, disciplinary thresholds and limits. In fact, Morley constructs the legitimate author function for a man of letters through a reading of a text by Diderot's contemporary, Raynal, who was credited with writing the narrative *History of the Indies*. Like Diderot's 'dispersive' writings, the Raynal text comprises a complex rhetorical medley – genres of discourse are 'poured in, almost by hazard . . . rhapsody and sober description, history and moral disquisition, commerce, law, physics and metaphysics' (*D*, vol. II, pp. 207–8). In order to construct a unifying author function for Raynal, Morley isolates one textual gesture above all others, or 'Raynal's habit . . . of incessantly measuring events by their consequences to western enlightenment and freedom, and of dropping out of sight all irrelevancies of detail' (*D*, vol. II, p. 213). Morley identifies this master-narrative of positivist historicism as 'the historic idea', and this becomes the monologic point of authorial unification around which the true significance of Raynal's text can be organised, while irrelevancies and trivialities are filtered out of sight.

Morley's strategy for isolating a tradition through an author function was used for evaluating the writings of English men of letters. As I have demonstrated, John Nichol's biography of Carlyle deploys a characteristic manoeuvre of author-function discourse, which individualises Carlylean rhetoric and frames it as interiorised thought rather than outwardly orientated rhetoric. Nichol's biography also has to come to terms with the fact that Carlylean rhetoric is materially produced and circulated through contradictory texts. In response, Nichol turns to the author function as a classificatory principle for highlighting 'approved' positions in these texts by simultaneously mobilising an ensemble of disciplinary thresholds and limits. It is by these means that Nichol foregrounds selected aspects of Carlyle's texts about emigration and labour, which enables Nichol to claim Carlyle as an 'author' whose 'many . . . suggestions have found a place in our code' (C, pp. 208–9). In this instance, the 'code' that Nichol claims to share with his readers is premised on the discipline of political economy, a 'science' whose 'natural' laws, it was claimed, had been progressively uncovered since Adam Smith's breakthrough discovery in the later part of the eighteenth century.[33]

In John Nichol's biography of Carlyle, the subject's value and significance as an English man of letters is produced through an assessment of his relationship to 'the historic idea' of political economy; this 'historic idea' produces an author function against which to measure the performance of a writer, and through which to discard aberrant, supplementary forms of signification. This is more apparent in Thomas Fowler's *Locke* for 'English Men of Letters', where an author function defined by the discipline of political economy is explicitly a regulating feature of the biographer's assessment of the authority of Locke's writings.[34] The same technique was used by other biographers to measure their subject's writings against other master-narratives of positive knowledge. In Leslie Stephen's biography of Pope for 'English Men of Letters', the biographer instructs readers of Pope's philosophical poem, the *Essay on Man*, that the writer is 'disqualified to speak as a philosopher' because the author function which defines authoritative pronouncements in the field of philosophy is governed by an 'historic idea' beyond Pope.[35] What remains is the author function which constructs an image of the writer who is characterised by subjectivity and the expression of inner feeling: 'As soon as Pope has a chance of expressing his personal . . . attitudes, his lines begin to glow'.[36]

When an English man of letters writes in this way his 'thoughts' do 'much to familiarise [the reader] with the genius of the language'. This 'genius of the language' will 'also supply constant solace and occupation in those moments of depression and vacuity which are only too sure to occur in every man's life'.[37] This is Thomas Fowler on the purpose of 'literary' instruction in his biography of John Locke. The main theme of Fowler's statement – that language is the property of all while the monoglot purity of *the* language is transmitted to the reader by an elite band of producers or genius authors – is by now familiar from the foregoing analysis of the liberal-Comtean fellowship of discourse and the hierarchical reading relations that it sought to establish. Fowler's statement also comments on the positive value of literature – that it works on the inward being of the reader and nourishes a mind tormented by the pressures and conflicts of modernity. This notion of 'literature' was inflated until it was enshrined in the Newbolt Report of 1921 as the principal discipline promoting national salvation, and it is the one that is foregrounded by demystificatory studies of the rise of the discipline of English studies in the later nineteenth century.[38]

However, this foregrounding is anachronistic, and it overlooks the diversity of practices and strategies that constituted 'literary criticism' in the late nineteenth century. The point about 'literature' that emerges from the 'English Men of Letters' series is the absence of a disciplinary status *per se*. 'Literature' is not really in possession of a concrete object of study. Rather, 'literariness' came into being through the complex movement of author functions across the thresholds delimiting other disciplines and constructed histories of their development. Liberal intellectuals who wrote the biographies comprising 'English Men of Letters' were most concerned to demonstrate the extent to which their subjects' writings anticipated or furthered the development of a master-narrative of positivist progress. While the 'literature' that came about could be morally uplifting and mentally soothing it was not inevitably so, and the biographers who commented on the writings of 'English Men of Letters' were ever vigilant against what they saw as deviant forms of 'literary' rhetoric which threatened to subvert 'the historic idea'.

Functions of criticism: the liberal police

'Literature' as deviant rhetoric was thought to be manifest in writings by an earlier generation of critic-intellectuals, specifically Carlyle and Macaulay, or the 'mere interpreters' designated by Comtean theory. A grasp of this enables us to distinguish between two different practices of 'literary' criticism that were vying for authority in the late nineteenth century. Essays like 'The function of criticism at the present time' (1864), in which Matthew Arnold defined the practice of criticism as the disinterested and positively 'literary' basis of culture, are often taken to be representative. Matthew Arnold's definition of criticism may be the one that we remember (or rather, have been taught), but there was another in circulation. Indeed, a consideration of this alternative definition of criticism helps to cast new light on Arnoldian practices and the way they participated in the broader contest over the ordering of discourse.

John Morley had approached Matthew Arnold in an attempt to recruit him for 'English Men of Letters' – Morley invited him to write the biography of Shakespeare – but Arnold declined, thereby distancing himself from this pedagogic project.[39] This also distanced Arnold from the intellectuals who were responsible for the elaboration of the project; Frederic Harrison was identified as one of the 'enemies' of Arnoldian 'culture' in *Culture and Anarchy*.[40] In fact, these intellectuals articulated the function of criticism in a very different vocabulary to Arnold's, as evidenced by the confrontational prose of T.H. Huxley in his life of David Hume for 'English Men of Letters':

> It is the business of criticism not only to keep watch over the vagaries of philosophy, but to do the duty of police in the whole world of thought. Wherever it espies sophistry or superstition they are to be bidden to stand; nay, they are to be followed to their very dens and there apprehended and exterminated, as Othello smothered Desdemona, 'else she'll betray more men'.[41]

Huxley is normally associated with popularising biological evolutionary theory; certainly he is connected with Victorian science so it is perhaps surprising to find him defining criticism, a term that Matthew Arnold's legacy has led us to associate with literature. Huxley's view of the function of criticism is as ambitious in scope as Arnold's; if Arnold's criticism promised to preserve 'the best that has been thought and said in the world', then Huxley's criticism promises to perform its activities in 'the whole world of thought'. For Huxley, however, the function of criticism is to 'police' aberrant forms of sophistry rigorously in whichsoever field they manifest themselves.

Aside from the implications of intellectual repression, the most striking aspect of Huxley's definition of the policing function of criticism is the gendered identity that is attached to the Other which it is criticism's duty to 'exterminate'. Huxley's allusion to *Othello* clearly posits Othello as 'criticism' and Desdemona as aberrant 'sophistry'. Clearly, femininity is associated with an unreliable use of language and the betrayal of manly values. Masculine criticism has to apprehend the effects of this wayward femininity and remove its effects from ways of thinking, speaking and writing where it has no business. Huxley's definition of the function of criticism points to the extent to which the liberal-Comtean fellowship of discourse was premised on gendered values in which masculinity was the privileged guardian of true knowledge. We should recall this scheme of values from A.P. Stanley's biographical construction of Dr Thomas Arnold's demeanour, which exemplified 'manliness and straightforwardness', Dr Arnold's masculinity being evident from his refusal to indulge in the 'wasting [of] words on trivial occasions'.

What did Matthew Arnold's and Huxley's definitions of criticism share, and how did they differ? And in what ways do the implications of Huxley's definition enable us to rethink the centrality of Arnoldian criticism in the order of late nineteenth-century cultural discourse? Huxley and other liberal intellectuals, like Morley, Stephen, Seeley and Harrison, developed a view of criticism which attempted to resist forms of 'literariness' which were seen as rhetorical and aberrant. As I shall demonstrate, Matthew Arnold's view of criticism was also opposed to rhetoric, and the apparently 'feminine' basis of its deviancy. But there were also differences between Matthew Arnold and the biographers who contributed to 'English Men of Letters'. Arnold developed a practice of criticism which identified rhetorical forms of critical language while attempting to place true 'literary' objects beyond their grasp in the authoritative but ethereal realm of 'culture'. However, the more combative biographers responsible for 'English Men of Letters' actually policed forms of popular writing like Macaulay's *The Lays of Ancient Rome* through biographical commentary, and attempted to discipline devious 'feminine' rhetoric by filtering it through an author function which stressed its ineffective 'literariness'. Two rather different understandings of the value of 'literariness' and strategies for dealing with it were thus implied. These similarities and differences can be illustrated by focusing simultaneously on reactions to Macaulay's writings and G.O. Trevelyan's biography of Macaulay.

Trevelyan's *Life of Macaulay* and rhetoric

Matthew Arnold stated a distaste for rhetoric when commenting on the first major biography of Macaulay to be published. Arnold begins his essay entitled 'A French critic on Milton' (1877) by referring to G.O. Trevelyan's biography, *The Life and Letters of Lord Macaulay* which had been published in 1876. Arnold speculates that the publication of this popular biographical text would in all likelihood tempt readers back to the original writings of Macaulay. The text of Macaulay's on which

Arnold focuses is his very first published essay, 'Milton', which appeared in 1825 in *The Edinburgh Review*. Arnold asserts that 'a reader who only wants rhetoric . . . will find what he wants. A reader who wants criticism will be disappointed.'[42]

There are three points that can be drawn from this. The first is that Arnold is alert to the power of biographical writing as the point of mediation between an intellectual with aspirations to direct culture, forms of critical writing produced by the biographical subject, and the object of this criticism (Macaulay's commentary on Milton). Arnold recognises that biography, as the centre of an intertextual network, can authoritatively shape reading relations. The second point relates specifically to Macaulay as a biographical subject whose writings have been pushed to the centre by this network. In Arnold's view, Macaulay's writings are simply not worthy of the attention that may be paid to them. Arnold anticipates John Morley's advice to the university extension students in London in 1887, to stay off the writings of Macaulay. In other words – and this is the third point – Arnold attempts to discredit the work of Macaulay. And this is because there is, in his view, something profoundly wrong with the language of commentary and interpretation used by Macaulay.

Macaulay's interpretive 'rhetoric' is held to be the Other of 'criticism'; Macaulay's essay on Milton might aspire to be criticism, but a language that approaches *Paradise Lost* (Arnold cites this) thus cannot claim the name of criticism: 'Milton's conception of love unites all the voluptuousness of the Oriental harem, and all the gallantry of the chivalric tournament, with all the pure and quiet affection of an English fireside'.[43] This discourse, which Arnold cites as problematic, mixes images of reserved 'English affection' with popular stereotypical images of the 'voluptuous' Orient and chivalric romance. The problem that Arnold has with this 'rhetoric' is not merely that it weaves together popular images of love as a means of commenting on Milton's high epic poem – though this is a problem for Arnold; rather, the main source of Arnold's objection is the obscurity of the connections that the rhetoric suggests, and the sense that its writer has not attempted to impose any control on the conditions of its consumption.[44] Arnold trips by accident on a connection between 'femininity' and rhetorical supplementarity. This is not because there is anything essentially 'feminine' about these images; rather, they are culturally linked to the sphere of the popular and gendered constructions of feminine desire. And their lack of direction renders them suspiciously deceitful and thus 'feminine' in the sense pointed to in Huxley's account of the policing function of criticism. It is important to remember that Arnold is dealing only with what he sees as an illegitimate language of criticism; once this has been disposed of through further commentary, *Paradise Lost* as the true language of poetic literature can safely ascend to the authoritative realm of 'culture' where no commentary at all is either necessary or possible.[45]

Liberal intellectuals like Leslie Stephen and James Cotter Morison were also perturbed by Macaulay's rhetoric. However, for them Macaulay's rhetoric posed a problem that was part of the general prospect of disorder threatened by 'literariness', and they went to elaborate critical lengths to resist this. In order to understand the drives and anxieties that underpinned the critical manœuvres that I will go on to discuss, it will be necessary first to look at Trevelyan's biography of Macaulay and the biographer's preoccupation with his subject's attachment to popular 'feminine' fictions, and then to look at the consequences of this predeliction for Macaulay's writings and their authoritative status. For Stephen and Morison, Macaulay's 'literariness' threatened to undermine the progress of the positivist 'historic idea'.

Although Trevelyan's biography represents Macaulay as a master of statesman-like speech,[46] the biographer's rhetorically double-voiced prose also represents Macaulay in a relationship to popular, fictional uses of language. This arises in connection with a particular kind of speech that Macaulay shares with his sister:

> The feeling with which Macaulay and his sister regarded books differed from that of other people in kind rather than in degree. When they were discoursing together about a work of history or biography, a bystander would have supposed that they had lived in the times of which the author treated, and had a personal aquaintance with every human being who was mentioned in his pages. . . . The past was to them as the present, and the ficticious as the actual. . . . On matters of the street or of the household, they would use the very language of Mrs Elton and Mrs Bennet . . . and other inimitable actors on Jane Austen's unpretending stage.[47]

This representation of Macaulay's and his sister's relationship to books and reading recognises a refusal to draw a binding distinction between fiction and the real. Fiction becomes performative, because once its pleasures have persuaded these readers to let it enter their lives, its discourses are imitated in subsequent acts and forms of articulation. For Macaulay and his sister, fictional rhetoric from the past comes actively to inhabit the present. This fictional rhetoric is identified in terms of the intertextual, in that it is not simply a subjectively 'imagined' world, but a shared network of references with precise cultural and generic locations (the novels of Jane Austen). Indeed, Macaulay's immersion in a multiplicity of popular literary genres – from romantic novels to street balladry – is a recurrent motif of Trevelyan's biography.

Macaulay's preoccupation with the language of popular entertainment and especially the rhetoric of romantic fiction was not, however, restricted to private interpersonal exchanges with his sister. We have already glimpsed the way in which it pervaded his *History of England* (see Chapter 2). It was also manifest in the public reviews that he submitted to the periodicals. These reviews were often organised around the biographical genre, and concerned representative figures from political, literary and intellectual history. Macaulay's 1837 essay on Bacon for *The Edinburgh Review* included a consideration of the question of style which involved a comparison between the stylistic trajectories of both Francis Bacon's writing in the early seventeenth century and Edmund Burke's writing in the second half of the eighteenth century. Macaulay's discourse on Burke needs quoting at some length:

> The treatise on the 'Sublime and the Beautiful', though written on a subject which the coldest metaphysician could hardly treat without being occasionally betrayed into florid writing, is the most unadorned of Burke's works. It appeared when he was twenty-five or twenty-six. When, at forty, he wrote the 'Thoughts on the Causes of the Existing Discontents', his reason and his judgement had reached their full maturity: but his eloquence was still in its splendid dawn. At fifty, his rhetoric was quite as rich as good taste would permit; and when he died at almost seventy, it had become quite ungracefully gorgeous. In his youth he wrote on the emotions produced by mountains and cascades, by the master-pieces of painting and sculpture, by the faces and necks of beautiful women, in the style of a parliamentary report. In his old age, he discussed treatises and tariffs in the most fervid and brilliant language of romance.[48]

This claims that the political may legitimately be articulated and enacted through 'gorgeous' rhetoric and the 'feminine' language of romance; for as the narrative effect signifies, Burke reaches this position *after* 'his reason and judgement had reached their full maturity'.

Macaulay's narrative construction of Burke's stylistic trajectory is worth considering for reasons which go beyond its inversion of a positivist ordering of discourse. This is because the narrative had the potential to undermine the very logic of historicist thinking that helped to hold such an order of discourse in place. The play here is upon the conventional opposition between impulsive, exuberant youth, and rational, sober maturity; playfulness is generated by inverting the order of the styles of writing that are normally associated with each life-stage; the writing of Burke's youth is plain, the writing of his old age, when immersed in the affairs of the state, is highly coloured. By inverting assumptions about the status of life-stages, Macaulay was undermining a much grander narrative – the 'historic idea' on which the positivist narrative of progress itself was constructed. A confident assessment of the progressive path of civilisation depended on a narrative framework that could organise clear distinctions between the theological, the metaphysical, and the positive stages. In addition, the narrative would demonstrate an unambiguous advance towards a positive epistemology from the point of view of the mature and scientistic industrial civilisations; the point of view and the selective process of demonstration involved splitting the wheat – positive knowledge – from the chaff – metaphysical error. Given this narrative frame of mind, Macaulay's portrait of Burke's 'gorgeous' rhetoric delivered on political topics in late life was hardly a supportive account.

The extent to which aspects of Macaulay's writing were perceived by liberal intellectuals to have the capacity to endanger the authority of 'the historic idea' of positivism can be seen if we look at Leslie Stephen's essay, 'Macaulay'. Like Matthew Arnold's essay 'A French critic on Milton', this essay was written in response to the publication of G.O. Trevelyan's biography of Macaulay. The writing that Stephen sought to illegitimise was Macaulay's review of Ranke's *Ecclesiastical and Political History of the Popes of Rome during the Sixteenth and Seventeenth Centuries* (1840). In order to explain why this was so, we need to look at Stephen's understanding of the rhetorical dimension of Macaulay's writing.

Stephen casts Macaulay as a 'rhetorician' in the sense that his writings are consistently 'soaking . . . the mind' of the reader.[49] In discussing Macaulay's handling of sources when composing the *History of England*, Stephen adds, 'his real authority was not this or that particular passage, but a literature'. The discovery of entire 'literatures' embedded in Macaulay's historical writings suggests to Stephen that Macaulay's rhetoric acts as a connotative generator, activating a multiplicity of intertextual networks in the 'soaked' mind of the reader. By such means, this rhetoric 'knows how to stir the blood of the average Englishman'.[50]

This casts light on Stephen's attempt to illegitimise Macaulay's essay on Ranke. For in meditating on the persistence of belief in Roman Catholic ritual in early modern and modern Europe, this essay advances an implicit theory of interpretation which offered no comfort to positivists and their 'historic idea':

> Natural theology . . . is not a progressive science . . . it seems to us, therefore, that we have no security for the future against the prevalence of any theological error that ever has prevailed among Christian men . . . when we reflect that Sir Thomas More was ready to die for the doctrine of transubstantiation, we cannot but feel some doubt whether the doctrine of transubstantiation may not triumph over all opposition. More was a man of eminent talents. He had all the information on the subject that we have, or that, while the world lasts, any human being will have. The text, 'This is my body', was in his New Testament as it is in ours. The absurdity of the literal interpretation was as great and as obvious in the sixteenth century as it is now. . . . We are, therefore, unable to understand why what Sir Thomas More believed respecting transubstantiation may not be believed to the end of time.[51]

Stephen's anxiety is that this discourse represents the modern intellect 'wandering in a labyrinth without a clue'.[52] Macaulay's discourse not only offers an interpretation; it is about interpretation. While recognising the 'absurdity' of More's literal interpretation of the biblical text supporting what should be a symbolic notion of transubstantiation, the discourse simultaneously acknowledges the impossibility of overturning the authority of this 'absurd' application of the literal. As such, the discourse recognises the customary basis of interpretive practices, particularly the power of rhetorical conventions that have won the following of whole communities while eschewing the need to ground their validity through inductive method. What is more, the discourse asserts that this following can be won at any moment in history. It has scant respect for the positive stage of knowledge. It envisages the possible irruption of rhetorically generated forms of belief and practice at any point in history. Stephen, Morley and Harrison were deeply troubled by the residual authority of religious organisations – a residual authority which was regenerating itself into an emergent power in the last quarter of the nineteenth century through an alliance between High Anglican ritualism and socialism.[53] While Eagleton has claimed that nineteenth-century critics mourned the collapse of religious authority, from the point of view of the liberal intellectual formation its re-emergence was ominous, especially when allied to socialism. We need to remember that positivists like Seeley constructed socialism and the forms of political protest generated by it as an erroneous, metaphysical form of belief.

It is in the context of these anxieties that we can read the collective drive of liberal intellectuals to produce a practice of criticism that would police forms of 'literariness' which, having stirred 'the blood of the average Englishman' might then 'unman' the reader. It is in this sense that I shall consider James Cotter Morison's biography of Macaulay for 'English Men of Letters', and the detailed critical reading of *The Lays of Ancient Rome* that the biographer undertakes.

Authorising *The Lays of Ancient Rome* for the fellowship of discourse

Macaulay's *The Lays of Ancient Rome*, a part-critical, part-poetic reconstruction of ancient Roman ballads, was published in 1842 during the decade when both Carlyle and Macaulay blended the 'historical' with the 'literary'. *The Lays* manifested a number of problems. The text seemed to belong neither to popular culture nor to high culture. Its relationship to the master-narrative of positive history was subversive in that while it claimed to be a critical text based on the authority of sources, the lays themselves were fabrications or inventions of the present. Finally, its rhetoric seemed wilfully to evade the authority of an author; it was instead a product of what we, in the late twentieth century, call intertextuality. This is not to conduct the argument on the basis of an anachronism; any study that follows in the tracks of Bakhtin and Foucault necessarily sees intertextuality and the problems of discursive order and authority that it poses as the definitive problems of print culture. Different versions of 'criticism' constitute different imaginative solutions for dealing with this problem and its effects on reading. It is significant that while Matthew Arnold's criticism denied commentary to writing such as *The Lays* and concentrated its reverent attentions on poetic 'touchstones' from Homer to Milton, James Cotter Morison's criticism confronted the problem of intertextuality posed by *The Lays* and subjected it to a rigorous evaluative system framed by an 'English Men of Letters' biography.

James Cotter Morison, an Oxford academic who was affiliated to liberal intellectuals such as Morley and Harrison,[54] wrote this biography in 1882.[55] In representing the life of Macaulay, the biography closely follows G.O. Trevelyan's narrative; the early life being a tale of infant prodigy, close-knit family life in an Evangelical household, and the imbalanced intellectual career at Cambridge, displaying brilliance in the study of classical languages, and total indifference to mathematics and other branches of science; leading to the later story of financial vicissitude and the necessity of a career in practical affairs of imperial administration and statesmanship, culminating in the prolonged devotion to the writing of the *History of England*.

There are, however, important aspects of this narrative which Morison's biography re-evaluates. This is particularly so in the case of Macaulay's relationship to popular literature, a relationship that was enthusiastically represented in the Trevelyan biography. Thus, in Morison's version of the story of family life, the young Macaulay is represented as 'being allowed to indulge almost without restraint his strong partiality for the lighter and more attractive forms of literature . . . there is no evidence that he . . . was ever submitted . . . to a mental discipline of a more bracing kind' (*M*, p. 6). In contrast to the Trevelyan biography, Morison's biography presents the relationship as a moral and intellectual failing. 'Literature' is presented as 'light' and 'attractive', and it is opposed to 'discipline'. The full implications of this opposition become clear when the biographer comments on Macaulay's intellectual predilections at Cambridge:

> His disproportionate partiality for the lighter sides of literature met with no corrective. . . . The poets, orators, and historians, read with a view chiefly to their language, formed a very imperfect discipline for a mind in which fancy and imagination rather needed the curb than the spur. . . .

We shall have repeated occasion in subsequent chapters to notice his
want of philosophic grasp . . . his deficient courage in facing intellectual
problems. (*M*, p. 9)

There is a recurrent concern with Macaulay's imbalanced 'partiality'
for 'light' or popular literature. 'Discipline' is invoked as the essential
means of restoring balance. The discipline that Macaulay lacks can be
traced in his reading of the texts which he was required to study;
instead of reading classical orators and historians with a view to
deriving concrete knowledge of 'things', he attends misguidedly to
their rhetoric. Macaulay's interpretation of history and politics sails
dangerously close to Seeley's idea of metapolitics; and this attention to
the constitutive powers of rhetoric is held to be a dangerously
'subjective' and fanciful indulgence of the imagination. What this habit
of interpretation lacks is 'philosophic grasp', or 'courage'. As we have
seen from Huxley's discourse on criticism, philosophic rigour is
defined as punitively masculine; lowly 'feminine' sophistry is 'bidden to
stand' and answer to it. According to Morison, Macaulay cannot stand
and face masculine 'intellectual problems'. The difficulty with *The
Lays of Ancient Rome* is that it attempts to confront intellectual problems
relating to questions of historical agency and epistemology without
reference to the disciplinary thresholds and limits maintained by the
liberal-Comtean fellowship of discourse.

The Lays of Ancient Rome

The Lays of Ancient Rome was highly popular. In the first ten years of
sale, 18,000 copies were bought; by 1862, the figure had reached
40,000, and by 1875, 100,000 copies were in circulation.[56] A late
feature of this wide circulation was the eventual institutionalisation of
the text in the education system; from their initial appearance, the
ballads, with their representations of acts of heroism and glory
celebrating the founding acts of Roman civilisation and history, were
considered to be good reading for the young, and from the 1890s,
specific editions designed for school use were produced.[57] Their
availability and accessibility prompted the need for a disciplined guide
to the reading strategies that might make use of them. However, the
need to provide a disciplined approach to their reading was also a
response to their nature. While some of the ballads were didactic and

patriotic elementary poems, the collection overall was a comment on the formation of 'historical' knowledge, and articulated a theory of the relationship between rhetorical acts and the historical process. This theory was articulated in a scholarly dissertation which bound together the verse texts. The dissertation states that 'a popular exposition of this theory and of the evidence by which it is supported, may not be without interest even for readers who are unacquainted with the ancient languages'.[58] The aim of this assertion would cause difficulties for the relations of exclusivity inscribed in the pedagogic hierarchy envisaged by a fellowship of discourse. Its commitment to popular exposition and translation, especially of theories relating to the classical languages, would have been frowned upon by Matthew Arnold, who in his essay 'On translating Homer' (1861) insisted that the only legitimate access to Homer was through an intimate knowledge of the Greek language developed by a university education. Such a commitment lifted restrictions on the circulation of discourse and it eroded the boundary between 'high' and 'low' culture. But what problems did the theory itself pose? The 'Preface' follows Niebuhr's theory of early Roman history: that episodes from the history of early Rome which had become familiar through being represented in the prose narratives of historians such as Livy, had their actual origins in anonymous oral vehicles in the form of lays and ballads. The early history of Rome was thus built on 'romance and drama' (*LAR*, p. 7).

The 'Preface' is in two minds as to the effects of 'romance and drama' on the political formation of modern societies. On the one hand it presents these effects as features of a faded, long-dead practice – 'a certain point in the progress towards refinement' (*LAR*, p. 9). On the other hand, in order to clinch its thesis concerning the transformation of oral, poetic memory into prosaic historiography, the scholarly dissertation raids 'scientific' historiography of the modern period in order to find its buried dependency upon oral modes of proliferation (*LAR*, pp. 21–2). The embedded residual effects of minstrelsy are not in the end confined to the distant past; and in the introduction to the ballad 'Virginia', songs are held to be 'by no means without influence on public affairs' in modern times (*LAR*, p. 85). For nineteenth-century society, which was beset by the problem of class relations and the potential for class unrest, this was not a source for comfort, given the subject matter of 'Virginia'; 'Virginia' is concerned with the conflict between patricians and plebeians. In fact, the violence between the classes that the ballad dramatises is overlaid by passions generated by gender relations and family politics; for the oppression of the plebeians is symbolised by the attempt of the patrician Appius Claudius to enthral the plebeian Virginia as a slave, which ends in the destruction of Virginia at the hands of her father, who chooses death for his daughter rather than sexual violation. Indeed, the introduction to the lay points to the capacity of the rhetoric of the ballad to make history repeat itself; the lay could be mobilised to create a similar reaction in moments of social crisis distant from the events recalled by the ballad (*LAR*, pp. 82–9). When *The Lays of Ancient Rome* became institutionalised as a school text, 'Virginia' was the ballad most likely to be cut from the collection.[59]

In *The Lays* the word does not function as a neutral unit furnishing historical representation, but rather as an agent generating historical acts at the same time as recalling past episodes to memory. All the introductions to the verses involve the reader by stressing the importance of imagining the context in which these restored ballads would be performed, and the effects that they might produce on their audience; in short, their rhetorical power. The scholarly introductions take as their theme the discursive effect which troubled Leslie Stephen in his reading of Macaulay; that is to say, the capacity of language to persuade and construct allegiances on the basis of interpretive conventions, rather than reason guided by inductive method. In the way that Macaulay's interpretation of Thomas More's attachment to transubstantiation seemed to militate against the 'necessity' of historical progress, the rhetoric of balladry in ancient Rome disorientated history and refused to allow it to run on a straight, progressive path. Unlike Macaulay's *History of England* where past and present are carefully separated, the line policing the difference and distance between past and present was not rigidly drawn by *The Lays*, producing the effect of the present as a cyclical repetition of the past, and the past as a domain consisting of instantly recognisable types, relationships and conflicts.

When it came to the acts of poetic reconstruction themselves, the voice conducting the 'Preface' declares that:

> In the following poems the author speaks, not in his own person, but in the persons of ancient minstrels who know only what a Roman citizen, born three or four hundred years before the Christian era, may be supposed to have known, and who are in nowise above the passions and prejudices of their nation. (*LAR*, pp. 23–4)

This act of denying the presence of a single authorial personality or style, which is performed to confirm and validate the 'pastness' of the ballads, also has the effect of inserting the texts into the heart of the present. For 'the author' sacrifices himself to the cause of historical veracity; he cannot speak in his own voice, but must subordinate himself, in the spirit of anonymous oral culture, to the reconstructed voices of the nameless carriers of the ballads. As these reading directives indicate, none of the ballads are controlled by the moralising gaze of an author in the present. Readers must enter into the Otherness they convey which will disrupt the public and private conventions, mores and discriminations constituting nineteenth-century culture. This has the effect of empowering the reader in relation to the verses, making the reader in the present the crucial element in their production.

As a consequence of empowering the mid-nineteenth-century reader, the verses had to offer that reader some familiar reference points; the 'Preface' states that 'it would have obviously been improper to mimic the manner of any particular age or country' to an extent that would render the verses undesirable to their main consumers. To compensate, the 'Preface' makes clear that it has 'borrowed' from more familiar generic sources, particularly 'our own old ballads', to make the artefacts amenable to certain cultural expectations (*LAR*, p. 24). In fact, these ballads borrow from a far more extensive pool of sources.

To take a specific instance, when confronted with the ballad 'Virginia', the reader is asked to enter sympathetically into the class conflicts of 'distant' antiquity. The sympathy demanded is to be wholly invested only in the plebeian side of the conflict, to which the ballad of 'Virginia' is addressed. The sympathy is generated by an intertextual network, consisting of an amalgam between the codes of mid-nineteenth-century English civic discourse, and popular melodrama, that are used to represent the heroine and her dilemma. To put this into broader conceptual terms, while the professed intention of the scholarly 'Preface' is to confine the object of its scholarship to the past, the actual effect of the verses at their moment of consumption might be very similar to the rhetorical function of ancient historical balladry. In being granted independence from the author figure, and invited to exercise interpretive powers in relation to an Otherness which is meaningful only in terms of combinations of recognisable nineteenth-century codes, the reader is confronted with a paradox: that is, an artefact that claims to respect the Otherness of the past, while simultaneously being cast in a form which makes 'the past present and the distant near' through the intertextual fabrications drawn from the present.

Biographical commentary: re-inscribing author functions

As a mediator between the late nineteenth-century reader and *The Lays*, Morison's biography of Macaulay seeks to inscribe that reader within the liberal-Comtean fellowship of discourse by securing the text to the figure of the author, even though *The Lays* foreground authorial absence as a purposeful strategy. Significantly, authorship is measured in relation to the thresholds and limits set by the discipline of history. This disciplinary mode of author-function discourse is in the end invoked to police the intertextuality of *The Lays*.

Necessarily then, Morison's biographical commentary on *The Lays* is attuned to their generic diversity. Morison's reading of *The Lays* is a sophisticated attempt to come to terms with the intersecting traditions, genres and codes that organise the text as a reading experience. First, as the commentary points out, the ballads are founded upon a 'descriptive' code:

> Line after line contains nothing but the most simple statement of fact in quite unadorned language. For instance: –

> But with a crash like thunder
> Fell every loosened beam,
> And, like a dam, the mighty wreck
> Lay right athwart the stream;
> And long a shout of triumph
> Rose from the walls of Rome,
> As to the highest turret tops
> Was splashed the yellow foam.

> Every statement might be made with propriety by a simple man . . . who had witnessed the event. . . . Each line might form part of a bald report, and yet the whole is graphic simply because it is literally true. (*M*, pp. 110–11)

What is striking about the commentary's treatment of the 'descriptive' code is its 'discovery' of a legitimate model of historical representation (as fetishised by the discipline from Ranke onwards); the lines are 'simple statements of fact', made up of verbal units that are 'unadorned'; indeed, the commentary goes on, the code connotes that these 'factual' units could have their origin in a 'simple man' who has been able to report what is 'literally true'. To take *The Lays* to be the authoritative account of a reliable and 'simple man' would be a mistake, for Morison points out how these are located amongst other contradictory codes which threaten to 'unman' the reader.

The reader would not be 'unmanned' by what Morison implicitly identifies as the civic code, which is very much to the fore: 'in Macaulay's ballads the State is everything' (*M*, p. 114). That is to say that it determines the celebrated heroic deeds, and is the essential frame within which the represented actions are justified. The civic code organises knowledge according to a framework of obligatory relations between a subject and state. There is a connection between the descriptive and civic codes; as I argued in the last chapter, 'referential' language was presented as the code for describing the historical growth of nations, and sought to discipline an understanding of the subject's inherited public obligations to the state. However, the weaving of the civic code into the ballad genre does not achieve this effect, and prompts Morison's commentary into an extended discussion. As the commentary notes, *The Lays* have as their most immediate generic ancestors the ballads of Sir Walter Scott – *The Minstrelsy of the Scottish Borders*, *Marmion* and *The Lay of the Last Minstrel* – and they clearly draw upon these influential performances. While drawing on these generic precursors, Macaulay's *Lays* at the same time mutate the genre in grafting it to the civic code. As the commentary points out, the Scott ballads are exclusively concerned with primitive feudal relationships; actions are played out in a 'private' world of interpersonal obligations. As such, *The Lays of Ancient Rome* appropriate the interpersonal generic base of Scott's performances for essentially 'public' or civic purposes. In escorting the reader through the various codes and genres that organise *The Lays*, the purpose of Morison's commentary is to point to what it deems to be incompatible combinations. For representing heroic deeds – Horatius's defence of the bridge, the Battle of Lake Regillus – in terms of civic obligations and duties owed to the state is one matter; but the interpersonal tragedy of a father's murder of his daughter represented through such language is another.

It is the problem of interwoven and incompatible 'public' and 'private' discourses that becomes concentrated on the ballad 'Virginia'. The figure of Virginia is obviously a construct drawn from popular fictional representations of Victorian innocent femininity, and is set in the domain of the 'private' (school/home):

> Just then, as though one cloudless chink in a black
>   stormy sky,
> Shines out the dewy morning star, a fair young girl
>   came by.
> With her small tablets in her hand, and her
>   satchel on her arm,
> Home she went bounding from the school,
>   nor dreamed of shame or harm;
> And past those dreaded axes she innocently ran,
> With bright, frank brow that had not learned to
>   blush at gaze of man . . . (*LAR*, p. 91)

The situation to which she is subjected – the threat of her sexual enslavement at the hands of the patrician leader, Appius Claudius – places her in a web of relations which escalates the ballad to a climax. The representation of this climax is crucial to the legitimacy of, first, the ballad's resolution, telling of plebeian crowd violence directed at the patricians; and second, the persuasiveness of the ballad as an incitement to act again in response to the rhetoric in which the crisis is resolved. So it is significant that the climax is represented in public-political language by the persuasive oratory of the young Icilius (*LAR*, pp. 92–3). It is also significant that the language of resistance to abuse of civic identity and civil rights that structures this central declamation permeates the language of the father, Virginius, as he reasons his way to the killing of his daughter (*LAR*, p. 96).

The point about Virginia is not just that she is merely an object of the ballad – though clearly she is, in that she never once attains the status of a speaking subject – but rather that she is an object whose dilemma can be seen simultaneously in terms of the 'private' language of popular literature, and the 'public' language of politics and the state. 'Virginia' depends for its effect on the intertextual meshing of, on the one hand, representations of 'private' femininity drawn from the language of popular literature and, on the other, the 'public' language of civic obligations and rights.

Morison's commentary constructs two author functions, 'the artist' and 'the liberal politician', in an attempt to contain the reader's involvement in the meshing between public and private rhetorics, and limit the ballad's 'meaning' to a monologic tension between opposed tendencies in Macaulay's career (*M*, p. 116). Furthermore, in the commentary on the supposedly interpersonal moment of Virginius's address to the daughter whose life he is about to take, Morison explains this mixed encoding as a deficiency in the sensibilities of the private author behind the text: 'in any case Macaulay seems to have been unusually incapable of, or averse to, the expression of tender and pathetic sentiment' (*M*, p. 117). The 'English Men of Letters' biography constructs an author flawed by warped capabilities of feeling and expression. In being made subject to a limit, the dangerous rhetoric of 'Virginia' is, to borrow Foucault's phrase again, 'modified in its efforts by the fact that it is recognised as literary', or to be more precise, flawed monologic 'literature'. This was to become a repeatable formula for witholding this text about crowd violence from readers in organised pedagogic contexts. W.J. Addis drew upon it to justify his exclusion of 'Virginia' from his school edition of Macaulay's *Lays* when it was published in 1902.[60]

In line with Foucault's claim about the workings of author-function discourse, the author function which reproduces and delimits 'Virginia' as monologic flawed 'literature' achieves its effects in relation to a wider field of texts and disciplinary thresholds. The field of historiography is invoked as a means of critically policing the wayward combination of codes that threaten to 'unman' the reader of *The Lays*. This is deployed against the contradictory invitations extended to the reader, that effectively make 'the past present and the distant near'; that is to say, strategies that render the Otherness of the past recognisable by casting it in the discourses and images of the present, while claiming to be exercises in truth seeking scholarship. Morison's commentary deems that a genuine lover of the truth would not issue such contradictory invitations (*M*, pp. 122–3). This places Macaulay beyond the pale of genuine lovers of truth – named as Hallam, Grote, Ranke, Freeman – who are presented as the founding fathers of a fellowship of historiographical discourse (*M*, p. 124). The disciplinary nature of this fellowship is strikingly articulated through juridical discourse – 'the court of history' (*M*, p. 74) – which is entitled to pass judgement on statements that stand before it; declaring that a 'simple unornate statement of the results obtained is the only style of treatment consonant with the dignity of genuine inquiry' (*M*, p. 140).

The disciplinary jurisdiction of 'the court of history' spread wide with regard to the circulation of Macaulay's *Lays*; certainly it was directed towards those editions of Macaulay's *Lays* prepared by R.L.A. du Pontet (1897), which appeared in the series 'Arnold's British Classics for Schools', the 'Preface' declares that readers of the *Lays* should be more interested in the verses than the scholarly apparatus that frames them. The latter should mainly be of interest to 'the historian', who should declare their conclusions to be spurious: 'there is nothing to show that any classical writer on Roman antiquity believed, or suspected, that poems of this kind contributed, in any material degree, to the formation of early Roman history'.[61] Despite this rejection of the theory of power attached to the act of historical representation by *The Lays*, there is an ambiguity here surrounding the term 'history' which cannot expel the insight of that theory. 'History' always slides between two meanings; first, the events that have happened, and second, the encoding of the events that have happened, which becomes an event, a release of energy, in itself. In referring to 'the formation of early Roman history', does the 'Preface' refer to the events brought about by temporality and the force and will of earnest individuals and the masses that follow them? Or does the 'Preface', through its own authority to articulate and pronounce, effect the formation and proliferation of rhetorical representations, tropes that have been authorised as neutral historiography? Perhaps there is no need to choose; perhaps the ambiguity is instructive because it points to an interdependence between the two senses that a late nineteenth-century ordering of discourse sought to repress.

At the base of this repression was an anxiety about the materiality of language, its modes of circulation and availability to appropriation, and a lurking uncertainty about the identity and make-up of the dissentient audience who might seize and reproduce textual rhetoric for their own radical purposes. In the light of this, it is appropriate to conclude with a very positive review of *The Lays of Ancient Rome* that appeared in the Tory *Blackwood's Magazine* (December, 1842). Pre-dating the mature emergence of the fellowship of discourse that I have been exploring in this chapter, it is a review that points to those very anxieties that propelled the formation of the liberal-Comtean pedagogic programme. The reviewer finds in the death of Virginia a representation of 'great natural affections' which is likely to generate pathos[62] – a judgement we have seen overturned by Morison's Comtean biographical reading of the text. The question of what readers beyond the community of *Blackwood's* readers will make of the oratory in 'Virginia' and its representation of class conflict is broached in frank but alarmist terms:

> No such mob-orator and poet, in our days, have our Tribunes of the people. Such spokesmen might do the state some mischief. . . . Thank heaven the history of our party feuds can show no comparable crime; yet there is no want of fuel in the annals of the poor, if there were fire to set it ablaze. What mean we by mob? The rabble? No! The rascal many? No! No! No! Burke never in all his days called the lower orders of Parisians, at any period of the Revolution, '*the* swinish multitude'. His words are '*that* swinish multitude' – at one particular hour. . . . Mob is *mobile*. It matters not much how it is composed, provided it be of the common men and women, and that they have, or think they have, wrongs to be redressed or avenged.[63]

The reviewer starts with an aesthetic judgement; the satisfactory representation of Virginia's plight which generates pathos. But this aesthetic judgement is intimately bound to a broader range of rhetorical considerations. These include a survey of the conventions supporting contemporary popular-political oratory, which suggests that the reviewer has an insight into the process through which 'Virginia' might be read or productively activated by a range of discourses 'external' to it. If the reviewer finds little in contemporary political oratory and the party political system to generate alarm, the conditions of existence of collective forms of protest are another matter. For in being both 'mobile' and time- and place-specific – in that space, at that particular moment, but with the potential to be elsewhere – the concept of the 'mob' is as mobile as discourse itself. It is in fact enabled by the mobility of discourse. It is precisely this which alarms the reviewer, rather than some stereotypical image of *the* mob as an irrational and monolithic mass – a manner of representing 'the mob' from which the reviewer distances himself. For this reviewer from the 1840s, the conditions of existence of a 'literary' discourse were far from simple. And although James Cotter Morison's contribution to the formation of a corrective fellowship of discourse was defensive and disciplined, the means by which he and other late nineteenth-century critic-biographers sought to limit and contain the 'literary' were equally complex.

Conclusion: Custodians of discourse

Terry Eagleton's account of the 'rise of English' in the nineteenth century is punctuated by ripostes parodying the thinking that structured the social mission of English studies in the nineteenth century. These are designed to sum up the naivety of the enterprise and to persuade us that, so far as the discipline of English literature is concerned, the game ought by now to be up: 'if the masses are not thrown a few novels, they may react by throwing up a few barricades' (*LT*, p. 25). But as we have seen, for the reviewer in *Blackwood's Magazine* of 1842, the random circulation of texts amongst a heterogeneous and indeterminable range of dissentient reading formations was the very source of the problem. The reviewer for *Blackwood's* asks: Which groups will gain access to and read 'Virginia'? Which signs and narratives of collective identification ('the annals of the poor') will they use to activate the text? What collective acts might follow from this act of reading? To be fair to Eagleton, in *The Function of Criticism* he saw that such questions were symptomatic of pressing anxieties about 'literacy' which beset nineteenth-century critics:

> What is most ideologically undermining is a literacy which is not literacy, a form of reading which transgresses the frontier between blindness and insight, a whole nation which reads but not in your sense of reading, and which is neither quite literate nor illiterate, neither securely within one's categories nor securely the other of them. It is at this deconstructive point, this *aporia* of reading, that the critic finds himself addressing an audience which is and is not his equal.[1]

157

Eagleton's vocabulary tantalisingly implies that the abstract critical preoccupations underwriting present-day deconstruction and post-structuralism once exerted a vital pressure which charged and challenged the social criticism of the nineteenth-century man of letters. This is an arresting insight, and an insight which my argument would endorse.

But Eagleton's metaphor of book-throwing suggests that in his view the response of nineteenth-century intellectuals to the social deconstruction of literacy norms was at once narrow and naive. A narrow romantic-expressivist notion of 'literary' transcendence, shared by successive generations of writers, came to prevail. This came to be enshrined in a practice of 'English' literary criticism which was both enormously ambitious in its social mission, and stupendously naive in its broader political reckonings; a criticism which believed that it could break down the barricades of class difference by throwing books at them. However, as we have seen, if the reviewer of Macaulay in *Blackwood's* identified a social process in which reading norms were deconstructed, then James Cotter Morison's 'English Men of Letters' biography of Macaulay participated in the construction of a far from naive criticism which attempted to discipline deconstructive acts at their social source, and that social source was language.

Morison's criticism was grounded in a theory of language elaborated by Auguste Comte. This theory of language held that whereas the relationship between the sign and the referent was fixed in nature, erroneous uses of language had blurred and perverted this relationship, leading to prolonged epistemological and social conflicts over the question of the direction of European polities. For Comteans this theory was demonstrated in practice by the workings of history. Previous epochs had been marked by 'theological' and 'metaphysical' uses of language, while the progressive march of history towards the 'positive' stage was increasingly characterised by disciplined uses of language which respected the fixity of the sign. But there were trends which held this progress back, and even within the regime of the 'positive', aberrant forms of language continued to be issued as invitations to shape utopian forms of political direction. It was precisely because J.R. Seeley was a positivist historian that he paid keen attention to language. Following Seeley, a formation of liberal-Comtean intellectuals defined these aberrant forms of language as 'literature'. For Seeley, 'literature' was not the transcendent healer of class conflicts; instead it was just as likely to fuel them. According to the liberal-Comtean formation, there was a 'literary' language of subjectivity and expressiveness, but it was to be treated warily, and framed for use in 'artistic' contexts which envisaged the proliferation of very limited effects. The legitimate and specialised 'positive' language of politics, which alone could ensure future progress along the tracks established by canonical positivism, had to be expunged of traces of 'literariness'. The positive language of politics was enshrined in the more authoritative discipline of history.

Canonical positivism was articulated by intellectuals through biographical writing representing significant individuals who advanced the master-narrative of positivism, gradually but progressively towards the final goal of the positive polity. In addition, Seeley's use of biography was envisaged as a bridge conveying the institutional authority of the History School of Cambridge University to his conception of a popular audience. Seeley, like other intellectuals of his generation, was preoccupied with questions concerning the circulation of discourse, and his rationale for the place of biography in historical writing was symptomatic of this. Liberal intellectuals such as Seeley, Morley, Harrison, Stephen and Morison confronted the mobility of discourse and the uncertain conditions under which it might be appropriated – and they attempted to impose restraint on these multiple energies through the maintenance of a fellowship of discourse which was disseminated through forms of popular pedagogic biography, especially the 'English Men of Letters' series. Thus Eagleton's quip about book-throwing does not do justice to the complexity of strategic thinking that late nineteenth-century intellectuals devised to deal with the problem of literacy that Eagleton himself identifies. We might say that late nineteenth-century historians and literary critics wrestled with the problem of what has come to be called distance learning – or more accurately, distance instruction – through a fellowship of discourse. It can also be argued that, given their strategic maintenance of a fellowship of discourse, nineteenth-century intellectuals had much in common with Eagleton's view of current-day literary theorists, critics and teachers, who are seen as 'custodians of discourse' (*LT*, p. 201). Nineteenth-century liberal intellectuals were also custodians of discourse – but the authoritative custody officer they nominated was the discipline of history, and it took 'literariness' into custody so that its aberrant tendencies could be policed.

From the perspective of the late nineteenth-century liberal-Comtean fellowship of discourse, the 'literariness' of Carlyle's early nineteenth-century writing was in special need of policing. Like his later liberal critics, Carlyle's 'teachings' often took the form of biographies; however, *Sartor Resartus, On Heroes and Hero-Worship* and *Oliver Cromwell's Letters and Speeches* were really metacommentaries on the problem of writing biography, and the sort of effects that writing would have when the inscribed life of a hero began to circulate in a print culture. Carlyle's writings embodied a practice of discourse as a rhetorical, constitutive act, and they displayed a fascination with the mobility of such rhetoric. The writings comprised, in Bakhtin's formulation, a 'novelistic' interrogation of disciplinary languages, arguing with the system that ordered them, and breaking the frames that conventionally separated them. Carlyle's writings significantly disrupt the ordering of early nineteenth-century discursive formations identified by Michel Foucault, and my analysis of this disruption has led to a reassessment of Raymond Williams's view of the fixity of 'literary' and 'historical' metalanguages. Williams argues that from the early nineteenth century, a metalinguistic division roughly corresponding to the 'literature' and 'history' division, reductive from the point of view of a social theory of writing, was accepted, and that it remained unchallenged for the duration of the century. However, the disciplinary practices devised by late nineteenth-century liberal intellectuals were an attempt to reconstruct lines of demarcation between discursive formations which had been challenged.

The challenge filtered into key cultural institutions which traditionally bestowed authority on the work of intellectuals. Charles Kingsley's writings appropriated Carlyle's practices, an appropriation which changed in prestige and status when it was framed by university authority – Kingsley held the Regius Chair of Modern History at Cambridge. Attempts to reaffirm the lines of separation between discursive formations were intimately linked to the concerns of a later generation of intellectuals with the condition of the universities, and key examples of late nineteenth-century biographical writing can be seen as attempts by intellectuals to renegotiate relations of authority between cultural institutions and heterogeneous audiences in a democratic culture. It is in this sense that I have argued against Ian Small's contention that the intellectual and the institutional should constitute two separate levels of an analysis when considering the emergence of a disciplinary culture in the nineteenth century.

It has been a consistent theme of my argument that the intellectual and the institutional are woven together. As I argued in the introduction to this book, the very questions that have prompted the processes of enquiry that led to its appearance were generated by institutional developments. This project would have found it difficult to ask the questions that it has without such journals as *Literature and History*, a publication of the 1970s and 1980s committed to exploring the historicity of writing and ideological formations. In fact the *raison d'être* of *Literature and History* was a critical interrogation of the separation of 'literary' from 'historical' metalanguages. This separation was interrogated by a new generation of teachers and critics, schooled in but critical of the uni-focal traditions of the disciplines of the older universities. Armed with a theoretical discourse of interdisciplinarity, they gained positions in the new institutions of higher education, the polytechnics. The intellectual project of these polytechnic-based critics and teachers was to let the 'literary' out of history's dubious custody; that is to say, 'literature' was no longer to be seen as an autonomous category of subjective expressiveness, and 'history' could no longer be seen to be independent of those representational strategies against which it had strained to define itself. Instead, the politics of disciplinary separation had to be interrogated and exposed. To return to that image from the Introduction, of myself sitting at a course-planning table, critically curious about the defensiveness of historians when the question of the status of representation in their discipline was broached, turning it into an object of research, it is quite clear that this book is a contribution to that process of interrogation and exposure. However, in becoming a custodian of the discourse of interdisciplinarity and its metalanguage, theory, one needs to ask a question: what sort of discourse is theoretical interdisciplinarity, and what sort of institutional framework supports its claims?

It may be the case that the institutional framework which now supports this discourse weighs heavily against the radical claims that were made for interdisciplinarity at its conception. It has been argued that what is being called institutional performativity undermines all attempts at radical programmes of intellectual questioning. Performative higher education is concerned to maximise the operational output of the system of knowledge production.[2] Under this logic the university teaches transferable skills, so that the content of a particular discipline is secondary to the acquisition of information retrieval skills. Similarly, research comes to mean what works best most quickly: the reproduction of successful theoretical 'tricks' which use, chew up and spit out the remnants of an ever-diminishing universe of disciplinary specialisms. In *The Function of Criticism*, Eagleton presents deconstruction as an ethically bankrupt practice of performative gaming, undertaken by the Anglo-American literary critical institution.[3] In a similar vein, Steven Connor's scepticism about the radical claims attached to interdisciplinarity needs to be considered:

> The forms of interdisciplinarity which result from [an] exchange of languages and concepts are often claimed as postmodern destabilisations of the structures of knowledge. But this argument could be put the other way round. The form of interdisciplinarity which has been fostered across the social sciences and humanities . . . can also be seen as attempts to master the field, coercing it into intellectual performativity.[4]

Connor's point may have a particular resonance in a British context; the polytechnics, birthplace of the interdisciplinary project, are currently being regraded. As new universities they are becoming the rapacious vanguard of the performative, market-orientated drive currently shaping the activities conducted in higher education. Interdisciplinarity merely accelerates this drive.

Connor's point has to be taken seriously, but it is possible to argue against his pessimistic reading. At the level of intellectual activity, it is not necessarily the case, as Connor suggests, that interdisciplinarity coerces a field into a seamless totality. My argument has been premised on the need to use theory to assert the differences between nineteenth-century biographers whose writings on 'literature' and 'history' participated in a complex struggle to define these terms. It is true that this will to differentiate simultaneously asserts patterns of identity between past and present, but again, the aim here has been to avoid condescension. I have argued that many of our so-called 'theoretical' preoccupations were the concerns of nineteenth-century intellectuals, and that they were deeply aware of a sophisticated theory and politics underwriting their intellectual activities.

The assertion of an identity between past and present can also cast a novel light on the broader question of present-day institutional developments that Connor raises. Connor assumes that performativity is the exclusive condition of the postmodern institution of higher education; but there are grounds for arguing that performativity was a condition of the institutionalisation of disciplines from a much earlier date. In 1909, C.H. Firth, Regius Professor of Modern History at Oxford and Fellow of the British Academy, wrote a paper entitled 'The faculties and their powers', which was a contribution to the continuing debate about university reform. In 1904, Firth produced a commentary on Carlyle's biography of Cromwell, urging that, instead of seeing it as 'history', it be seen as 'literature' or an inferior form of 'imaginative' discourse (see Chapter 4). In his paper on 'The faculties and their powers', Firth states that 'English literature and Modern History' are 'the two subjects with which I am personally concerned'.[5] The point of Firth's intervention is to argue the need for a faculty structure that will bind these two subjects together: 'the system of self-governing Faculties has been adopted everywhere, because it allows each separate study to develop itself with freedom, and it is yet compatible with a certain amount of control exercised by some central body representing the common interest'.[6] In many respects, this way of overseeing 'literature' and 'history' bore a strong resemblance to the British Academy's epistemological management of disciplinary research (see Chapter 5), so this 'new' institutional framework was connected to the liberal-Comtean fellowship of discourse.

This new institutional framework facilitated a performative drive. Firth makes the point that Oxford – the target of his advocacy – is being left behind, for the structure of self-governing faculties has been 'adopted eveywhere'. 'Everywhere' refers to the new universities of late nineteenth-century Britain, particularly Manchester and Liverpool, which are a part of 'a reorganisation of higher education producing research and publications based on scientific lines and inspired by a definite purpose'.[7] Firth warns of the danger of Oxford failing to compete in a productive, scientifically rational, national higher education system whose performance is to be measured economically: 'at present the richest university in the country does not perform its educational duty as efficiently as England expects it to do'.[8] Firth's advocacy of the faculty structure points to the university on the threshold of the twentieth century adopting a performative function, its culture of disciplinary differentiation being deployed in order to maximise the production of research in specialised fields, in line with models of economic efficiency.

There is no necessary relationship of determination between the performative drive of present-day higher educational institutions and a theoretical discourse of interdisciplinarity. C.H. Firth's text of 1909 suggests that intellectual and institutional performativity could follow from disciplinary specialisation. There is no great surprise in this; in the sense that discourse is culturally constitutive – a central argument of this book – then all forms of discourse which work through institutions would tend to be performative in aspiration and effect. There is, however, a difference between those discourses which reflect on their performativity, and those which systematically neglect to do so. A theoretical discourse of interdisciplinarity which reflects on its own reading practices and acts of textual selection, in short its own will to constitute and perform an argument as a rhetorical act, casts a critical light on those disciplines which have historically occluded their constitutive powers. Theoretical discourses of interdisciplinarity may not be able to transcend performativity itself, but they have the capacity to interrogate established interests which have previously been advanced by occluded performativity. Analyses of the present also need to take into account the role of the intellectual formation. Present-day intellectual formations which produce criticism from an interdisciplinary, theoretical perspective tend to resist identification with the dominant ideological aims of present-day higher education; and they carry out their projects semi-independently of their institutional employers.[9]

Contrary to Eagleton's advice in *Literary Theory*, we ought not to abandon our custodianship of apparently defunct disciplines like 'English literature' and turn to a political criticism based on rhetoric. This is an either/or formulation which comes to terms with neither historical nor present-day complexities. Instead, present-day custodians of interdisciplinary discourse need to help others to become more alert to the political relationship that exists between centripetal and centrifugal energies at work in language, and the implications that this has for attempts to possess rhetoric in the cause of social struggles – both within and beyond the academy.

Notes

Introduction: Historicising academic disciplines

1. See Ira Bruce Nadel, *Biography: Fiction, fact and form* (Macmillan, London, 1984).
2. John Morley, *The Life of Gladstone*, 3 vols (Macmillan, London, 1903), vol. I, p. 4; for the contribution of an apparently singular tradition of Victorian biography to the construction of 'Victorianism' see W.E. Houghton, *The Victorian Frame of Mind: 1830–1870* (Yale UP, New Haven and London, 1957), ch. 12, pp. 318–30.
3. G.M. Trevelyan, *An Autobiography* (Longmans, London, 1949), p. 48. Trevelyan was surprised at the success of *English Social History* (1944) given that it was 'less adapted to the examination system' (p. 49) than his other writings on political history.
4. Chris Baldick's book, *The Social Mission of English Criticism: 1848–1932* (Clarendon, Oxford, 1983) has been influential; best known, however, is perhaps Peter Widdowson (ed.), *Re-Reading English*, New Accents (Methuen, London, 1982); Brian Doyle wrote an essay for Widdowson's collection – 'The hidden history of English studies', pp. 17–31 – which has recently been expanded into the much more ambitious and sophisticated *English and Englishness*, New Accents (Routledge, London, 1989); Terry Eagleton has written two very influential accounts in *The Function of Criticism* (Verso, London, 1984), and *Literary Theory: An introduction* (Blackwell, Oxford, 1983). In the field of historical studies, Christopher Parker's 'Academic history: Paradigms and dialectics' appeared in *Literature and History*, 5:2 (Autumn, 1979), pp. 165–82; this has been expanded into *The English Historical Tradition since 1850* (John Donald, London, 1990). The Birmingham Centre for Contemporary Cultural Studies has produced a radical critique of the English tradition of historical studies – see Richard Johnson *et al.* (eds), *Making Histories* (Hutchinson, London, 1982).

5. I shall refer quite closely to Eagleton's *Literary Theory*; when I do, the reference will be given in the main text in parenthesis (*LT*) followed by a page number.

6. Ian Small, *Conditions for Criticism: Authority, knowledge and literature in the late nineteenth century* (Clarendon Press, Oxford, 1990). Small's project is not without precedent; in the late 1960s Perry Anderson attempted a structuralist Marxist reading of the emergence of nineteenth-century academic disciplines which was most concerned with determining absences; see 'Components of the national culture', *New Left Review*, **50** (May/June, 1968). For an example of a uni-focal approach to the emergence of history as an academic discipline in the nineteenth-century university sector, see Peter R.H. Slee, *Learning and a Liberal Education: The study of modern history in the universities of Oxford, Cambridge and Manchester 1800 – 1914* (Manchester UP, Manchester, 1986).

7. Michel Foucault's work is not just concerned with the way in which discursive formations or domains of statements play a constructive role in organising culture; rather it is concerned with the historicality of various perceptions surrounding this theme: see *The Order of Things*, 1966 (Tavistock, London, 1970) which is particularly exemplary in this respect. Foucault's work also examines the way in which disciplines and bodies of knowledge are generated by institutional sites; see *The Birth of the Clinic*, 1963 (Tavistock, London, 1973), which looks at the relationship between the emergence of the clinic and the production of medical knowledge; also, *Discipline and Punish*, 1975 (Penguin, Harmondsworth, 1979), which examines the relationship between the prison and penal discourses of criminal 'reform'. Foucault's work also provides a methodology for examining the organisation of academic discourse; more of this in the Introduction to follow.

8. Raymond Williams, *Marxism and Literature* (OUP, Oxford, 1977), pp. 145–50; *Keywords: A vocabulary of culture and society* was published in 1976. *Culture and Society 1780–1950* (Penguin, Harmondsworth, 1982), the text which initiated the project, was published in 1958. Raymond Williams's work cannot be assimilated to a Foucauldian perspective without problems; in fact Williams's late work was squarely against the conse-quences of certain uses of this language-centred theory (see for instance his posthumously collected essays *The Politics of Modernism*, ed. T. Pinkney, Verso, London, 1989, which is ominously subtitled *Against the new conformists*). However, Williams's more recent work has set itself against the conventional organisational lines of academic disciplines, and like Foucault, his work has been preoccupied with the historic 'burial' of an understanding of language as a constitutive social force; see *Marxism and Literature*, pp. 24–5. Williams's perspective on this problematic remains a thoroughly humanist one – and this is where he differs markedly from Foucault.

9. Terry Eagleton, *The Function of Criticism*, pp. 39–40.

10. Jonathan Culler, 'Problems in the "history" of contemporary criticism', *Journal of Midwestern Modern Languages Association*, **17**:1 (1984), pp. 3–15.

11. Ian Small, *Conditions for Criticism*, p. 30; future references will be given in parenthesis (*CC*) in the main text, followed by a page number.

12. The case for refusing to see the current intellectual crisis in English studies primarily in terms of the institutional is developed most forcefully by Ian Small in collaboration with Josephine Guy in 'English in crisis?', *Essays in Criticism*, **39**:3 (July, 1989), pp. 185–95. *Textual Practice* is singled out as the offending journal which sanctions the connection opposed by Small and Guy; see Terence Hawkes, 'Editorial', *Textual Practice*, 1 (1987); Terry Eagleton, 'End of English', *Textual Practice*, 1 (1987), pp. 1–9; Peter Widdowson, 'Terrorism and literary studies', *Textual Practice*, 2 (1988), pp. 1–21.

13. *DNB*, Buckle, Thomas Henry (entry by Leslie Stephen), vol. VII, 1886, p. 211.

14. For a more detailed account of the *DNB* and the relationship between cultural institutions and intellectuals, see D. Amigoni, 'Life histories and the cultural politics of historical knowing: *The Dictionary of National Biography* and the late nineteenth-century political field', in Shirley Dex (ed.), *Life and Work History Analyses: Qualitative and quantitative developments* (Routledge, London, 1991), pp. 144–66.

15. Williams, *Marxism and Literature*, p. 119.

16. For Antonio Gramsci's conception of the intellectual as a social function, see *Selections from the Prison Notebooks* (Lawrence and Wishart, London, 1971), p. 9.

17. Mikhail Bakhtin, 'The problem of the text in linguistics, philosophy and the human sciences', in his *Speech Genres and Other Late Essays* (Texas UP, Austin and London, 1986), pp. 125–6. This is, as I have said in the main text, an example of Bakhtin's late work. Bakhtin's *œuvre* creates a certain number of problems for any writer who claims it as an authority. These problems need to be seen in the context of Bakhtin's complex life, which was lived out in the dangerous cultural and political climate of the Soviet Union between the 1920s and 1970s. The biography, by Katerina Clark and Michael Holquist (Harvard UP, Cambridge, Mass., and London, 1984), is the best guide here. The later work which embraces *Speech Genres* also includes the better-known essays collected as *The Dialogic Imagination Four essays* (Texas UP, Austin and London, 1981), *Rabelais and His World*, 1965 (Indiana UP, Bloomington, 1984), and *Problems of Dostoevsky's Poetics*, 1963 (Minnesota UP, Minneapolis, 1984). All of these writings were, it seems, produced by Bakhtin. There are in existence, however, a number of earlier texts where the authorship is less certain. These include early papers and short dissertations, such as 'Discourse in life and discourse in poetry' (1926), which have recently been collected and translated by Ann Shukman in *The Bakhtin School Papers* (Russian Poetics in Translation, Oxford, 1988); *Freudianism* (1927); *The Formal Method in Literary Scholarship* (1928); and *Marxism and the Philosophy of Language* (1929; Seminar Press, New York, 1973). The main problem is that these latter texts originally appeared under different names – P.N. Medvedev (*Freudianism: a Marxist Critique*, 1927 (Seminar Press, New York, 1973)) and V.N. Volosinov (*The Formal*

Method in Literary Scholarship: A critical introduction to sociological poetics, 1928 (Harvard UP, Cambridge, Mass., 1985)) – they have since been claimed as the writings of Bakhtin. This is a very difficult, some would argue impossible, problem to solve. It raises uncomfortable questions because both Volosinov and Medvedev, whose names were attached to these unorthodox texts, disappeared during the Stalinist purges of the 1930s. Those who hold definite positions on the question include Clark and Holquist in their biography, and Tvetzan Todorov in *Mikhail Bakhtin: The Dialogical Principle* (Manchester UP, Manchester, 1984). I am not competent to enter into the debate. However, where in the forthcoming argument I refer to Bakhtin/Volosinov, I am citing those texts where authorship is disputed. Where I refer to Bakhtin only, I am citing those texts which have been ascribed unproblematically to Bakhtin.

18. Harold Nicolson, *The Development of English Biography* (Hogarth Press, London, 1927), pp. 8–9. In order to explain 'the development of English biography' through this distinction between 'pure' and 'impure' biography, Nicolson borrowed a model of historical understanding which has since become a crucial periodising device of English literary critical discourse. For Nicolson, biographies written during the English Civil War were for the most part 'impure' in the sense that they lacked the adequate degree of detachment and objectivity demanded by Nicolson's notion of 'pure' biography. This evaluation is very similar to T.S. Eliot's watershed notion of the 'dissociation of sensibility', a concept for structuring the literary history of English poetry which derives from Eliot's historical view of the linguistic and affective legacy of the later seventeenth century (see Eliot's essay 'The metaphysical poets', 1921). In the same way that this historical understanding of Eliot's ('something which had happened to the mind of England') enables him to construct a tradition of canonical poets and dramatists, Nicolson's historical understanding shapes the formation of a canon of 'pure' biographers – Johnson, Boswell and Froude, for instance. Although he was affiliated to the Bloomsbury group and its avant-garde sense of distance from the nineteenth century, Nicolson uses this device supporting the master-narrative of English modernist cultural criticism to reach conclusions which run counter to Eliot's (and Bloomsbury's) generally dismissive approach to the biographical legacy of nineteenth-century literary criticism.

19. Nicolson, *English Biography*, pp. 129–31

20. Hayden White's seminal work is *Metahistory: The historical imagination in nineteenth-century Europe* (Johns Hopkins UP, Baltimore, 1973), which uses a framework of rhetorical analysis derived from Northrop Frye and Kenneth Burke, the purpose of which is to collapse the classical distinction between 'fictional' literary narratives and 'factual' historiographical narratives. A very useful and brief exposition of Hayden White's project, which includes an analysis of the emergence of positivistic history, can be found in his essay 'The fictions of factual representation', in *Tropics of Discourse* (Johns Hopkins UP, Baltimore and London, 1978), pp. 121–34.

21. For other manifestations of this anxiety, see for example Christopher J.W. Parker, 'Academic history: Paradigms and dialectics', *Literature and History*, 5:2 (Autumn, 1979), pp. 165–82; Parker begins his essay by quoting Stubbs belligerently denying the literariness of his discipline, history. A more recent and sophisticated exponent of history as a discipline distinct from the text-based methods of literary analysis can be found in the person of Sir Geoffrey Elton; for Elton's notion of 'the event' as a concrete fact embedded in a source, see the debate he has with Fogel in R.W. Fogel and G.R. Elton, *Which Road to the Past? Two views of history* (Yale UP, New Haven and London, 1983).

Chapter 1   Biography and the ordering of discourse

1. Williams, *Marxism and Literature*, p. 149.
2. *Ibid.*, pp. 45–54.
3. *Ibid.*, pp. 145–50.
4. See Williams's introduction to the series 'English Literature in History', in Roger Sales, *Pastoral and Politics: 1780–1830* (Hutchinson, London, 1983), pp. 9–12.
5. For a history of rhetoric as a discipline, as well as a history of the various suspicions registered in connection with its powers of influence, see Brian Vickers, *In Defence of Rhetoric* (OUP, Oxford, 1988); for a good introduction to rhetorical terms and genres, see Dick Leith and George Myerson, *The Power of Address: Explorations in rhetoric* (Routledge, London, 1989).
6. Michel Foucault, 'The order of discourse', 1970, in *The Archaeology of Knowledge*, 1969 (Tavistock, London, 1972). For a discussion of Foucault's thinking on rhetoric as aberrant language, see Christopher Norris in his comparison between Foucault and Paul De Man, *Paul De Man: Deconstruction and the critique of aesthetic ideology* (Routledge, London, 1988), pp. 93–5.
7. See Richard D. Altick, *The English Common Reader: A social history of the mass reading public 1800–1900*, 1957 (Chicago UP, Chicago and London, 1963), pp. 122–3.
8. For the programmatic aims eventually embodied in the SDUK, see Henry Brougham, *Practical Observations Upon the Education of the People*, 1825 (E.J. Morton, Manchester, 1971). For the relationship between Charles Knight and the SDUK, see R.K. Webb, *The British Working-Class Reader 1790–1848* (Allen and Unwin, London, 1955).
9. See David Vincent, *Bread, Knowledge and Freedom: A study of nineteenth-century working-class autobiography* (Europa, London, 1978), p. 145.
10. Nicolson, *Development of English Biography*, pp. 129–31.
11. For this broad definition of ideology, see John B. Thompson, *Studies in the Theory of Ideology* (Polity, Cambridge, 1984), p. 5.
12. See Louis Althusser, 'Ideology and the state' in *Lenin and Philosophy and Other Essays* (NLB, London, 1977).

13. For Gramsci's theory of intellectual activity, hegemony and ideology, see *The Prison Notebooks*, especially section 2, 'State and civil society' and 'The study of philosophy', pp. 325–36. Gramsci also undertook masses of detailed empirical and theoretical work on the relationship between popular texts, linguistic disciplines, and ideological practices in the Italy of the 1920s and 1930s, which has recently been collected in *Selections from the Cultural Writings* (Lawrence and Wishart, London, 1985).

14. See V.N. Volosinov (Bakhtin/Volosinov), *Marxism and the Philosophy of Language*; see also Raymond Williams's adaptation of this model in his conceptualisation of language in *Marxism and Literature*, pp. 21–44.

15. Charles Knight, *William Caxton: The First English Printer* (Charles Knight and Co., London, 1844), p. 14.

16. Mikhail Bakhtin, *The Dialogic Imagination*; see the essay 'Discourse and the novel', pp. 325, 354.

17. Bakhtin, 'Discourse and the novel', p. 354.

18. For the view of discourse as a productive act which resolves a situation and projects a plan for its future organisation, see V.N. Volosinov (Bakhtin/Volosinov), 'Discourse in life and discourse in poetry', *Bakhtin School Papers*, p. 11.

19. Tony Crowley, *The Politics of Discourse: The standard language question in British cultural debate* (Macmillan, London, 1989), ch. 1.

20. Whether this threat could have materialised into a revolutionary crisis through Chartist politics is currently being debated by historians. Taking a challenging and language-centred view, Gareth Stedman Jones has recently advanced the thesis that many Chartists shared a discourse of old-style political Radicalism born of the eighteenth century which could not adapt itself to the subtly changing interventionist practices of the state between 1838 and 1842. Quite simply, the diverse activities of the utilitarian state left the Chartist analysis behind it. See Stedman Jones, 'The language of Chartism' in James Epstein and Dorothy Thompson (eds), *The Chartist Experience: Studies in working-class radicalism and culture, 1830–1860* (Macmillan, London, 1982).

21. See Crowley, *Politics of Discourse*, pp. 120–4.

22. For the relationship between epic and absolute past, see Mikhail Bakhtin, 'Epic and novel', in *The Dialogic Imagination*, p. 16. See also: 'Epic language is not separable from its subject, for an absolute fusion of subject matter and spatial-temporal aspects with valorized (hierarchical) ones is characteristic of semantics in the epic' (p. 17).

23. See Tony Crowley, 'Bakhtin and the history of the language' in Ken Hirschkop and David Shepherd (eds), *Bakhtin and Cultural Theory* (Manchester UP, Manchester, 1989), p 71.

24. Mikhail Bakhtin, *Rabelais and His World*, 1965.

25. For the emergence and function of Menippean satire, see Mikhail Bakhtin, *Problems of Dostoevsky's Poetics*, 1963, pp. 101–20.

26. Crowley, *Politics of Discourse*, p. 9.

27. See Richard McKeon's (ed.) commentary: Aristotle, *The Basic Works of Aristotle* (Random House, New York, 1941), pp. xxix-xxxii.

28. Graham Pechey, 'Bakhtin, Marxism and post-structuralism' in Francis Barker *et al.* (eds), *Literature, Politics and Theory: Papers from the Essex conference 1976–1984* (Methuen, London, 1986), p. 123.
29. See Michael Holquist, *Dialogism: Bakhtin and his world*, New Accents, (Routledge, London, 1990); see especially Holquist's point about the dialogue that Bakhtin was engaged in with Georg Lukacs over the history of the novel, pp. 70–3.
30. See McKeon, *Aristotle*, p. xxxi.
31. Pechey, 'Bakhtin, Marxism and post-structuralism', p. 123.
32. Katerina Clark and Michael Holquist, *Mikhail Bakhtin*, p 276.
33. Ben Knights, *The Idea of the Clerisy in the Nineteenth Century* (CUP, Cambridge, 1978), pp. 76–7.
34. Samuel Taylor Coleridge, *On the Constitution of the Church and State*, 1830 (Dent, London, 1972), p. 36.
35. J.C. Hare, *John Sterling's Essays and Tales, Collected and Edited with a Memoir of His Life*, 2 vols (J.W. Parker, London, 1848), vol. I, p. xv.
36. Thomas Carlyle, *The Life of John Sterling*, 1851, in *The Centenary Edition of the Works of Thomas Carlyle*, 30 vols, edited by H. D. Traill (Chapman and Hall, London, 1896–1899), vol. XI, p. 55.
37. Foucault, 'The order of discourse', p. 218.
38. The status of 'man' as both subject and object of discourse arises out of Foucault's work on language, representation and subjectivity elaborated in *The Order of Things*, 1966 (Tavistock, London, 1970); Mark Cousin helps to formulate the anxieties that this can generate for the historicist discourses of the human sciences in his essay 'The practice of historical investigation', in Derek Attridge *et al.* (eds), *Post-structuralism and the Question of History* (CUP, Cambridge, 1987), pp. 126–36.
39. Foucault, 'The order of discourse', pp. 222–6.
40. See 'The functions of literature' in Michel Foucault, *Politics, Philosophy, Culture: Interviews and other writings 1977–1984* (Routledge, London and New York, 1988), p. 311. Although it is possible to look at this question as a methodological opening enabling the examination of 'literature' as an institutionally sanctioned 'object' – the path I take – Foucault is asking the question in a rather different sense here, which follows from his *I, Pierre Rivière, Having Slaughtered my Mother, my Sister, my Brother . . .* , 1973 (Peregrine, London, 1978). Foucault came to see Rivière's memoir of the murders that he committed, and the events that led to them, as an act of 'beauty'. This means that for Foucault, Rivière's writing evaded the thresholds and limits established by the disciplines of the human and medical sciences that attempted to appropriate it and explain his behaviour. It is notable that Foucault should look to the language of aesthetics to articulate this point; for Foucault, Rivière's memoir was beautiful because it evaded these disciplines, so therefore it was 'literary'. Foucault is quite close to Bakhtin at this point. None the less, it is perfectly legitimate and necessary to use Foucault's methodology to examine the *institutionalisation* of literary criticism; for a very recent example, see Simon During, *Foucault and Literature: Towards a genealogy of writing* (Routledge, London, 1992), especially ch. 9.

41. John Gross, *The Rise and Fall of the Man of Letters: Aspects of English literary life since 1800* (Weidenfeld and Nicolson, London, 1969); Terry Eagleton has written a critical history of the term and the functions it supposes in *The Function of Criticism*, ch. III.
42. Carlyle, *Sterling*, in *Works*, p. 54.
43. See Hubert L. Dreyfus's and Paul Rabinow's reading of Foucault's famous account of Velásquez's *Las Meninas* which prefaces *The Order of Things*: 'What is not represented is a unified and unifying subject who posits these representations and makes them objects for himself. This subject will emerge, in Foucault's account, with the emergence of man, with Kant' *Michel Foucault: Beyond structuralism and hermeneutics* (Harvester, Brighton, 1982), p. 25.
44. John Morley, 'Carlyle', in *Nineteenth-Century Essays*, edited by Peter Stansky (Chicago UP, Chicago and London, 1970), pp. 41–4.
45. Foucault, 'Order of discourse', pp. 225–6.
46. Morley, 'Carlyle', p. 33.
47. See Christopher Harvie, *The Lights of Liberalism: University liberals and the challenge of democracy 1860–1886* (Allen Lane, London, 1976).
48. Christopher Kent, *Brains and Numbers: Elitism, Comtism and democracy in nineteenth-century England* (Toronto UP, Buffalo, 1978), p. xiii.
49. See Auguste Comte, 'Philosophical considerations on the sciences and the savants', 1825, in *The Crisis of Industrial Civilisation: The early essays of Auguste Comte*, edited by Ronald Fletcher (Heinemann, London, 1974), especially pp. 209–13.
50. J.R. Seeley, *Classical Studies as an Introduction to the Moral Sciences* (Macmillan, London, 1864), p. 19.

Chapter 2   Re-reading the rhetorical hero in Carlylean biography

1. A good example would be Rosemary Jann, *The Art and Science of Victorian History* (Ohio State UP, Columbia, 1985) who devotes a chapter to Carlyle which focuses on *Cromwell* and *Frederick*. For Geoffrey Hartman's points about Carlyle, see *Criticism in the Wilderness: The study of literature today* (Yale UP, New Haven and London, 1980); see especially pp. 50, 150–1, 136–7. Terry Eagleton, *The Function of Criticism*, pp. 39–40.
2. Raymond Williams, *Politics and Letters: Interviews with the 'New Left Review'*, (NLB, London, 1979), pp. 105–6. If the sort of questioning that Williams is challenged with exemplifies a reading of Carlyle which emphasises his authoritarianism, there are readings of Carlyle which foreground the more radical tendencies in his writings; see for instance Philip Rosenberg, *The Seventh Hero: Thomas Carlyle and the theory of radical activism* (Harvard UP, Cambridge, Mass., 1974). Rosenberg develops a thesis about Carlylean radicalism through a close engagement with the

ideas of his texts – for instance, Rosenberg argues convincingly that Carlyle was not against 'election' as a social act, rather the institutions and instrumental practices of bourgeois democracy (p. 194). Because of the thesis of Rosenberg's book – that the seventh hero in the Carlylean cosmology is the ordinary reader of the text – Rosenberg's account is implicitly alert to questions of form, the very structure of Carlylean address. More recently, Gillian Beer has brilliantly analysed the breathtaking formal energies of Carlyle's writings; see her 'Carlylean transports' in *Arguing with the Past: Essays in narrative from Woolf to Sidney* (Routledge, London, 1989). My argument is centred more on the radical possibilities that are opened up by the formal characteristics of Carlyle's writings. I draw upon a Bakhtinian analysis – a framework that Beer gestures towards but pulls away from (pp. 79–80).

3. V.N. Volosinov (Bakhtin/Volosinov), 'Discourse in life and discourse in poetry', *Bakhtin School Papers*, pp. 15 and 17.

4. Thomas Carlyle, 'The hero as divinity' in *On Heroes and Hero-Worship*, 1841, *Works*, vol. V, pp. 27–8.

5. Carlyle, 'The hero as man of letters', *On Heroes and Hero-Worship*, pp. 160–1.

6. Carlyle's *The Life of Schiller* (1825) is a case in point. Schiller is represented in this biography as dramatist, novelist and philosopher of history. The commentaries that represent these styles of intellectual endeavour place them in different domains of the multiplicity of writing. See *Works*, vol. XXV, pp. 66–7, 100–1.

7. See Carlyle, 'Count Cagliostro: First flight', *Fraser's Magazine*, XLIII, vol. IX (July, 1833), p. 19.

8. Bakhtin, 'Forms of time and chronotope in the novel', *Dialogic Imagination*, p. 131.

9. Carlyle, 'Cagliostro: First flight', p. 26.

10. The serialisation was continuous bar two interruptions – January and May 1834. Although *Sartor* appeared in 1833–34, Carlyle actually composed the text in 1830–31. It proved to be a difficult text to get published, and in the end, *Fraser's* took it – reluctantly. Throughout this section of the chapter, the text of *Sartor Resartus* that I shall cite from is vol. I of the *Centenary Edition of the Works*; I shall abbreviate the citation in the following way: (*SR*, p. 1), and the citations will appear in the main text.

11.
    Man has not been able to describe himself as a configuration in the *episteme* without thought at the same discovering, both in itself and outside itself, at its borders yet also in its very warp and woof, an element of darkness, an inert density in which it is embedded, an unthought which it contains entirely, yet in which it is also caught. (Foucault, *The Order of Things*, p. 326)

    It is striking that Foucault should call upon a weaving metaphor to highlight this problem.

12. For *Fraser's* Tory politics, see for instance the editorial address on 'The state and prospects of Toryism', which is simultaneously an attack on the

Benthamite radicalism of *The Westminster Review*; XLIX, vol. IX, (January, 1834), p. 1; for its counter-modern stance on economics and social investigation see in the same issue 'The present condition of the people: Labourers in cities and towns'. Strikingly, the 'social' is a phenomenon constructed less through a discourse of observation and reportage as with the later Henry Mayhew, and more through a discourse grounded in admittedly modern associationist psychology, which is anxious about the loss of oral communication, community and the problem posed by teaching words through the 'empty' written text:

> The faculty of uttering words can be of no benefit to any individual – they serve not to convey ideas to the mind. All acquire a sufficient number of words, and the ideas of which they are the signs, to enable them to express their wants, their pleasures and their pains, in some way intelligible to their fellow men; mere words, then, for the performances of the common offices of life and labour, desires and wants, are obtained by oral communication – while living in a social state of existence . . . [the teaching of reading and spelling is here implicated] not only taught boys plain words, but subsequently to live without thinking . . . (p. 77).

13. See 'The Miller correspondence', where literary London is lampooned through letters written in parodies of the styles of figures including Coleridge, Edgeworth and Henry Hallam; *Fraser's Magazine*, XLVIII, vol. VIII, (November, 1833), pp. 624–6.

14. Carlyle's early biographical sketches and critical commentaries on Goethe, Novalis and Jean-Paul Richter are collected in vols XXVI and XXVII of the *Works*; Carlyle's translation of *Wilhelm Meister's Apprenticeship* can be found in vols. XXIII and XXIV; the translations of Johann Musaeus, Friedrich de la Motte Fouque, Ludwig Tieck, E.T.W. Hoffman and Jean-Paul Richter can be found in vols XXI and XXII, *Works*, collected under the title of *German Romances*.

15. René Wellek, *Confrontations: Studies in the intellectual and literary relations between Germany, England and the United States during the nineteenth century* (Princeton UP, Princeton N.J., 1965); see especially ch. 2.

16. See Kathleen M. Wheeler's (ed.) anthology, *German Aesthetic and Literary Criticism: The Romantic ironists and Goethe* (CUP, Cambridge, 1984), p. 8.

17. *Ibid.*, p. 8.

18. Friedrich Schlegel, 'Letter about the Novel', 1800, from *Dialogue on Poetry and Literary Aphorisms* and trans. E. Behler and R. Struc, Pennsylvania State UP, (Pennsylvania and London, 1968), pp. 94–105; taken from Wheeler, *German Aesthetic*, pp. 73–80, 78 and 79.

19. Jean-Paul Richter, 'On the Novel', 1804, from *Horn of Oberon: Jean-Paul Richter's School for Aesthetics*, trans. Margaret Hale (Wayne State UP, Detroit, 1973); taken from Wheeler, *German Aesthetic*, p. 199.

20. Bakhtin, 'Epic and novel', *Dialogic Imagination*, p. 3.

21. James Boswell, *Life of Johnson*, 1791, 5 vols, edited by John Wilson Croker (John Murray, London, 1831). Croker outlines his editorial philosophy

and methods in vol. I, p. viii; the reasons for editorial interventions can be traced to a complicated publishing history – see Pat Rogers's introduction to the World's Classics (Oxford University Press, Oxford, 1980) edition of Boswell's *Life of Johnson*, pp. xvii-xviii (for details, see n. 22). Macaulay was a contributer to the debate about the nature of biography; his review of Croker's edition appeared in *The Edinburgh Review*, September 1831.

22. See James Boswell, *Life of Johnson*, 1791 (OUP, Oxford, 1980); for symposia-style textual organisation, see for instance pp 606–8. For Bakhtin's point about the place of the Socratic/Platonic dialogue in the early formation of prose genres, see 'Epic and novel', *Dialogic Imagination*, pp. 22–3.

23. Boswell, *Life of Johnson*, p. 600.

24. Johnson makes it into Samuel Smiles's *Self-Help* as one who advocated looking on the bright side of life; for a rendering of the life into a full-blooded self-help narrative, see for instance Thomas Cooper, *Triumphs of Perseverance and Enterprise in Learning, Science, Art, Commerce and Adventure* (Ward Lock, London, 1879), p. 29.

25. Boswell, *Life of Johnson*, p. 598.

26. *Ibid.*, pp. 7–8.

27. In Foucauldian analytics, history 'is that fundamental arrangement of knowledge, involving notions of time, development, "becoming", that is common to all the empirical sciences that arose in the closing years of the eighteenth century'. See Alan Sheridan, *Michel Foucault: The will to truth* (Tavistock, London, 1980), p. 65.

28. The lordly right of giving names extends so far that one should allow oneself to conceive the origin of language itself as an expression of power on the part of the rulers: they say 'this *is* this and this,' they seal every thing and event with a sound and, as it were, take possession of it. (Friedrich Nietzsche, *On the Genealogy of Morals*, 1887 (Vintage, New York, 1969), p. 26)

29. Roland Barthes, 'The death of the author' (1968) in *Image-Music-Text*, edited by Stephen Heath (Fontana/Collins, London, 1977).

30. Graham Pechey, 'On the borders of Bakhtin: Dialogisation, decolonisation', in Hirschkop and Shepherd (eds), *Bakhtin and Cultural Theory*, p. 41.

31. For Beer, Carlylean discourse is marked by an insistence upon the 'simultaneity of reading and writing as sense experience . . . the reader's sense experience *while reading* is brought to our attention. In this way, synchrony with the initial activity of the writer writing is emphasised', 'Carlylean transports', p. 86.

32. Thomas Carlyle, *Oliver Cromwell's Letters and Speeches*, in *Works*, vols VI–IX; for the purpose of citation, vol. VI d I and vol. IX d IV, and all future references will be given as follows (*OCLS*, vol. no., p. no.) in the main text.

33. Williams, *Marxism and Literature*, p. 148.

34. Stephen Bann, *The Clothing of Clio: The representation of history in nineteenth-century Britain and France* (CUP, Cambridge, 1984), pp. 8–11.

35. Mr Macaulay has, with an instinctive sense, both of truth and of power to realise it, perceived that a true story may be, and should be, as agreeably told as a fictitious one; that the incidents of real life, whether political or domestic, admit of being so arranged as, without detriment to accuracy, to command all the interest of an artificial series of facts; that the chain of circumstances which constitute history may be as finely and gracefully woven as any tale of fancy. (Review of *The History of England*, *The Edinburgh Review* (July 1849), CLXXXI, no. XC, p. 251)

36. Thomas Babington Macaulay, *The History of England from the Accession of James II*, 1849–61, 3 vols (Dent, London, 1906), vol. I, p. 165.

37. *Ibid.*, vol. I, pp. 476–8.

38. *Ibid.*, vol. I, p. 269.

39. *Ibid.*, vol. I, p. 297.

40. Bakhtin, 'Epic and novel', in *Dialogic Imagination*, pp. 13–14.

41. Macaulay, *History of England*; see for instance vol. I, p. 251 especially fn, and p. 302.

42. Foucault, 'The order of discourse', p. 218.

43. See Tony Bennett, 'Text, readers and reading formations', *Literature and History*, 9:2 (Autumn, 1983), pp. 214–27.

44. See Karl Marx, 'The Eighteenth Brumaire of Louis Bonaparte' (1851) in *Surveys from Exile*, edited by David Fernbach (Penguin, Harmondsworth, 1973), pp. 147–8.

45. For an example of the way in which a late nineteenth-century British socialist described his debt to Carlyle, see Keir Hardie in 'The Labour Party and the books that helped to make it', *The Review of Reviews* (June, 1906), no. 33, pp. 570–1; for a specific and fascinating discussion of Hardie's 'against the grain' reading of the 'Carmagnole complete' episode in Carlyle's *The French Revolution*, see Fred Reid, *Keir Hardie: The making of a socialist* (Croom Helm, Beckenham, 1978), pp. 121–3. Hardie criticised British trade union officials for attempting to bar a group of syndicalist French socialists from a London conference in 1888. The response of the French was to disrupt the conference hall by singing and dancing, which Hardie 'read' sympathetically by drawing upon Carlyle's representation of the power of popular carnival and dance in the French Revolution.

46. I am referring to the Everyman edition of the novel (Dent, London, no date). References will be prefixed by (*AL*) in the main text, followed by a page number.

47. See Brian Maidment, 'Essayists and artisans: The making of nineteenth-century self-taught poets', *Literature and History*, 9:1 (Spring 1983), pp. 74–91.

Chapter 3   The Comtean ordering of discourse

1. See Sheldon Rothblatt, *The Revolution of the Dons: Cambridge and society in Victorian England*, 1967 (CUP, Cambridge, 1981), p. 166.
2. *Ibid.*, pp. 170–1.
3. See Christopher Kent, *Brains and Numbers*, p. 7, and Peter R.H. Slee, *Learning and a Liberal Education*; see Slee's chapter on the practices of the Oxford History School from the late 1840s. In Chapter 5, I will look at Thomas Arnold's role as one of the founders of a liberal-Comtean fellowship of discourse.
4. See Kent, *Brains and Numbers*, pp. 71–2.
5. It is really only in the context of twentieth-century historiographical theory that 'presentness' – the idea that the significance of the past is assessed only through an artificially restrictive focus organised by the present – has come to be seen as a 'heresy', particularly through the work of Herbert Butterfield; see *The Whig Interpretation of History*, 1931, (Penguin, Harmondsworth, 1973). Even so, 'presentness' began to be construed as a problem amongst scholars who helped to form History as an English university discipline in the nineteenth century. For instance, Charles Harding Firth complained that Carlyle was a present-centred historian in the introduction to the 1904 edition of *Cromwell's Letters and Speeches*, edited by S.C. Lomas (Methuen, London, 1904), p. xlvii; I shall refer again to this text in the next chapter. For a recent and stimulating rethink of Butterfield and 'presentness' where the concept of 'present-centred history' is coined, see Adrian Wilson and T.G. Ashplant, 'Whig history and present-centred history', in *The Historical Journal*, **31**:1 (1988), pp. 1–16. I am indebted to this essay.
6. Kent, *Brains and Numbers*, p. xiii.
7. Mill's approach to Comte can be gathered from two texts: Comte's influence on the earlier writings of John Stuart Mill is most in evidence in Book VI, 'On the logic of the moral sciences' of *A System of Logic*, 1843; Mill uses Comte's distinction between social statics and social dynamics, but the theory of the 'inverse deductive (or Historical) method' is an elaboration of Mill's based on Comte's system. See *A System of Logic* (Longman, London, 1961), pp. 594–8. Mill's *Logic* acquired a reputation as being the text most widely read by free-thinking Oxford undergraduates in the 1840s and 1850s. The text in which Mill expounded Comte's theory while distancing himself from the ritualistic aspects is *Auguste Comte and Positivism* (Trübner, London, 1865) which appeared originally in *The Westminster Review*. In this text, Mill advances a judgement which asserts the importance of Comte in British intellectual culture: 'The great treatise of M. Comte was scarcely mentioned in French literature or criticism, when it was already working powerfully on the minds of many British students and thinkers' (p. 2).
8. Auguste Comte, *The Crisis of Industrial Civilisation*, pp 77–8.
9. *Ibid.*, p. 78.

10. Sheridan, *Foucault*, p. 43.
11. Michel Foucault, *Archaeology of Knowledge*, p. 164.
12. Kent, *Brains and Numbers*, p. 58.
13. Detailed empirical accounts of this intellectual formation, its aims and practical involvement in the questions and debates that structured late Victorian cultural and political life, can be found in Kent, *Brains and Numbers*, and Christopher Harvie, *The Lights of Liberalism*.
14. See Kent, *Brains and Numbers*, p. 72.
15. Frederic Harrison, 'The use of history', in *The Meaning of History*, (Macmillan, London, 1894), pp. 19–20.
16. *Ibid.*, p. 6.
17. Auguste Comte, *General View of Positivism and Introductory Principles*, vol. I of *The System of Positive Polity* (Longman and Green, London, 1875), p. 223; this volume translated by J.H. Bridges.
18. *Ibid.*, p. 58.
19. Auguste Comte, *Social Statics*, vol. II of *The System of Positive Polity* (Longman and Green, London, 1875), p. 213.
20. *Ibid.*
21. *Ibid.*, p. 214.
22. Norris, *Paul De Man*, pp. 93–5.
23. Comte, *Social Statics*, p. 217.
24. *Ibid.*, p. 213.
25. Comte, *General View*, p. 252.
26. *Ibid.*, p. 226.
27. Foucault, 'Order of discourse', pp. 225–6.
28. Harrison, 'Some great books of history', *The Meaning of History*, p. 123.

Chapter 4   Biographies of statesmen and the epistemology of positive political history

1. When in the early part of the twentieth century the historical profession came to reflect on the way in which it had formed during the nineteenth century, one prominent commentator pointed out that Seeley had forced a connection between politics and history which was institutionalised by the establishment of political science in the Historical Tripos; it was also clear to this commentator that for Seeley, history was a demarcated field – 'no historian of his time took a more limited view of the province of history than Seeley'. Furthermore, this 'limited province' was powerful because it could organise detail into disciplined principles – 'Historical details were worth nothing to him but as a basis for generalisation.' See G.P. Gooch, *History and Historians in the Nineteenth Century*, 1913, new edition (Longman, London, 1952), pp. 344–9.
2. See Christopher J.W. Parker, 'Academic history: Paradigms and dialectics', pp. 165–82.
3. *Ibid.*, pp. 168 and 175.

4. For an exposition of this theme in White's work, see 'The fictions of factual representation' in *Tropics of Discourse*, pp. 121–34.

5. Rothblatt, *Revolution of the Dons*, pp. 155–6.

6. Deborah Wormell, *Sir John Seeley and the Uses of History* (CUP, Cambridge, 1979), pp. 12–22.

7. Rothblatt, *Revolution of the Dons*, p. 177.

8. See Owen Chadwick, 'Charles Kingsley at Cambridge', *Historical Journal*, vol. XVIII (June, 1975), pp. 303–26.

9. Foucault, 'Order of discourse', p. 224.

10. J.R. Seeley, 'The teaching of politics', in *Lectures and Essays*, 1870 (Macmillan, London, 1895), pp. 319–48.

11. See Knights, *Idea of the Clerisy in the Nineteenth Century*, ch. 6.

12. Rosemary Jann, *The Art and Science of Victorian History*, p. 232.

13. J.R. Seeley, *The Life and Times of Stein*, 3 vols., (CUP, Cambridge, 1879): all future references to this work (*S*, vol. no., p. no.) will appear in the main text in parenthesis.

14. Wormell, *Seeley and the Uses of History*, p. 77.

15. J.R. Seeley, 'Introduction', *The Life and Adventures of E.M. Arndt*, (Seeley and Jackson, London, 1879), pp. v–vi.

16. *Ibid.*, p. vi.

17. Foucault, 'Order of discourse', p. 216.

18. Williams, *Marxism and Literature*, p. 148.

19. Unpublished manuscript, quoted in Wormell, *Seeley and the Uses of History*, pp. 128–9; K. Marx and F. Engels, *The Manifesto of the Communist Party*, 1848, in *Basic Writings in Politics and Philosophy*, edited by L. S. Feur (Fontana, London, 1969), p. 43. I am indebted to John Storey for the point about the opening words of *The Manifesto of the Communist Party*.

20. Edward Gibbon, *Autobiography*, 1796 (Dent, London, 1948), p. 110.

21. John Morley, *The Life of Richard Cobden*, 1878, new edition (Chapman and Hall, London, 1883), p. 114.

22. For Morley's biography, I have used a number of sources: the most detailed is D.A. Hamer's *John Morley: A liberal intellectual in politics* (Clarendon Press, Oxford, 1968); Jeffrey Paul von Arx's *Progress and Pessimism: Religion, politics and history in late nineteenth-century Britain* (Harvard UP, Cambridge, Mass., 1985) provides a good sketch of Morley's early career (ch. 4); Kent's *Brains and Numbers* also devotes a chapter (ch. 8) to Morley's career.

23. See John Morley, 'The expansion of England' (review of Seeley's book of the same title) in *Critical Miscellanies*, 3 vols (Macmillan, London, 1886), vol. III, pp. 291–335; see especially p. 294, where Morley cites the offending passage from Seeley's *Expansion* which claims that the 'real' history of England in the eighteenth century was being forged in the Americas and in Asia.

24. For the impact of the Home Rule Crisis on late nineteenth-century political and intellectual culture, see J. Roach, 'Liberalism and the Victorian intelligentsia', *Cambridge Historical Journal*, **13** (1957), pp. 58–81.

25. John Morley, *Oliver Cromwell* (Macmillan, London, 1900), p. 42.
26. For an account of the history of the university extension movement, see N.A. Jepson, *The Beginnings of English University Adult Education* (Michael Joseph, London, 1973).
27. Much of this information about the careers and positions of these intellectuals is taken from *The Dictionary of National Biography*. This is not simply a neutral 'source' – excellent and astonishing scholarly project though it is; rather, it is more appropriate to see the *DNB* as a sophisticated bid for, and consolidation of, cultural power, recording the careers of the compilers along with the lives of those whom the compilers celebrated. For an account of the *DNB*'s editorial policy, its aims and ambitions, see Amigoni, 'Life histories and the cultural politics of historical knowing: The *DNB*', in Shirley Dex (ed.), *Life and Work History Analyses*.
28. See Christopher Harvie, *Lights of Liberalism*, p. 183.
29. For an account of the 'Higher Journalism', see John Gross's account of the Victorian and Edwardian literary intelligentsia, *The Rise and Fall of the Man of Letters*.
30. See S. Collini, J. Winch and J. Burrow, *That Noble Science of Politics: A study in nineteenth-century intellectual history*, (CUP, Cambridge, 1983), ch. 7, on the place of the Comparative Method in nineteenth-century intellectual history.
31. See John Burrow, *A Liberal Descent: Victorian historians and the English past*, (CUP, Cambridge, 1981), pp. 163–4.
32. Archibald Primrose (Lord Rosebery), *Pitt*, Twelve English Statesmen (Macmillan, London, 1891), p. 52.
33. H.D. Traill, *William the Third*, Twelve English Statesmen (Macmillan, London, 1888), pp. 38–9.
34. Goldwin Smith, *Three English Statesmen: A course of lectures on the political history of England* (Macmillan, London, 1868).
35. Morley, *Cromwell*, p. 23.
36. *Ibid.*, p. 343.
37. Ian Small, *Conditions for Criticism*, pp. 94–5.
38. Morley, *Cromwell*, p. 3.
39. *Ibid.*, p. 218.
40. E.A. Freeman, *William the Conqueror*, Twelve English Statesmen (Macmillan, London, 1888), p. 2.
41. *Ibid.*, pp. 104, 125.
42. Frederic Harrison, *Oliver Cromwell*, Twelve English Statesmen (Macmillan, London, 1888), pp. 82–3.
43. Frederic Harrison, *Chatham*, Twelve English Statesmen (Macmillan, London, 1905), p. 35.
44. *Ibid.*, p. 23.
45. C.H. Firth's Introduction to Carlyle's *Oliver Cromwell's Letters and Speeches*, edited by S.C. Lomas (Methuen, London, 1904), p. xxviii.
46. *Ibid.*, p. xxxvi.

Chapter 5   Limiting the literary: biography and the construction of a fellowship of discourse

1. Michel Foucault, 'The functions of literature', in *Politics, Philosophy, Culture*, p. 311.
2. Arthur P. Stanley, *The Life and Correspondence of Thomas Arnold*, 1844, 2 vols, 14th edn (John Murray, London, 1887), vol. I, p. 157.
3. This is actually Matthew Arnold, recalling through his lecture 'Culture and its enemies' what Thomas Arnold would have done with the Hyde Park rioters of 1868. 'Culture and its enemies' was later moulded into *Culture and Anarchy*. Dr Arnold's solution to problems of disorder was left out in this version. See Raymond Williams, 'A hundred years of culture and anarchy', *Problems in Materialism and Culture: Selected essays*, (Verso, London, 1980), p. 7.
4. Stanley, *Arnold*, vol. I, pp. 157–8.
5. See Christopher Kent, *Brains and Numbers*, pp. 5–6.
6. Stanley, *Arnold*, vol. I, p. 121.
7. *Ibid.*, p. 135.
8. *Ibid.*, p. 162.
9. The Church of England lost a great deal of its symbolic power upon the passing of the Tests Act, 1871; see Michael Sanderson (ed.), *The Universities in the Nineteenth Century* (RKP, London, 1975), pp. 148–9.
10. Although Stephen was required to leave his teaching post, the active intervention of Henry Fawcett meant that he was allowed to keep his fellowship – though the fact that Fawcett had to intervene suggests that this was not a standard concession; see the entry for Leslie Stephen, *DNB*. Early in his time at Oxford (1851), Morley was exposed to a view of the activities of reactionary clerical fellows who kept Mark Pattison – a radical in the debate over the reform of university resources and practices – from becoming the Rector of Lincoln College; see the entry for John Morley, *DNB*.
11. See 'Presidential address', *Proceedings of the British Academy 1903–1904* (Frowde, Oxford, 1905), p. 8.
12. *Ibid.*, p. 12.
13. Publicity material, marketing 'English Men of Letters'; taken from the publicity pages from the rear of William Minto's *Defoe*, English Men of Letters (Macmillan, London, 1879).
14. The first effective year of the extension movement as organised by Oxford and Cambridge was 1885–86. Eighty courses at 48 centres were organised; 8,500 students attended lectures. The two most popular and widely taught disciplines in extension classes were History and Literature; these disciplines accounted for 75 per cent of all extension classes organised by Oxford University between 1889 and 1902; see Jepson, *Beginnings of English University Adult Education*, p. 236.
15. See J.F.C. Harrison, *Learning and Living: 1790–1960* (RKP, London, 1961), p. 219.

16. The form of the extension lecture itself (since it was rarely possible to back this up with close reading of a series of agreed texts) meant that there was a tendency for the lecturer merely to expound the peculiar beauties of one author or another in a more or less biographical manner. (Chris Baldick, *The Social Mission of English Criticism: 1848–1932*, pp. 74–5)

17. See 'On the study of literature' in John Morley, *Studies in Literature*, 1890 (Macmillan, London, 1904), p. 223.

18. John Nichol, *Carlyle*, English Men of Letters (Macmillan, London, 1892), pp. 170–1; further references will be given as (*C*, p. no.).

19. Morley, 'Study of literature', pp. 221–5.

20. Graham Pechey, 'Bakhtin, Marxism and post-structuralism' in Barker *et al.*, *Literature, Politics and Theory*, p. 123.

21. See Diane McDonell, *Theories of Discourse* (Blackwell, Oxford, 1986), pp. 15–16.

22. Michel Foucault, 'What is an author?', in J. V. Harari (ed.), *Textual Strategies: Perspectives in post-structuralist criticism* (Methuen, London, 1980), p. 154.

23. *Ibid.*, p. 147.

24. *Ibid.*, p. 148.

25. *Ibid.*, p. 159.

26. *Ibid.*, p. 157.

27. Ira Bruce Nadel, *Biography: Fiction, fact and form*, p. 35.

28. John Morley, letter to Macmillan, 9 November 1877, Macmillan Archive, MS 5505, vol. CLLX.

29. John Morley, *Diderot*, 2 vols (Macmillan, London, 1878). References to this work will be given as (*D*, vol. no., p. no.) in the main text.

30. Ira Bruce Nadel, *Biography*, p. 37.

31. For the extent to which organised religion figured as a source of anxiety in the writings and other activities of Morley, Stephen and W.E.H. Lecky, see Jeffrey Paul von Arx, *Progress and Pessimism*; for the significance of Morley's 1873 pamphlet, *The Struggle for National Education* – a contribution to the debate on national, elementary education, and an attack on the Church of England – see pp. 146–51.

32. Foucault, 'What is an author?', p. 151.

33. For this orthodox position, see Leslie Stephen's entry on Adam Smith in the *DNB*.

34. Thomas Fowler, *Locke*, English Men of Letters (Macmillan, London, 1880), pp. 186–93.

35. Leslie Stephen, *Pope*, English Men of Letters (Macmillan, London, 1880), p. 164.

36. *Ibid.*, p. 186.

37. Fowler, *Locke*, p 173.

38. I am thinking of Eagleton's account of 'the rise of English' in *Literary Theory*. For a recent account of the Newbolt Report, see Brian Doyle,

English and Englishness, ch. 2. For a revisionary assessment of the significance of the Newbolt Report, the way in which it was received by its contemporaries, and the way it has been selectively used in recent accounts of the rise of English studies, see Noel King, 'The teacher must exist before the pupil: *The Newbolt Report on the Teaching of English in England*, 1921', *Literature and History*, **13**:1 (Spring 1987), pp. 14–37.

39. See Alexander Macmillan to Malcolm Macmillan, 2 October 1877, in C.L. Graves (ed.), *The Life and Letters of Alexander Macmillan* (Macmillan, London, 1910), p. 342; see also Nadel, *Biography*, pp. 31–2.

40. Harrison became the object of Arnold's criticism in *Culture and Anarchy* because of Harrison's parody of Arnold's discourse on 'culture'; see Harrison's 'Culture: A dialogue', which originally appeared in Morley's *Fortnightly Review* (November, 1867); the essay was reprinted in Frederic Harrison's collection, *The Choice of Books* (Macmillan, London, 1886).

41. T.H. Huxley, *Hume*, English Men of Letters (Macmillan, London, 1879), p. 58.

42. Matthew Arnold, 'A French critic on Milton', in *The Oxford Authors: Matthew Arnold*, edited by M. Allott and R.H. Super, (OUP, Oxford, 1986), p. 394.

43. *Ibid.*, p. 395; the offending discourse can be found in Macaulay's essay on Milton, reprinted many times during the course of the nineteenth century. I cite from a popular edition; see *Macaulay's Lays of Ancient Rome: With selections from the essays* (Richard E. King, London, 1893), p. 354.

44. Arnold, 'A French critic on Milton', p. 396.

45. For Matthew Arnold's view of the literary authority which resides in certain 'touchstones' of poetry, see 'The study of poetry', in *Essays in Criticism: Second series*, 1888 (Macmillan, London, 1958), p. 11. The 'touchstone' from Milton's *Paradise Lost* that Arnold cites is from Book I, ll. 599–602.

46. G.O. Trevelyan, *The Life and Letters of Lord Macaulay*, 1876, 2 vols (OUP, Oxford, 1932), vol. I, pp. 158–60.

47. *Ibid.*, pp. 121–2.

48. Macaulay, 'Bacon', in *Works: Albany edition*, 12 vols (Longman, London, 1898), vol. VIII, pp. 641–2.

49. Leslie Stephen, 'Macaulay', in *Hours in a Library*, 3 vols (Smith and Elder, London, 1892), vol. II, pp. 336–7.

50. *Ibid.*, p. 369.

51. Macaulay, 'Ranke', *Works*, vol. IX, pp. 291–2.

52. Stephen, 'Macaulay', p. 356.

53. In his *Reminiscences*, John Morley records in 1891 a representative set of anxieties on the relationship between Anglicanism, regressive theological knowledge 'disguised' as progressive science and criticism, and socialism:

> T. Fowler [biographer of Locke for 'English Men of Letters'] and I dined at Club together. Very interesting talk about the current drift of things in Oxford. How the Anglicans were trying to capture the spirit of science, criticism, philosophy and the new social spirit. Told

me about *Lux Mundi* – the famous attempt to reconcile Anglicanism *alias* Catholicism with the most advanced Biblical criticism. . . . Fowler assigns the beginning of this movement to T.H. Green, and the revival in his teaching of Transcendental Philosophy.

See Harvie, *Lights of Liberalism*, p. 236.

54. A tutor at Lincoln College, Oxford, Morison had been an Oxford undergraduate at the same time as his friend John Morley who, as editor of 'English Men of Letters' for Macmillan, commissioned the volume on Macaulay. Like Morley, Morison wrote for *The Saturday Review*. Like J.R. Seeley, Morison was trained as a classicist, while his intellectual commitments moved increasingly in the direction of positivist science. Whereas Seeley distanced himself from organised positivism upon securing his academic appointments in London and Cambridge, Morison divided his life between tutoring at Oxford and lecturing at Frederic Harrison's Newton Hall in London. For a detailed account of Morison's career, see the *DNB*.

55. James Cotter Morison, *Macaulay*, English Men of Letters (Macmillan, London, 1882); all future references to this work will be given as (*M*, p. no.) in the main text.

56. For an account of the sales and publication history of these ballads, see Donald Gray, 'Macaulay's *The Lays of Ancient Rome* and the publication of nineteenth-century British poetry', in J.R. Kinkaird and A.J. Kuhn (eds), *Victorian Literature and Society: Essays presented to R.D. Altick* (Ohio State UP, Ohio, 1984), pp. 74–93.

57. *Ibid.*, p. 82. I will refer to the construction of two such school editions in the course of this argument: *Macaulay's Lays: Horatius, Lake Regillus, the Spanish Armada and Imry*, edited by W.J. Addis (Allman and Son, London, 1902); and *Macaulay's Lays of Ancient Rome and Other Poems*, edited by R.L.A. du Pontet, Arnold's Classics for Schools (Edward Arnold, London, 1897).

58. Macaulay, *The Lays of Ancient Rome*, in *Macaulay's 'Lays of Ancient Rome':* *With selections from the essays*, p. 7; future citations from the poetry and its framing statements will be given from this edition as (*LAR*, p. no.) and will appear in the main text.

59. See *Macaulay's Lays*, edited by Addis; 'Virginia' is excluded from this edition.

60. *Ibid.*, p. 7.

61. R.L.A. du Pontet (ed.), *Macaulay's Lays*, p. xix.

62. Review of Macaulay's *Lays*, *Blackwood's Magazine*, vol. CCCXXVI (December, 1842), p. 820.

63. *Ibid.*, p. 821.

Conclusion: Custodians of discourse

1. Terry Eagleton, *The Function of Criticism*, p. 52.
2. Steven Connor, *Postmodernist Culture: An introduction to theories of the*

contemporary (Blackwell, Oxford, 1989); Connor defines performativity during a discussion of Lyotard, pp. 32–3.

3. Eagleton, *Function of Criticism*, ch. 5.

4. Connor, *Postmodernist Culture*, pp. 42–3.

5. C.H. Firth, 'The faculties and their powers: A contribution to the history of university organisation' (Blackwell, Oxford, 1909), *Tracts on Education: 1907–9*, British Library, Bloomsbury; p. 26.

6. *Ibid.*, p. 28.

7. *Ibid.*, p. 26.

8. *Ibid.*, p. 42.

9. The intellectual formations that I have in mind here are the (now unfortunately disbanded) Literature, Teaching, Politics (LTP) Group; and more recently, Oxford English Limited's metamorphosis into the formation grouped around the journal *News from Nowhere*.

References

Only works which have been cited directly in the notes appear in this list of references. Dates in parenthesis refer to the publication date of the edition used; dates not in parenthesis refer to original year of publication. Where an essay is a contribution to a collection of essays or a Festschrift, only the full work in which it appears is cited here, under the name of the editor(s). Recent (non-nineteenth-century) essays which have appeared in scholarly journals are cited in their own right.

Abbreviations used:

UP   University Press
CUP   Cambridge University Press
NLB   New Left Books
OUP   Oxford University Press
RKP   Routledge and Kegan Paul

Archival collection

The Macmillan Archive, British Library, Bloomsbury, London

Nineteenth-century periodicals

Blackwood's Magazine
The Edinburgh Review
Fraser's Magazine
The Review of Reviews

Printed books

Althusser, Louis, *Lenin and Philosophy and Other Essays* (NLB, London, 1977)

Altick, Richard D., *The English Common Reader: A social history of the mass reading public 1800–1900*, 1957 (Chicago UP, Chicago and London, 1963)

Anderson, Perry, 'Components of the national culture', *New Left Review*, 50 (May/June, 1968), pp. 1–57

Aristotle, *The Basic Works of Aristotle*, edited by Richard McKeon (Random House, New York, 1941)

Arnold, Matthew, *Culture and Anarchy*, 1869, popular edition (Smith and Elder, London, 1889)

Arnold, Matthew, *Essays in Criticism: Second series*, 1888 (Macmillan, London, 1958)

Arnold, Matthew, *The Oxford Authors: Matthew Arnold*, edited by M. Allott and R. H. Super (Oxford UP, Oxford, 1986)

Arx, Jeffrey Paul von, *Progress and Pessimism: Religion, politics and history in late nineteenth-century Britain* (Harvard UP, Cambridge, Mass., 1985)

Attridge, Derek, Geoff Bennington and Robert Young (eds), *Post-structuralism and the Question of History* (CUP, Cambridge, 1987)

Bakhtin, M. M., *The Dialogic Imagination: Four essays* (Texas UP, Austin and London, 1981)

Bakhtin, M. M., *Problems of Dostoevsky's Poetics*, 1963 (Minnesota UP, Minneapolis, 1984)

Bakhtin, M. M., *Rabelais and His World*, 1965 (Indiana UP, Bloomington, 1984)

Bakhtin, M. M., *Speech Genres and Other Late Essays* (Texas UP, Austin and London, 1986)

Baldick, Chris, *The Social Mission of English Criticism: 1848–1932* (Clarendon Press, Oxford, 1983)

Bann, Stephen, *The Clothing of Clio: The representation of history in nineteenth-century Britain and France* (CUP, Cambridge, 1984)

Barker, Francis, Peter Hulme, Margaret Iverson and Diana Loxley (eds), *Literature, Politics and Theory: Papers from the Essex Conference 1976–1984* (Methuen, London, 1986)

Barthes, Roland, *Image–Music–Text*, edited by Stephen Heath (Fontana/Collins, London, 1977)

Beer, Gillian, *Arguing with the Past: Essays in narrative from Woolf to Sidney* (Routledge, London, 1989)

Bennett, Tony, 'Texts, readers and reading formations', *Literature and History*, 9:2 (Autumn 1983), pp. 214–27

Boswell, James, *Life of Johnson*, 1791 (OUP, Oxford, 1980)

Boswell, James, *The Life of Johnson*, 1791, 5 vols, edited by John Wilson Croker (John Murray, London, 1831)

Brougham, Henry, *Practical Observations upon the Education of the People*, 1825 (E. J. Morton, Manchester, 1971)

Burrow, John, *A Liberal Descent: Victorian historians and the English past* (CUP, Cambridge, 1981)

Butterfield, Herbert, *The Whig Interpretation of History*, 1931 (Penguin, Harmondsworth, 1973)

Carlyle, Thomas, *The Centenary Edition of the Works of Thomas Carlyle*, 30 vols, edited by H. D. Traill (Chapman and Hall, London, 1896–1899)

Carlyle, Thomas, *Oliver Cromwell's Letters and Speeches*, edited by S. C. Lomas and introduced by C. H. Firth (Methuen, London, 1904)

Chadwick, Owen, 'Charles Kingsley at Cambridge', *Historical Journal*, vol. XVIII (June, 1975), pp. 303–26

Clark, Katerina and Michael Holquist, *Mikhail Bakhtin* (Harvard UP, Cambridge, Mass., and London, 1984)

Coleridge, Samuel Taylor, *On the Constitution of the Church and State*, 1830 (Dent, London, 1972)

Collini, Stephan, J. Winch and J. Burrow, *That Noble Science of Politics: A study in nineteenth-century intellectual history* (CUP, Cambridge, 1983)

Comte, Auguste, *The Crisis of Industrial Civilisation: The early essays of Auguste Comte*, edited by Ronald Fletcher (Heinemann, London, 1974)

Comte, Auguste, *The System of Positive Polity*, 4 vols, 1851–54 (Longman and Green, London, 1875–77)

Connor, Steven, *Postmodernist Culture: An introduction to theories of the contemporary* (Blackwell, Oxford, 1989)

Cooper, Thomas, *Triumphs of Perseverance and Enterprise, in Learning, Science, Art, Commerce and Adventure* (Ward Lock, London, 1879)

Creighton, Mandell, *Cardinal Wolsey*, Twelve English Statesmen (Macmillan, London, 1888)

Crowley, Tony, *The Politics of Discourse: The standard language question in British cultural debate* (Macmillan, London, 1989)

Culler, Jonathan, 'Problems in the "history" of contemporary criticism', *Journal of Midwestern Modern Languages Association*, **17**: 1 (1984), pp. 3–15

Dex, Shirley (ed.), *Life and Work History Analyses: Qualitative and quantitative developments* (Routledge, London, 1991), pp. 144–66

The Dictionary of National Biography, 1885–1900, 22 vols (Smith, Elder and Co., London, 1909 reprint)

Doyle, Brian, *English and Englishness* New Accents (Routledge, London, 1989)

Dreyfus, Hubert L., and Paul Rabinow, *Michel Foucault: Beyond structuralism and hermeneutics* (Harvester, Brighton, 1982)

During, Simon, *Foucault and Literature: Towards a genealogy of writing* (Routledge, London, 1992)

Eagleton, Terry, 'End of English', *Textual Practice*, **1** (1987), pp. 1–9

Eagleton, Terry, *The Function of Criticism* (Verso, London, 1984)

Eagleton, Terry, *Literary Theory: An introduction* (Blackwell, Oxford, 1983)

Epstein, James and Dorothy Thompson (eds), *The Chartist Experience: Studies in working-class radicalism and culture, 1830–1860* (Macmillan, London, 1982)

Firth, C. H., 'The faculties and their powers: A contribution to the history of university organisation' [pamphlet] (Blackwell, Oxford, 1909)

Fogel, R. W. and G. R. Elton, *Which Road to the Past? Two views of history* (Yale UP, New Haven and London, 1983)

Foucault, Michel, *The Archaeology of Knowledge*, 1969 (Tavistock, London, 1972)

Foucault, Michel, *The Birth of the Clinic*, 1963 (Tavistock, London, 1973)

Foucault, Michel, *Discipline and Punish*, 1975 (Penguin, Harmondsworth, 1979)

Foucault, Michel, *I, Pierre Rivière, Having Slaughtered my Mother, my Sister, my Brother . . .*, 1973 (Peregrine, London, 1978)

Foucault, Michel, 'The order of discourse', 1970, appendix to *The Archaeology of Knowledge*

Foucault, Michel, *The Order of Things*, 1966 (Tavistock, London, 1970)

Foucault, Michel, *Politics, Philosophy, Culture: Interviews and other writings 1977–1984*, (Routledge, London and New York, 1988)

Foucault, Michel, 'What is an author?', in J. V. Harari (ed.), *Textual Strategies: Perspectives in post–structuralist criticism* (Methuen, London, 1980) pp. 141–60

Fowler, Thomas, *Locke*, English Men of Letters (Macmillan, London, 1880)

Freeman, E. A., *William the Conqueror*, Twelve English Statesmen (Macmillan, London, 1888)

Gibbon, Edward, *Autobiography*, 1796 (Dent, London, 1948)

Gooch, G. P., *History and Historians in the Nineteenth Century*, 1913, new edition (Longman, London, 1952)

Gramsci, Antonio, *Selections from the Cultural Writings* (Lawrence and Wishart, London, 1985)

Gramsci, Antonio, *Selections from the Prison Notebooks* (Lawrence and Wishart, London, 1971)

Graves, C. L. (ed.), *The Life and Letters of Alexander Macmillan* (Macmillan, London, 1910)

Gross, John, *The Rise and Fall of the Man of Letters: Aspects of English literary life since 1800* (Weidenfeld and Nicolson, London, 1969)

Hamer, D. A., *John Morley: A liberal intellectual in politics* (Clarendon Press, Oxford, 1968)

Hare, J. C., *John Sterling's Essays and Tales, Collected and Edited With A Memoir of His Life*, 2 vols (J. W. Parker, London, 1848)

Harrison, Frederic, *Chatham*, Twelve English Statesmen (Macmillan, London, 1905)

Harrison, Frederic, *The Choice of Books* (Macmillan, London, 1886)

Harrison, Frederic, *The Meaning of History* (Macmillan, London, 1894)

Harrison, Frederic, *Oliver Cromwell*, Twelve English Statesmen (Macmillan, London, 1888)

Harrison, J. F. C., *Learning and Living: 1790–1960* (RKP, London, 1961)

Hartman, Geoffrey, *Criticism in the Wilderness: The study of literature today* (Yale UP, New Haven and London, 1980)

Harvie, Christopher, *The Lights of Liberalism: University liberals and the challenge of democracy 1860–1886* (Allen Lane, London, 1976)

Hawkes, Terence, 'Editorial', *Textual Practice*, 1 (1987)

Hirschkop, Ken and David Shepherd (eds), *Bakhtin and Cultural Theory* (Manchester UP, Manchester, 1989)

Holquist, Michael, *Dialogism: Bakhtin and his world*, New Accents, (Routledge, London, 1990)

Houghton, W. E., *The Victorian Frame of Mind: 1830–1870* (Yale UP, New Haven and London, 1957)

Huxley, T. H., *Hume*, English Men of Letters (Macmillan, London, 1879)

Jann, Rosemary, *The Art and Science of Victorian History* (Ohio State UP, Columbia, 1985)

Jepson, N. A., *The Beginnings of English University Adult Education* (Michael Joseph, London, 1973)

Johnson, Richard, Gregor McLennan, Bill Schwarz and David Sutton (eds), *Making Histories* (Birmingham Centre for Contemporary Cultural Studies/Hutchinson, London, 1982)

Kent, Christopher, *Brains and Numbers: Elitism, Comtism and democracy in nineteenth–century England* (Toronto UP, Buffalo, 1978)

King, Noel, 'The teacher must exist before the pupil: *The Newbolt Report on the Teaching of English in England*, 1921', *Literature and History*, **13**: 1 (Spring 1987), pp. 14–37

Kingsley, Charles, *Alton Locke*, 1850 (Dent, London, no date)

Kinkaird, J. R. and A. J. Kuhn (eds), *Victorian Literature and Society: Essays presented to R. D. Altick* (Ohio State UP, Ohio, 1984)

Knight, Charles, *William Caxton: The first English printer* (Charles Knight and Co., London, 1844)

Knights, Ben, *The Idea of the Clerisy in the Nineteenth Century* (CUP, Cambridge, 1978)

Leith, Dick and George Myerson, *The Power of Address: Explorations in rhetoric* (Routledge, London, 1989)

McDonell, Diane, *Theories of Discourse* (Blackwell, Oxford, 1986)

Macaulay, Thomas Babington, *Works: Albany edition*, 12 vols (Longman, London, 1898)

Macaulay, Thomas Babington, *The History of England from the Accession of James II*, 1849–61, 3 vols (Dent, London, 1906)

Macaulay, Thomas Babington, *Macaulay's Lays of Ancient Rome: With selections from the essays* (Richard E. King, London, 1893)

Macaulay, Thomas Babington, *Macaulay's Lays: Horatius, Lake Regillus, the Spanish Armada and Imry*, edited by W. J. Addis (Allman and Son, London, 1902)

Macaulay, Thomas Babington, *Macaulay's Lays of Ancient Rome and Other Poems*, edited by R. L. A. du Pontet, Arnold's British Classics for Schools (Edward Arnold, London, 1897)

Maidment, Brian, 'Essayists and artisans: The making of nineteenth–century self-taught poets', *Literature and History*, **9**:1 (Spring 1983), pp. 74–91

Marx, Karl, *Surveys from Exile*, edited by David Fernbach (Penguin, Harmondsworth, 1973)

Marx, Karl, and Frederick Engels, *Basic Writings in Politics and Philosophy*, edited by L. S. Feur (Fontana, London, 1969)

Medvedev, P. N., *The Formal Method in Literary Scholarship: A critical introduction to sociological poetics*, 1928 (Harvard UP, Cambridge, Mass., 1985)

Mill, John Stuart, *Auguste Comte and Positivism* (Trübner, London, 1865)

Mill, John Stuart, *A System of Logic*, 1843 (Longman, London, 1961)

Minto, William, *Defoe*, English Men of Letters (Macmillan, London, 1879)

Morison, James Cotter, *Macaulay*, English Men of Letters (Macmillan, London, 1882)

Morley, John, *Critical Miscellanies*, 3 vols (Macmillan, London, 1886)

Morley, John, *Diderot*, 2 vols (Macmillan, London, 1878)

Morley, John, *The Life of Gladstone*, 3 vols (Macmillan, London, 1903)

Morley, John, *The Life of Richard Cobden*, 1878 (Chapman and Hall, new edn, London, 1883)

Morley, John, *Nineteenth-Century Essays*, edited by Peter Stansky (Chicago UP, Chicago and London, 1970)

Morley, John, *Oliver Cromwell* (Macmillan, London, 1900)

Morley, John, *The Struggle for National Education* (Macmillan, London, 1873)

Morley, John, *Studies in Literature*, 1890 (Macmillan, London, 1904)

Nadel, Ira Bruce, *Biography: Fiction, fact and form* (Macmillan, London, 1984)

Nichol, John, *Carlyle*, English Men of Letters (Macmillan, London, 1892)

Nicolson, Harold, *The Development of English Biography* (Hogarth Press, London, 1927)

Nietzsche, Friedrich, *On the Genealogy of Morals*, 1887 (Vintage, New York, 1969)

Norris, Christopher, *Paul De Man: Deconstruction and the critique of aesthetic ideology* (Routledge, London, 1988)

Parker, Christopher J. W., 'Academic history: Paradigms and dialectics', *Literature and History*, 5:2 (Autumn, 1979), pp. 165–82

Parker, Christopher J. W., *The English Historical Tradition since 1850* (John Donald, London, 1990)

Primrose, Archibald P. (Lord Rosebery), *Pitt*, Twelve English Statesmen, (Macmillan, London, 1891)

Proceedings of the British Academy 1903–4 (Frowde, Oxford, 1905)

Reid, Fred, *Keir Hardie: The making of a socialist* (Croom Helm, Beckenham, 1978)

Roach, John, 'Liberalism and the Victorian intelligentsia', *Cambridge Historical Journal*, 13 (1957), pp. 58–81

Rosenberg, Philip, *The Seventh Hero: Thomas Carlyle and the theory of radical activism* (Harvard UP, Cambridge, Mass., 1974)

Rothblatt, Sheldon, *The Revolution of the Dons: Cambridge and society in Victorian England*, 1967 (CUP, Cambridge, 1981)

Sales, Roger, *Pastoral and Politics: 1780–1830* (Hutchinson, London, 1983)

Sanderson, Michael (ed.), *The Universities in the Nineteenth Century* (RKP, London, 1975)

Seeley, J. R., *Classical Studies as an Introduction to the Moral Sciences* (Macmillan, London, 1864)

Seeley, J. R., *The Expansion of England* (Macmillan, London, 1883)

Seeley, J. R., *Lectures and Essays*, 1870 (Macmillan, London, 1895)

Seeley, J. R., *The Life and Adventures of E. M. Arndt* (Seeley and Jackson, London, 1879)

Seeley, J. R., *The Life and Times of Stein*, 3 vols (CUP, Cambridge, 1879)

Sheridan, Alan, *Michel Foucault: The will to truth* (Tavistock, London, 1980)

Slee, Peter R. H., *Learning and a Liberal Education: The study of modern history in the universities of Oxford, Cambridge and Manchester, 1800–1914* (Manchester UP, Manchester, 1986)

Small, Ian, *Conditions for Criticism: Authority, knowledge and literature in the late nineteenth century* (Clarendon Press, Oxford, 1990)

Small, Ian and Josephine Guy, 'English in crisis?' *Essays in Criticism*, **39**:3 (July, 1989), pp. 185–95

Smiles, Samuel, *Lives of the Engineers, with an Account of their Principal Works*, 3 vols (John Murray, London, 1861)

Smiles, Samuel, *Self-Help, with Illustrations of Conduct and Perseverance*, 1859 (John Murray, London, 1910)

Smith, Goldwin, *Three English Statesmen: A course of lectures on the political history of England* (Macmillan, London, 1868)

Stanley, Arthur P., *The Life and Correspondence of Thomas Arnold*, 1844, 2 vols, 14th edn (John Murray, London, 1887)

Stephen, Leslie, *Hours in a Library*, 3 vols (Smith and Elder, London, 1892)

Stephen, Leslie, *Pope*, English Men of Letters (Macmillan, London, 1880)

Thompson, John B., *Studies in the Theory of Ideology* (Polity, Cambridge, 1984)

Todorov, Tvetzan, *Mikhail Bakhtin: The dialogical principle* (Manchester UP, Manchester, 1984)

Traill, H. D., *William the Third*, Twelve English Statesmen (Macmillan, London, 1888)

Trevelyan, G. M., *An Autobiography* (Longmans, London, 1949)

Trevelyan, G. O., *The Life and Letters of Lord Macaulay*, 1876, 2 vols (OUP, Oxford, 1932)

Vickers, Brian, *In Defence of Rhetoric* (OUP, Oxford, 1988)

Vincent, David, *Bread, Knowledge and Freedom: A study of nineteenth-century working-class autobiography* (Europa, London, 1978)

Volosinov, V. N., 'Discourse in life and discourse in poetry: Questions of sociological poetics', 1926, in Ann Shukman (ed.), *The Bakhtin School Papers* (Russian Poetics in Translation, Oxford, 1988)

Volosinov, V. N., *Freudianism: A Marxist Critique*, 1927 (Seminar Press, New York, 1973)

Volosinov, V. N., *Marxism and the Philosophy of Language*, 1929 (Seminar Press, New York, 1973)

Webb, R. K., *The British Working–Class Reader 1790–1848* (Allen and Unwin, London, 1955)

Wellek, René, *Confrontations: Studies in the intellectual and literary relations between Germany, England and the United States during the nineteenth century* (Princeton UP, Princeton N.J., 1965)

Wheeler, Kathleen M. (ed.), *German Aesthetic and Literary Criticism: The Romantic ironists and Goethe* (CUP, Cambridge, 1984)

White, Hayden, *Metahistory: The historical imagination in nineteenth-century Europe* (Johns Hopkins UP, Baltimore, 1973)

White, Hayden, *Tropics of Discourse* (Johns Hopkins UP, Baltimore and London, 1978)

Widdowson, Peter (ed.), *Re-reading English* (Methuen, London, 1982)

Widdowson, Peter, 'Terrorism and literary studies', *Textual Practice*, 2 (1988), pp. 1–21

Williams, Raymond, *Culture and Society 1780–1950*, 1958 (Penguin, Harmondsworth, 1982)

Williams, Raymond, *Marxism and Literature* (OUP, Oxford, 1977)

Williams, Raymond, *Politics and Letters: Interviews with the 'New Left Review'*, (NLB, London, 1979)

Williams, Raymond, *The Politics of Modernism: Against the new conformists*, edited by T. Pinkney (Verso, London, 1989)

Williams, Raymond, *Problems in Materialism and Culture: Selected essays* (Verso, London, 1980)

Wilson, Adrian and T. G. Ashplant, 'Whig history and present-centred history', *The Historical Journal*, 31:1 (1988), pp. 1–16

Wormell, Deborah, *Sir John Seeley and the Uses of History* (CUP, Cambridge, 1979)

Index